T0301648

Innovation in the Service Economy

Innovation in the Service Economy

The New Wealth of Nations

Faïz Gallouj

Associate Professor of Economics, Clersé-Ifrési, University of Lille I, France

Edward Elgar
Cheltenham, UK • Northampton, MA, USA

Published by
Edward Elgar Publishing Limited
The Lypiatts
15 Lansdown Road
Cheltenham
Glos GL50 2JA
UK

Edward Elgar Publishing, Inc.
William Pratt House
9 Dewey Court
Northampton
Massachusetts 01060
USA

This book has been printed on demand to keep the title in print.

A catalogue record for this book
is available from the British Library

ISBN 978 1 84064 670 2

Contents

Figures

Tables

Acknowledgements

This book as a whole and, more specifically, some of its individual chapters, have benefited from the comments, criticisms or encouragement offered by many colleagues, friends and family members, in particular Cristiano Antonelli, André Barcet, Joël Bonamy, Michel Callon, Patrick Cohendet, Jacques De Bandt, Faridah Djellal, Jean Gadrey, Camal Gallouj, Mike Hales, Ian Miles, Marie-Christine Monnoyer, Keith Pavitt, Jon Sundbo and Olivier Weinstein. I thank them all warmly.

I am also grateful to the following institutions that funded the empirical investigations that laid the foundations for the book: the European Commission (DG XII, TSER program), the Commissariat Général du Plan, the French Ministry of Education, the French Ministry of Research and Technology, the French Post Office and the Union des Assurances de Paris.

I express my sincere gratitude to my friends Marianne Kleim (financial management), Kourosh Saljoghi (computer expert), Véronique Testelin (administration) and Andy Wilson (translation) whose professionalism and creativity make them real case studies in innovation in service provision.

For allowing me to draw upon previously published material I also thank the publishers of *Research Policy* (for material appearing in Chapter 3, section 1), *Science and Public Policy* (for material used in Chapter 4, Section 3) and *Economies et Sociétés* (Chapter 5, Section 2).

Finally I must express my loving thanks to Faridah, Naïm, Naïla and Nassim, for their patience and encouraging cheerfulness. It is to them that this book is dedicated.

Introduction

For several decades, modern economies have been service economies, and the point of no return has long been passed. The theoretical disputes as to how to explain and assess the expansion of the service sector, which pitted advocates of 'post-industrialism' against 'neo-industrialists', have gradually become blurred.[1] While services (as a sector) and the service relationship (as a mode of coordination between economic agents) are now essential characteristics of contemporary economies, innovation is another (Baumol, 2002). Thus modern economies are both service economies and economies of innovation. Paradoxically, they are not regarded as economies of innovation *in* services, that is as economies in which service firms' innovation efforts are proportional to their contribution to the major economic aggregates. It is as if services and innovation were two parallel universes that coexist in blissful ignorance of each other.

This paradox reflects the old concepts of services and the controversies that used to surround them (some of which have become myths) and, more generally, the inertia of our analytical and conceptual apparatus.

1. SERVICES: OLD MYTHS, NEW MYTHS, SPECIFICITIES

In order to understand properly the failure to recognize or the underestimation of innovation in services, we need, firstly, to reconsider certain myths (that is simplified and illusory images) associated with services and, secondly, to examine in a more analytical and concrete manner the specificities generally attributed to service activities. These two points are of course closely linked.

1.1 The Myths

Most of the views outlined here are relatively old. Some are rooted in the history of economic thought. There would be no difficulty at all in demonstrating that they continue to exert influence through those present-day economic and political discourses that incessantly warn us of the risks and limits of the service economy.

To simplify somewhat, three myths (artificially separated out here, but obviously linked) can be said still to be causing confusion in the analysis of innovation in services (for a detailed analysis of these myths, see Gallouj, 2001):

1. the myth of the unproductive, 'third' sector,
2. the myth of low productivity and low capital intensity in services, and
3. the myth of the service society as a society of 'servants'.

The first of these myths is a (negative) general judgement on the nature of an activity and of a sector; the other two are (equally negative) assessments of the factors of production (capital, labor) that service activities draw on.

1.1.1 Unproductive services and the 'third' sector

The notion of services as an unproductive activity with no economic value has its origins in the history of economic thought, and in particular in the work of Adam Smith (1960), who makes a distinction between the productive work of manufacturing and the unproductive work that characterizes service activities, which fade away at the very moment they are realized. This analysis, developed for services reduced to little more than the work of domestic servants, servants of the state and artists, continues to influence many present-day approaches. While the accounting concerns of the first theorists of the service sector (particularly Fisher, 1935; Clark, 1940) led to a residual, negative definition of services (everything that is not agriculture or manufacturing) that does not constitute a value judgement on the economic worth of the tertiary sector, the same most definitely cannot be said of other, more recent analyses. These analyses contain a number of negative assessments of the service sector ('peripheral', 'pathological'...) which, taken as a whole, contribute to what, by analogy with the third world, we describe as the myth of the 'third sector'. There are numerous studies deploring the growth of the service sector. We will confine ourselves here to citing just a few particularly suggestive examples. In a study revealingly entitled 'Manufacturing matters', Cohen and Zysman (1987) take the view that services are 'peripheral' activities that impede the functioning of manufacturing industry, which is regarded as the only engine of economic growth. Adam Smith's vision of services as unproductive also lies at the heart of the study by Bacon and Eltis (1978) entitled 'Too few producers'. The service sector is also suspected of having been the culprit in the economic crisis of the early 1970s (Aglietta and Brender, 1984; Lorenzi et al., 1980) and the image of services as a 'pathology' flourishes in the economic literature (cf. in particular Attali, 1981).

1.1.2 Low capital intensity and low productivity

The second myth conveys the notion that the service sector is characterized by low capital intensity and low productivity. The myth of low capital intensity is linked to the absence of factories and large-scale production lines in the service sector. This myth is very resistant even to those statistical investigations which, from the studies of Kutscher and Mark (1983) onwards, have concluded that capital intensity in services is in fact high. This has always been the case in some activities (particularly energy distribution and transport in its various forms) and has become so in others that are now the main users of information and communication technologies (banking and insurance, for example). When these analyses do bow to the statistical evidence, it is to reveal a new syndrome that condemns services. This is Solow's paradox, according to which increasing technological intensity is accompanied by a stagnation or even a decline in productivity. Now it is likely that a less 'industrialist' definition of productivity would cause us to revise our opinion of productivity in services and its evolution (Gadrey, 1996c).

1.1.3 A society of servants

The third myth concerns the quality of labor as a production factor in the service economy. It constitutes an attack on what might be considered one of the strengths of services, namely their job creating ability. The literature contains a large number of studies warning against such an error. Once again, we will not examine these studies in detail but confine ourselves to singling out a few particularly telling phrases. Thus as far as job creation is concerned, the service society is said to be nothing other than a 'society of servants', a 'hamburger society' and a 'bad jobs society' (Bluestone and Harrison, 1986; Cohen and Zysman, 1987; Gorz, 1988; Thurow, 1985; Mahar, 1992). Once again, there is no difficulty in adducing statistical evidence to give the lie to these analyses. While it is true that the service society creates deskilled jobs, it is equally true that it is now the main source of jobs for managerial staff and high-level professionals (Noyelle, 1986; Gadrey, 1996a; Meisenheimer, 1998; Illeris, 1996).

All these various myths, in their different ways and to differing extents, contribute to the underestimation of innovation in services. After all, innovation, the main engine of wealth creation, and such undervalued activities surely have little in common.

1.2 The Specificities of Services

The various myths outlined above can be regarded as the general context that helps to sustain the underestimation of innovation in services. Over and above this general context, there are also a certain number of particular concrete analytical problems (which will be examined in greater detail in

Chapter 2) that also (through the way in which they are apprehended) contribute to this underestimation.[2] They arise out of the ill-defined nature of the output of service activities, the interactive nature of the act of service delivery and the heterogeneity of services.

1.2.1 The product is a 'nebulous' process

The first analytical problem raised by services is the relatively fuzzy and unstable nature of their product. Indeed a service is a process, a sequence of operations, a formula, a protocol, a mode of organization. It is difficult, in many cases, to locate the boundaries of a service in the same way as those of a good can be fixed.

They have to be considered within a three-dimensional space:

1. the time horizon of the service provided, which is made up of the delivery of the service in the short term, what Gadrey (1996a) calls the 'service in actuality', and its long-term effect;
2. the reference universe or 'world', in the sense of the term developed by Boltanski and Thévenot (1991), i.e. the 'value system' used to evaluate the 'product' in all its various dimensions;[3]
3. the degree of materiality or tangibility in the service (which is often linked to its technological content).

1.2.2 Services are interactive

Services are consumed as they are being produced and involve some degree of customer participation. This characteristic has several theoretical consequences for the definition and the organization mode of innovation in services. For example, it would seem to prohibit a linear conception of innovation. On the other hand, it is particularly consistent with an interactive model, like that advanced by Kline and Rosenberg (1986).

1.2.3 The service sector is one of extreme diversity

Differences in respect of innovation sometimes seem greater within the service sector than between some service industries and some manufacturing industries. For example, the innovation behavior of computer services and telecommunications companies is relatively close to that of manufacturing firms and may, to some extent, be captured by the same survey arrangements. On the other hand, the types of 'products' vary widely from one service activity to another. Thus the content of product innovation is not necessarily the same for a hotel service, a consultancy service or a financial service. The difficulty of applying the traditional definitions seems to increase in the case of services whose target is information, knowledge or individuals. Customized or ad hoc innovation occupies an important place in consultancy services, for example. Particular attention should be focused on this type of activity and, more generally, on knowledge-intensive business services. They pose particular methodological problems, in that the providers of such services, while producing innovations in their own right, are also participants in the innovations produced by their clients.

It might well be asked whether the notion that services are activities with a high degree of specificity has not itself become a myth. After all, there are many exceptions to the characteristics outlined above, but in particular they also manifest themselves in the process of producing goods. Intangible elements and interactivity are becoming increasingly important in manufacturing. Thus an investigation into innovation in services should help not only to reconcile the two basic features of modern economies but also to enrich analysis of innovation in manufacturing.

2.   IN SEARCH OF A THEORY OF INNOVATION IN SERVICES

The myths referred to above and the theoretical problems inherent in the very nature of services have conspired to produce a situation in which innovation in services is not properly recognized.

The predominant approach to innovation in services is one that draws on the myth of the 'third sector'. Manufacturing industry, the driving force in the economy, produces technical systems from which service activities may indeed benefit. From this perspective, services are subordinate and dependent: they adopt, but they create nothing. In this respect, the 'third sector' behaves like the 'third world'. This is not an entirely false notion. It is, as we will see, simply incomplete and unable fully to account for innovation in services in all its diversity.

The technological bias alluded to above can be avoided. Some studies have achieved this by emphasizing the specific forms of innovation in particular parts of the service sector or by producing local analyses or theories of innovation in services. Thus there are typologies of forms of innovation in consultancy, theories of commercial innovation and theories of financial innovation. These various studies adopt approaches that might be described as 'service-oriented', as opposed to technologist (or industrialist) approaches.

Our objective here must be to go beyond these local analyses in order to develop a more general interpretative framework that can account for technological and non-technological innovation in services and in manufacturing. Such a synthesis is necessary because of a tendency for goods and services to become increasingly similar in nature. This phenomenon manifests itself in various ways and in opposite directions, including an increase in the intangible component of the production of agricultural and industrial goods and the industrial rationalization taking place in certain service activities. This convergence reflects the transition from the service economy to an economy based on the *service relationship* as a mode of coordination between economic agents (De Bandt and Gadrey, 1994). A characteristics-based approach derived from Lancaster's work would appear to be capable of bringing about this synthesis or integration and of accounting for the diversity of forms of innovation.

It is precisely such an approach that is being advanced in this book. We will be drawing in particular on a certain number of our own studies, both empirical and theoretical, individual and collective. Since texts, as Callon (1991) suggests, are networks, we will of course be drawing also – directly or indirectly – on much of the economic, sociological and management literature devoted to innovation in services. Nevertheless, it is not the aim of this book, or at least not the principal one, simply to synthesize the various strands of this literature. More fundamentally, this literature will inform our attempts to develop a theory of innovation in services that takes account of the specificities of services without excluding goods. In the light of this objective, the paradoxical nature of the book's title does not elude us. It seeks to register our particular interest in services rather than being a plea for a specific theory of innovation in the tertiary sector.

Our main sources of inspiration in this book are certain concepts and methodologies associated with two rapidly developing schools of thought: evolutionary theory and convention theory.

These two schools have developed independently of each other and of any reference to services. The first has its origins largely in the English-speaking world, while the second is predominantly French. Both constitute attempts to break into the 'black box' of the firm. They challenge the neo-classical notion of substantive rationality and expose the limitations of market-based coordination as the basis of economic behavior. They recognize and construct conceptually the heterogeneity of productive organizations (sectoral taxonomies of forms of technical change in evolutionary theory; cities and worlds of production in convention theory). In the course of the book, we will examine in greater detail the various elements of these theories and the exact nature of any actual or potential convergence between them. However, the principal object of investigation here is the way in which, as they converge, these two schools of thought can provide the foundations for an analytical framework, a theory even, of innovation in services.

3. AN OUTLINE OF THE BOOK

The book is divided into six chapters. The first chapter provides an ordered and critical survey of the literature devoted to innovation in services. Although such a survey is essential in order to reveal the gaps in this literature and to lay the foundations for the construction of our theory, it was our desire to keep it relatively short and readers are referred to earlier, more comprehensive studies (Gallouj, 1994a; C. Gallouj and F. Gallouj, 1996). It will be remembered, for example, that a significant part of this literature takes the process or process innovation as a starting point and that such (technological) innovation tends to be considered in terms of how it contributes to the codification of the service relationship, thereby reducing, as it were, the degree of freedom or variety in that relationship.

In Chapter 2, conversely, we adopt the 'product' as our starting point, which is more consistent, as we will see, with an evolutionary and neo-Schumpeterian analysis. Thus this chapter is given over to an examination of the notion of the product and of the ways in which Lancaster's characteristics-based approach[4] might be transposed to services and the service relationship. We will see that, in reality, the approach adopted and the amendments we propose do not exclude the possibility of taking processes into account.

The various modes and models of innovation derived from this approach are then outlined, illustrated and linked to each other in Chapter 3. These are the radical, incremental, ad hoc, ameliorative, recombinative and objectifying (or formalization) modes of innovation. As we will see, these various models encompass a set of *basic mechanisms for processing* the technical and services characteristics as well as the competences that go to make up the 'product', namely addition, removal, association, dissociation, formalization (or formatting), evolution or variation, and so on.

Chapter 4 examines the actual conditions in which these various types of innovation are produced (sources and determining factors, modes of organization, examined from the perspective of the actors involved and of the processes brought into play, appropriation and protection regimes, etc.).

Chapter 5 seeks to demonstrate that the characteristics-based approach adopted and the models of innovation derived from it fall within the scope of an evolutionary approach to innovation. The main aim of this chapter is not merely to make this observation and to illustrate it in various ways but, more fundamentally, to enrich evolutionary analyses and thereby push them in new directions. For example, our approach opens up opportunities for constructing richer sectoral taxonomies of innovation (and not just of technical change in the strict sense of the term) that are closer to the reality of service firms and industries.

However, these 'evolutionary' concepts, which constitute an important step forwards in our understanding of the mechanisms of innovation in services, are still unable to account for the various justifiable forms of the product, which are more diverse in services than elsewhere. Thus Chapter 6 examines the way in which conventionist approaches might help to enrich the evolutionary approaches to the product and to innovation.

NOTES

1. For an overview of these debates, cf. Delaunay and Gadrey (1992); Petit (1986).
2. For a detailed analysis of the analytical and methodological consequences of these characteristics on the definition and measurement of innovation, cf. Djellal and Gallouj (1999).
3. Boltanski and Thévenot's approach emphasizes the diversity of 'worlds' i.e. of value systems and of criteria of legitimacy. According to the nature of the dominant value system it distinguishes six 'worlds': the industrial world, the market world, the domestic world, the civic world, the creative or inspirational world, the opinion-based world (in which the values are those of reputation and self-esteem).
4. Some of the developments presented in this book are an extension of an initial investigation conducted in collaboration with O. Weinstein (Gallouj and Weinstein, 1997).

1.   Innovation in Services: a Brief Survey

INTRODUCTION

No serious theoretical investigation of innovation in services can dispense
with a survey, however brief and scholarly, of the 'state of the art'. Although
such an exercise is undeniably useful (innovation in services being indeed a
new 'art', if not in the workplace at least as far as researchers and governments
are concerned), we will confine ourselves here to the bare minimum and refer
the reader to other, more extensive surveys (see in particular Gallouj, 1994a;
C. Gallouj and F. Gallouj, 1996; Sundbo, 1998; Boden and Miles, 2000;
Flipo, 2000; Dumont, 2001; Warrant, 2001).

A not insignificant share of the literature on innovation in services can be
accounted for by identifying three basic approaches to research:

1. a *technologist* approach that equates or reduces innovation in services to
    the introduction of technical systems (material transport and processing
    systems and, above all, information and communication systems) into
    service firms and organizations;
2. a *service-oriented* approach that seeks to identify any possible particulari-
    ties in the nature and organization of innovation in services;
3. an *integrative* approach which, taking as its starting point the trend to-
    wards convergence and the blurring of the boundaries between goods and
    services, favors a similar analytical approach to innovation in both cases.

These three approaches fit neatly into what might be described as a natural life
cycle of theoretical concerns.[1] The technologist approach is in a phase of relative decline (the pioneers of research into innovation in services naturally
adopted a technologist 'gaze' that had its roots in a manufacturing economy
and manufacturing economics); the service-oriented approach is in its mature
phase (the next generation of researchers attempted to highlight the specificities of services, possibly even overplaying their hand to some extent); the
integrative approach is emerging and expanding (attempts are now being made
to bring goods and services together in a unified approach to innovation). The
point of view adopted in this book falls within the scope of this last approach.
It must be stressed that our concept of integration in no way implies aban-

donment of the search for specificity or of a concern with the technological aspects of innovation in services.

1. THE TECHNOLOGIST APPROACH

Those studies that equate innovation in services with technological innovation (adopted by services) are by far the oldest and most numerous, which has contributed to some extent to the overestimation of the technological dimension or, more precisely, to the underestimation of other aspects of innovation in services.

Over and above theoretical interpretations (and in particular the implicit or explicit acceptance of the assumptions of standard neoclassical theory which, through the notion of the production function, give pride of place to process innovations), the main argument in favor of such an approach is that service industries are becoming increasingly technology and capital-intensive. It may also be that, over the course of the 20th century, innovation in services was often driven primarily by the adoption of industrial technologies and goods (this was the case, for example, with all forms of transport) and that non-technological innovations did not begin to assert themselves and become important until relatively recently.

As Table 1.1 shows (see also Amable and Palombarini, 1998), service industries are now the main users of capital goods in the principal OECD countries.

Table 1.1 Share of total national investment in capital goods by sector in the G7 countries*

Country Sector	USA	GB	Japan	France	Germany	Italy	Canada
Primary	4.6	3.9	2.4	6.8	2.6	3.3	3.6
Secondary	30.9	32.3	42.0	42.4	47.0	46.4	51.9
Tertiary	*64.5*	*63.8*	*55.6*	*50.8*	*50.4*	*50.3*	*44.5*

Note: *in 1985 for Italy and in 1990 for the other countries.
Source: After OECD (1996).

If we take just information technologies, the data show that their share in capital expenditure (what is known as technological intensity) has for several decades been considerably greater in services than in manufacturing (on this point, see particularly the studies by Guile and Quinn, 1998, which refer to the USA). While it is hardly surprising that financial services or telecommunications services, for example, should have high technological intensities (see Table 1.2), it should be noted that technological intensities have also been increasing steadily in service industries traditionally described as non-informational (cleaning, transport and hotels, for example). Thus as Djellal (2000) puts it, deliberately pointing up the paradox, 'information technologies are playing an increasingly important role in non-informational services'.

Table 1.2 IT investment as a share of total equipment spending: selected industries

Sector/Industry	1973	1979	1981	1990	1993	1994
Manufacturing	3.9	10.2	17.1	30.3	38.4	40.0
Services	20.6	27.4	34.9	43.3	52.1	54.2
Transport	1.2	2.8	12.2	28.2	35.1	36.4
Communications	85.9	87.5	85.7	82.8	81.9	83.1
Wholesale trade	7.1	26.2	39.4	55.8	64.4	66.5
Retail trade	3.7	20.0	30.1	42.3	49.6	51.8
Finance, insurance and real estate	23.4	26.1	28.5	41.9	54.4	56.7
Misc. Services :	17.9	15.3	21.0	34.2	43.7	46.7
Personal services	30.0	20.3	26.2	38.0	49.7	50.2
Business services	12.5	8.5	11.1	19.8	32.3	38.4
Auto repair, parking	0.1	5.8	14.9	23.8	33.1	36.0
Health services	55.6	50.4	51.8	50.7	55.7	56.2
Legal services	8.6	24.8	38.5	56.8	66.5	68.0

Source: Bureau of Economic Analysis, U.S. Department of Commerce (1996).

The first (technologist) approach can be broken down for convenience's sake into three groups of studies of varying size and differing degrees of theoretical ambition. The technologist approach is dominated in quantitative terms by a group of studies that focus on the consequences of the introduction of technical systems into service firms or industries (impact analyses). The second group consists of studies that draw on the evolutionary approach in order to map out innovation trajectories in services. The last group contains just one study (Barras' reverse life cycle model), which in our view is an extremely important one, since its aim is to advance a theory of innovation in services. Our task here is to summarize very rapidly the main issues addressed by these various groups of studies.

1.1. The Impact of (Informational) Technologies on Services

A considerable proportion of the literature devoted to innovation in services is concerned with the economic consequences of the expansion of the informational paradigm and with its manifestations at the micro, meso and macroeconomic levels. For simplicity's sake, it will be assumed here that the expansion of this paradigm can be described by means of two models of innovation (which may either succeed each other or overlap): centralized or mainframe computer systems, on one hand, and decentralized computer systems and networks, on the other. One convenient way of summarizing if not the findings then at least the main general questions addressed in these numerous studies[2] is to construct a 'matrix' that combines these two models with a set of economic variables, such as employment, skills and work organization, productivity, the tradability of the service 'product' or 'output' and its nature (or quality).

Thus the main theoretical questions raised can be formulated as follows: what consequences does the introduction of each of these two innovation models have for employment, skills, productivity, tradability and quality in service firms and industries?

The centralized or mainframe model is said to have a positive effect on productivity and tradability but a negative impact on employment and skill levels. This model of innovation does not seem to have any particular influence on the quality of the service provided. It equates to the computerization of back-office functions and its primary objective is to reduce the cost of service delivery through the standardization of tasks and the exploitation of economies of scale.

The decentralized or network model, for its part, is said to have positive effects on employment, skill levels and tradability and possibly also on productivity and quality. This second model of innovation brings about fundamental changes in front-office functions. It gives rise to economies of scope and reduces routine tasks in favor of sales and advisory activities, which generate more value added.

These statements are neither definitive answers nor findings but rather hypotheses. Whatever the model of innovation under consideration, a significant proportion of the literature is concerned to present (in the case of a given firm, activity or group of activities, or even for the whole of the service sector) one, several or all of these theoretical hypotheses and their mechanisms, to compare them with reality and to attempt to interpret any discrepancies that might emerge.

One important theoretical question, which is common to both models and to many research studies, is expressed in the following terms by Solow (1987): 'You can see the computer age everywhere but in the productivity statistics'. This paradox reflects the fact that, at the same time as the pace of technological change is growing ever quicker, productivity as currently measured is stagnating or even declining. However, impact analyses are not sufficient to capture the multiple links between technological innovation and service(s). There may in fact be many other types of relation between technology and services (in particular those based on substitution, identity, determination, diffusion and production), which are defined and illustrated in Table 1.3.

Table 1.3 Technologies and services: mutual relations of greater complexity

Type of relation	Definition	Illustrations
Substitution relation	The (innovative) technical tool replaces, in whole or in part, in the front or back office, the service or service provider.	ATMs, information and advice terminals in banks, guidance and promotion terminals in large retail outlets, viewing of transport timetables, reservation systems.
Identity relation	The service provided constitutes the use value of the technology.	Speed, safety, comfort, etc. in the case of cars.
Determination relation	The technological innovation determines the emergence of new service functions.	Computer services and consultancy, determined by the development of IT. Finance, insurance, consultancy, maintenance and rental services determined by the development of the automobile.
	Services (and innovation in services) determine the technological innovation.	Service providers putting pressure on producers of equipment or software. Large retailers putting pressure on the food industry and other sectors in respect of the quality, packaging and environmental friendliness of products.
Diffusion relation	Some services contribute to the diffusion of technological innovations.	High tech consultants and the diffusion of new technologies.
Production relation	Service firms themselves design and produce technological innovations. However, this relation is usually based on coproduction.	The electronic document management systems produced by some insurance companies, ATMs in some banks, production of robots by some cleaning firms.

These relations reflect a fact that is frequently ignored in impact studies, namely that technology can replace services, in whole or in part, that it can determine innovation in services (and vice versa), that it can itself provide services and, conversely, that services can contribute to the diffusion, production or coproduction of technological innovation (Miles et al., 1994; Djellal, 1995; Bessant and Rush, 1995; Antonelli, 1997; Den Hertog, 2000; Hales, 1997).

1.2. Taxonomies of Sectoral Technological Trajectories

By defining innovation as a cumulative and specific process rather than as a disembodied outcome, evolutionary theory paved the way for a number of taxonomic studies that sought to establish sectoral technological trajectories. The most important and highly developed of these taxonomic studies is K. Pavitt's now well-known article 'Sectoral Patterns of Technical Change: Towards a Taxonomy and a Theory', published in the journal *Research Policy* in 1984. One of the principal limitations of this seminal taxonomy is that it locks the whole of the service sector into a single trajectory. Other studies have adopted the same theoretical perspective in order to identify a diversity of trajectories in services; they include those of Soete and Miozzo (1990), which draws directly on Pavitt's taxonomy and adopts its criteria, and of Lakshmanan (1987).

1.2.1. Pavitt's taxonomy and the service economy
Although it is based on a huge empirical study carried out in Great Britain, particularly on a database of nearly 2000 significant innovations introduced there between 1945 and 1979, Pavitt's taxonomy is intended to be universally applicable. Using a number of criteria and characteristics (particularly sources of technology, types of user and their needs, regimes of innovation appropriation, size of firm, degree of technological diversification, etc.) it breaks the economy down into four categories of firm (Figure 1.1): supplier-dominated firms, scale-intensive firms, specialized suppliers and science-based firms, each of which represents a sectoral model of technical change.

The category of 'scale-intensive firms' includes continuous-process activities (steel and glass industries) and mass-production activities (automotive, consumer durables); 'specialized suppliers' include (high precision) instrumentation and mechanical engineering, whilst the category of 'science-based firms' contains firms in the electronics, electrical and chemical industries.

In this taxonomy, professional, financial and business services belong for the most part to the category of 'supplier-dominated firms' (that is supply of instruments and technical systems). Services are thus assigned to a category which also includes manufacturing activities such as textiles, clothing, leather, publishing and printing. The main characteristics of this type of firm are as follows: they tend to be small, have no R&D function and they may have difficulty in appropriating innovation through technical means, which forces them to fall back on non-technical procedures such as branding, marketing, etc.; their clients are likely to be more conscious of price than performance, and their technological trajectory obeys a logic of cost-cutting.

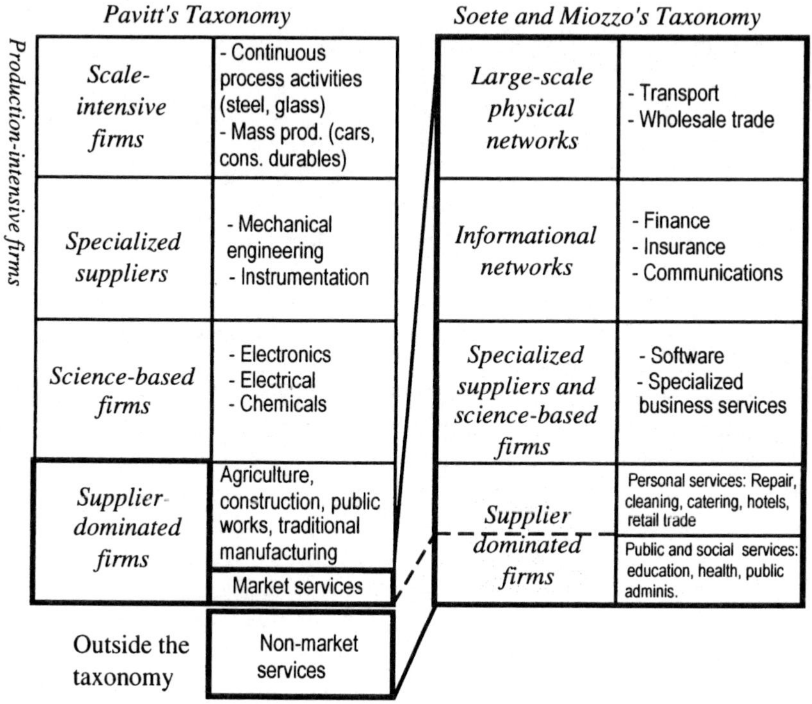

Pavitt's Taxonomy		*Soete and Miozzo's Taxonomy*	
Scale-intensive firms	- Continuous process activities (steel, glass) - Mass prod. (cars, cons. durables)	*Large-scale physical networks*	- Transport - Wholesale trade
Specialized suppliers	- Mechanical engineering - Instrumentation	*Informational networks*	- Finance - Insurance - Communications
Science-based firms	- Electronics - Electrical - Chemicals	*Specialized suppliers and science-based firms*	- Software - Specialized business services
Supplier-dominated firms	Agriculture, construction, public works, traditional manufacturing	*Supplier dominated firms*	Personal services: Repair, cleaning, catering, hotels, retail trade
	Market services		Public and social services: education, health, public adminis.
Outside the taxonomy	Non-market services		

Production-intensive firms (vertical label, left margin)

Figure 1.1 The correspondences between Pavitt's taxonomy and Soete and Miozzo's taxonomy

However interesting it may be, Pavitt's taxonomy does not, in our view, account for the variety of innovation trajectories in services. This is mainly due to a number of traits peculiar to services (whether the sector as a whole or the 'product') and to innovation in services. The following arguments will highlight the limitations of Pavitt's taxonomy as an instrument for dealing with innovation in this type of activity.

1. The various categories in the taxonomy are highly disproportionate in that the industries which generate more than 70 per cent of wealth and employment in our economies are assigned, for the most part, to a single

category, that of 'supplier-dominated firms'. Furthermore, non-market services are excluded from the analysis.

2.   The taxonomy does not account for the heterogeneity of behavior within industries, whether in the manufacturing or service sectors. It seems to assume that a given industry is made up of identical firms; in other words, it can be represented by a 'typical' firm. Moreover, it does not account for heterogeneous behavior within firms.

3.   It underestimates the greatly heterogeneous nature of service activities, a heterogeneity which is evident from the diversity of relationships which the various activities have with technology, differences in firm size, the different appropriation regimes, etc. Indeed, a large bank would be unlikely to behave in the same way as a transport or contract cleaning SME, and within an industry as heterogeneous as consultancy, computer consultancy would be unlikely to follow the same trajectory as legal consultancy.

4.   It is becoming increasingly evident today that some high-level services (i.e. skill-intensive activities employing large numbers of engineers and managerial staff) are strategic suppliers of information and knowledge (including technological expertise), to both the manufacturing and service sectors. The competitive advantage which these service providers have in terms of expertise has, to a certain extent, helped reverse the balance of power to such an extent that, today, certain service industries can be said to dominate the other sectors, including in the diffusion of new information technologies. This highlights what has been called an 'interactional innovation model' in which innovation is co-produced by the client and the service provider (Gallouj, 2002a). The existence of such a model makes allocating a given trajectory to a given firm all the more difficult, as some innovation trajectories could be said to be co-produced (use of consultants, inter-firm collaboration, etc.).

5.   The taxonomy presupposes that distinguishing between product innovation and process innovation is straightforward, involving discrete variables which can be easily identified, described, enumerated[3] and entered into a database (at least by an expert). Apart from the fact that such a conception marks a break with the evolutionary hypothesis of innovation viewed as a process rather than a definitive outcome, this distinction, which is difficult to put into practice in the case of goods, proves to be more difficult when it comes to services, a fact which can largely be explained by the intangible and interactive nature of a large number of services (cf. Djellal and Gallouj, 1999).

6.   It is concerned only with technological trajectories despite the fact that, in services (as in manufacturing) other types of trajectory are operating, particularly those which we will term service trajectories. Admittedly, Pavitt (1984, p. 344) recognizes that his data 'do not take into account the in-

cremental and social innovations which often accompany significant technical innovations'. In reality, they do not account either for social innovations produced independently of technical innovations, the importance of which is highlighted by Freeman (1991). Recent works (see in particular Gallouj and Gallouj, 1996; Sundbo, 1998; Hauknes, 1999; Howells, 2000; Pilat, 2000; Preissl, 2000) have highlighted particular forms and modalities of innovation in services not covered by Pavitt's approach, such as tailor-made or ad hoc innovations, intangible products, incremental or combinatory innovations, or simply organizational innovation. The content of the latter can be quite different in services, since it can be assimilated by the 'product' it incorporates and, in a way 'materializes' (e.g. a new type of shop, a new method, etc.).

7. It considers size of firm measured by numbers employed (and this applies to firms outside the service sector as well) as a structural given, representative of a type of trajectory, when in fact this variable evolves over the course of the trajectory. It is as if the size of firms remains static for a given trajectory, to the point where it is size alone that determines the trajectory. In reality, however, progression along an innovation path has repercussions on this variable. For example, the innovation trajectory in the retail trade has for some forty years been characterized by a trend away from small-scale towards large-scale retailing.

Pavitt himself tries to respond to some of these limitations and objections in later works. Thus, within services, another trajectory, designated 'knowledge-intensive', is highlighted (Pavitt et al, 1989). The fact remains, however, that even in this new trajectory services are still dominated by suppliers, although this time, new dominators enter the picture, namely suppliers of information technologies.

1.2.2. A specific taxonomy for the service sector, in the tradition of Pavitt

Soete and Miozzo (1990) reject the hypothesis that technological behavior in the service sector is homogeneous. The taxonomy they advance does indeed use Pavitt's criteria, but draws on them in order to release services from their confinement to a single category. Thus it would seem that services themselves follow different technological trajectories and that they can belong to different types of the taxonomy rather than to just one.

Thus Soete and Miozzo identify three types of firm or industry (see Figure 1.1, Section 1.2.1):

1. Firms 'dominated by suppliers' of equipment and technical systems, which are not very innovative and are content merely to acquire their process technologies from industrial suppliers. This first category can be

further divided into two groups: personal services (repair services, cleaning, hotel and catering, retailing, laundry services, etc.) and public and
social services (education, health, public administration). The first group
is made up of small firms whose customers are sensitive to performance
and whose modes of innovation appropriation are non-technological (professional know-how, aesthetic design, branding, advertising). The second
group is made up of large firms and organizations, whose customers are
conscious of quality in the wider sense and whose innovations constitute
public goods that they cannot claim to appropriate for themselves.
2. 'Network firms' can also be divided into two groups depending on the
principal medium of service delivery. Thus the taxonomy makes a distinction between physical networks, which are made up of firms whose
services are based on tangible mediums (transport, wholesale trade) and informational networks, in which codified information is the medium of
service delivery (finance, insurance, communications). Network firms in
both groups follow a technological trajectory characterized by cost reduction and the implementation of a networking strategy. They tend to be
large in size. Standards and norms constitute their main modes of innovation appropriation. Their customers are extremely price-sensitive. These
firms may turn to outside suppliers for their technologies, but always do
so from a position of strength. Where appropriate, it is possible to speak
of industrial firms dominated by services.
3. 'Specialized suppliers and science-based services' are particularly active in
terms of technological innovations (which may be based on their R&D
activities). This category includes all service providers that have particular relationships to R&D, information technologies and telecommunications. They are usually small firms whose technological trajectory is
based on systems design. Their clients are more concerned with the performance of the technologies than with their cost, while the innovation
appropriation regime is dominated by R&D know-how, copyright and
product differentiation.

As an extension of Pavitt's taxonomy, therefore, that of Soete and Miozzo
constitutes an important step forward in our understanding of diversity of
innovation trajectories in services. It does, however, introduce some new
difficulties. Thus the notion of network (and the corresponding technological
trajectory), which here constitutes one of the taxonomic 'types' is, in fact,
common to several of them. Awareness of this difficulty also leads us to
reconsider the question of the relative size of firms.

For all that, most of the criticisms of Pavitt's taxonomy outlined above
still apply to this later taxonomy. Thus, even though it rejects the notion,
explicitly postulated in Pavitt's analysis, that technological behavior in services is homogeneous and although it captures the diversity of behavior within

this heterogeneous sector, it does not explain the diversity of the forms of innovation and the corresponding trajectories. In other words, just as in Pavitt's analysis, only the technological trajectory is considered. In services, however, other trajectories have a particularly important place, as suggested by several recent studies (those that adopt the service-based and integrative approaches that we are going to examine later in this book).

Furthermore, in Pavitt's taxonomy, as in that of Soete and Miozzo, firms and industries are locked into given trajectories. The possibility of shifting from one trajectory to another or of combining trajectories is not considered. However, as we shall see in Chapter 5, a change of analytical perspective means that such developments can be envisaged.

1.2.3 Technological and institutional trajectories according to Lakshmanan

Lakshmanan (1987) shares the same theoretical (evolutionary) approach as the previous two endeavours. On the other hand, he differs from them in that he does not construct his various trajectories on the basis of predefined criteria (determinants) but by using a pre-existing typology of services, namely that developed by Mills (1986), in which the various categories are differentiated from each other by their technological behavior as well.

Mills' typology, as used and adapted by Lakshmanan, comprises three groups of service activities whose principal distinguishing characteristics are the degree of interaction with the customer and the degree of informational asymmetry within the service relationship; they are known, respectively, as service-dispensing activities, task-interactive services and personal-interactive services.

Service-dispensing activities (distribution, telecommunications, fast-food industry, etc.) are characterized by a low level of interaction and an absence of informational asymmetry. The technological trajectory at work in this first type of service activity is characterized by a tendency towards increasing mechanization and the exploitation of economies of scale (Nelson and Winter's (1982) 'natural' technological trajectory). The technologies deployed are those involving the processing of large volumes of information and materials (cash registers in supermarkets, the technologies used for processing mail, the various aspects of mechanization in the fast-food industry, etc.).

Task-interactive services (accountancy, legal and financial services) are characterized by an intermediate level of interaction and a high degree of uncertainty as to the outcome of the service, while personal-interactive services (health, social security) have a high degree of interaction and considerable informational asymmetries (adverse selection and moral hazard). The technologies at work in these two categories of service activities are intended to reduce communication costs. It is hardly surprising, therefore, that the favored technologies are the various information and telecommunications technologies.

Lakshmanan does not confine his analysis to technological innovations. He also acknowledges (although without investigating them any further) the existence of institutional innovations that might enter into synergy with technological innovations. Self-service, coproduction, the monitoring of service providers and the practice known as 'bonding' (demonstrating the quality of the service provider and the service through the holding of references and certificates) are examples of institutional innovations. They are in effect rules governing the modes of interaction between individuals. With the exception of these rules, Lakshmanan's analysis, like the previous one, ignores certain forms of innovation specific to services.

1.3 Barras' Model: a Theory of Innovation in Services?

Barras' model (1986, 1990), the merits and limitations of which will be examined here, marks a new stage in the maturing theoretical ambitions of those approaches we have described as technologist. The objective is explicitly stated and amounts to nothing less than the construction of a theory of innovation in services following in the tradition of Schumpeter.[4]

1.3.1 A reverse cycle

Barras' argument is based on a large-scale empirical study carried out in the area of financial (banking and insurance), accountancy and administrative services. Innovation in these service activities is said to follow a product life cycle that is the reverse of the traditional industrial cycle which begins, we scarcely need to point out, with product innovations and continues with process innovations (Abernathy and Utterback, 1978).

The various phases of Barras' cycle are launched by the introduction within a service firm or organization of a data processing system. The learning processes triggered by the implementation of this new technology are said to provide the impetus for various successive types of innovation. The first of these are incremental process innovations whose objective is to improve the efficiency of service delivery. The second comprise more radical process innovations leading to the improvement of service quality, while the final phase of the cycle involves product innovations, that is new services (see Table 1.4).

As Table 1.4 shows, the three phases of the reverse cycle are initiated, respectively, by the adoption and introduction of mainframe computer systems, of mini and microcomputers and, finally, of networks.

The innovation does not lie in these technical systems themselves (which constitutes an important advance over most 'impact studies') but rather in the changes they make possible across the whole range of learning processes (learning by doing, using, interacting, consulting).

Table 1.4 The principal characteristics of the reverse product cycle

Phase of the cycle	Main forms of innovation	Competitive effort	Enabling technologies	Examples
Phase I	Incremental process innovation	Improvement of service efficiency (cost decrease)	Mainframe	Computerization of insurance policy records, personnel records and payrolls
Phase II	Radical process innovation	Improvement of service quality	Mini and micro computers	Computerized management of housing waiting lists in local public adminis-tration, on-line insurance policy quotations, ATMs
Phase III	Product innovation	New services	Networks	Home banking

The incremental process innovations that predominate during the first phase of the cycle are back-office innovations, for example the computerization of insurance policies records and and of personnel and wage records.

The radical process innovations that take place in the second phase of the cycle mainly affect front-office functions. Examples include the computerized management of housing waiting lists in town halls, the 'on line' registration of policies in the offices of some insurance companies and computerized book-keeping in accountancy firms. The installation of ATMs in banks also be-longs in this category.

Product innovations are still relatively rare, for the moment at least. Home banking is the most obvious example. However, there are also new services, still at the experimental stage, such as interactive and completely computeri-zed auditing and accounting procedures in auditing firms or the entirely 'on line' services being introduced by insurance companies. The growth of this type of innovation depends on the existence of a public informational infras-tructure able to harness the capabilities of the enabling technologies.

1.3.2 What is the sphere of validity of such a model?

The question of the validity of Barras' model (whether it is to be curtailed or extended) can be posed in several ways. It is not certain, firstly, that Barras' argument can be extended to all service activities. As already noted, it is based empirically on particular service activities involving the processing of codified information: banking, insurance, accountancy, public services. This model would probably lose a good deal of its explanatory power if applied to service activities less sensitive to informational technologies.

Secondly, the fact that the model confines itself to information and tele-communications technologies might well be seen as restricting its possible sphere of application. Other technologies are at work in services: logistics and material handling technologies (transport vehicles, refrigeration, cooking, cleaning equipment) and life technologies (genetics, biotechnologies, etc.), for example. Might these various types of technologies not also act as enabling technologies? In other words, is it so difficult to envisage them initiating a reverse cycle in which process innovations give way to quasi-product innovations?

Another question that Barras does not raise is that of the validity of the reverse cycle model if applied to service functions within firms (including manufacturing firms). A positive response to this question would make it possible to extend the model's sphere of application considerably.

1.3.3 A model of the diffusion within services of technological innovations derived from manufacturing industry

Barras' model is above all a theory (and a satisfying one, within the limits laid down by our earlier observations) of the diffusion to service firms and industries of technological innovations derived from manufacturing industry. If it is to have any claim at all to being a real theory of innovation in services, it must take account of the various forms and mechanisms of innovation that elude it. Can we really address the question of innovation in banking if we disregard new financial products or, in the case of insurance, new kinds of policies or the new aid or support services?

In other words, the reverse cycle model is essentially technologist in that its concept of innovation does not extend beyond the 'technological possibilities'. Even in those service activities to which it seems best suited (informational service activities), there are (significant) categories of innovations that continue to elude it.

Table 1.5 shows the diversity of types of possible innovation in insurance services (although the typology can be applied to all financial services). It highlights those not captured by Barras' model. Thus it can be said that:

- most of the process innovations taken into account by Barras' model are in categories D2 (innovations associated with a service product that remains unchanged in its formal specifications and mode of delivery) and D3 (innovations associated with a service product whose formal specifications remain unchanged but whose mode of delivery, perceived quality and marketing are improved);

- 'product' innovations in the form of new policies and services (categories A, B and C), which are insurance companies' core activities, largely elude Barras' model, which adopts a very restrictive definition of 'new products';
- 'product' innovations (in the forms of new policies and services) can give rise to process innovations. In this case, Barras' cycle can be said to have been reversed, since product innovation now precedes process innovation (return to the traditional cycle).

Table 1.5 The main forms of innovation in financial services

Types of innovation	Sub-categories		Definition
A: Product/service innovations	A1: 'Absolute' product/service innovations		New service, concept or policy for the whole market
	A2: 'Relative' product/service innovations		New service, concept or policy for the company concerned
	A3: Tailor-made product/ service innovations	1) Adaptive tailor-made innovations	Adaptation of a standard policy for a particular client through changes in pricing or the addition of certain supplementary clauses
		2) Fully tailor-made innovations	Design of a genuinely specific policy for a given client
		3) Cover for special risks	Cover for a new risk affecting only small populations
B: Architectural innovations	B1: Product/service bundling innovations		Combination of existing products/services
	B2: Product/service unbundling innovations		Isolation of one element in a product/service for sale as a separate item
C: Innovations based on modifications to a product or service			Certain specifications and options are modified, leaving the basic formula unchanged

Innovation in the Service Economy

D: Process and organizational innovations, Innovations in methods and management	D1: Innovations introduced in support of product/service innovations	Process and organizational innovation following a product/service of type A, B or C and indissociable from it
	D2: Innovations associated with a product/service that remains unchanged in terms of both formal specifications and mode of delivery	Significant change in process (technology, work organization), leaving the final service unchanged
	D3: Innovations associated with a product/service whose formal specifications remain unchanged but whose mode of delivery, perceived quality and marketing are to be improved	Significant change in process (technology, work organization) leaving the product 'formally' identical but improved in quality
	D4: Formal management innovations	Innovations relating to financial, actuarial, legal, HR management
	D5: Informal management innovations (ad hoc or makeshift innovation)	Differentiated from the forms outlined above by their informal nature

Source: Gadrey and Gallouj (1994).

1.4 The Technological Content of Innovation in Services: the Results of a Survey

It has been apparent for some time that the explanatory power of technologist analyses has reached the point of diminishing returns. Following the emergence of new approaches that focus less single-mindedly on the technological aspect of innovation (and which will be examined in the following sections), the technologist approach now has its rivals.

In order to conclude this conspectus of technologist analyses, and to put the role of technology in the dynamic of innovation in services into context, we can draw on the results of a postal survey we conducted recently in France (Djellal and Gallouj, 1998, 2002).

In the course of this survey, which was concerned primarily with the technological content of innovation in services, we were able to gather more than 900 examples of actual innovations introduced between 1992 and 1997 in the 324 firms in our sample. Adopting a Schumpeterian perspective, four types of innovation were identified:

1.   innovations in service product, defined sufficiently broadly to include both tangible and 'intangible' products (for example, a new training method, a new area of consultancy, etc.);
2.   process innovations, whether linked to technical systems or more intangible processes (such as consultants' methods);
3.   (internal) organizational innovations, which differ from the previous type in that they constitute the structure within which activities and processes unfold. The introduction of a matrix structure, for example, falls into this category;
4.   innovations in external relations, defined as the establishment of particular relationships with a firm's partners, whether they be clients, suppliers, public authorities or competitors. Examples would include strategic alliances, new types of interface, the setting up of a mediator, etc.

As Table 1.6 shows, 35 per cent of all the innovations cited, of whatever type, are 'innovations in which technology plays no role', 37 per cent are 'non-technological innovations, but ones that could not have been realized without technology' and 28 per cent are 'technological innovations'. Overall, therefore, no less than 72 per cent of the examples of innovations cited (of all types) are non-technological innovations in the narrow or broad sense of the term.

Examination of each type of innovation separately reveals that:

1.   only 22 per cent of the examples of product innovations are technological innovations, whereas one third are innovations in which technology plays no role and 45 per cent are non-technological innovations but ones that could not have been realized without technology. Overall, non-technological innovations broadly defined account for 78 per cent of the examples of product innovations cited;
2.   the majority (54 per cent) of the examples of process innovations are technological innovations. However, 46 per cent of them can be regarded as non-technological innovations in the broad sense of the term;
3.   the organizational innovations, which differ from the previous types in that they involve changes in the organizational structures and not in the organization of service delivery (processes), are mostly (90 per cent) non-

technological innovations in the broad sense of the term. However, there is nothing surprising in this observation;

4. the vast majority (82 per cent) of innovations in external relations are non-technological innovations in the broad sense.

Table 1.6 The technological intensity of the example of innovations cited

Type of innovation	Product		Process		Organiza- tional		External Relations		Total	
Techological content	n	%	n	%	n	%	n	%	n	%
Non-technological (strict sense)*	91	33	33	13	110	54	84	50	318	35
Non technological (wide sense)**	121	45	84	33	73	36	55	32	333	37
Technological	60	22	140	54	21	10	30	18	251	28
Total	272	100	257	100	204	100	169	100	902	100

Source: Djellal and Gallouj (1998).
Notes:
*'Innovations in which technology plays no role'.
**'Non-technological innovations, but ones that could not have been realized without techno-logy'.

Thus these results provide quantitative indications of the existence and scale of non-technological innovation trajectories in services. In the second part of this chapter, we are going to tackle this question from the qualitative point of view, that is by examining the actual content of possible types of specific innovations.

2.   THE SERVICE-BASED AND THE INTEGRATIVE AP- PROACHES

As we have just established (notably through the volume of studies that have been carried out and the number of topics addressed), technology is undeniably a key element in innovation in services. However, it cannot by itself account for the full range of innovations (as is suggested, for example, by the statistics cited above).

In the second part of this chapter, we seek to outline some of the new ana-lytical concerns that have emerged recently. Whether they adopt the service-based or the integrative approach, the studies in question have a certain number of points in common, in particular a desire not to reduce innovation in services to technological innovation alone without for all that ignoring or underestimating it.

2.1 The Service-Based Approach

The service-based approach is adopted in a group of studies (small in number but growing) that share one (or both) of the following two objectives:

1. to highlight the existence of particular forms of innovation in services. These studies criticize the technologist approaches for their short-sightedness, which leads them to privilege technological innovation over other forms of innovation. They draw on the Schumpeterian tradition to develop an extended approach to innovation that includes technological innovation but also embraces other forms, such as ad hoc innovations, intangible products and processes, etc.
2. to attempt to produce 'local theories' of innovation more closely tailored to particular service industries.

2.1.1 Specific forms of innovation in services

It is no surprise to discover that some of the studies that adopt a service-based approach focus on services with a high cognitive or informational component. Indeed, the hypothesis that implicitly underlies these studies is that the 'purest' services (consultancy activities fall into this category) constitute the best 'laboratory' for exploring the possible specificities of innovation in services.

Consultancy activities have much in common with research activities: a high 'grey matter' content, similar problem-solving objectives, etc. Paradoxically, however, it is difficult to investigate and evaluate research and innovation in this area with the traditional analytical tools. Some researchers have no hesitation in concluding that there is little innovation in this type of activity and that what innovation does exist is confined largely to the technical systems put in place (technologist approaches). Consultants themselves can often be divided into one of two camps: those who underestimate their capacity for innovation and those who regard any service transaction as an innovation because each one is new and unique. For our part, we are not persuaded by either of these conclusions, which merely demonstrate the unsuitability of our analytical tools for the task of apprehending the nature of innovation within service firms. One of the major difficulties lies in the existence and importance of the interface in this type of activity. Along with other characteristics of services (namely their intangibility and immediacy), the interface, that is the interactive nature of services, calls into question the traditional distinction between product and process innovation. Innovation certainly exists in this type of activity, but it can take different forms.

On the basis of our empirical studies (Gallouj 1991, 1994c, 1995), three types of innovation can be identified, which we denote by the following terms: ad hoc innovation, anticipatory innovation (or innovation involving a new sphere of knowledge) and objectifying or formalization innovation.

1) Ad hoc innovation can be defined as the process of constructing a (new) solution to a problem being experienced by the client firm. This process is interactive in that it requires the participation of the client organization itself. It is described as ad hoc because it is 'unprogrammed' or 'emergent'; in other words, it is coterminous with the process of service delivery and can only be dissociated from it a posteriori. In many cases, the problem for which a solution has to be found is itself a new one. It may concern any aspect of the client firm's activity, not just the technical aspects. In other words, the solutions thus developed may be legal, fiscal, organizational, strategic, social, computer-related, etc. Ad hoc innovation cannot be reduced simply to processes of learning or adaptation to various situations, even though it may draw on such processes (accumulated knowledge and experience) and help to enrich individual and organizational learning processes and memories. Ad hoc innovation cannot be reduced to mere learning phenomena because new solutions are produced (innovations brought about in the client firm) and at least partially 'incorporated' or 'registered'. The particular nature of this activity raises a certain number of theoretical questions concerning its appropriation and reproducibility. Its appropriation raises problems, on both the substantive level (how can it be protected effectively?) and the normative level (since ad hoc innovation is co-produced, emergent and unprogrammed, it is difficult to determine ownership). Reproducing it in exactly the same form is equally difficult. However, there is nothing to prevent indirect reproduction, that is the use of ideas, 'tricks of the trade' and methods in similar situations.

2) Anticipatory innovation. This particular form of innovation could equally well be described as a '*new field of knowledge or expertise or an expertise-field innovation*'. It can be regarded as a particular manifestation (that is, one adapted to knowledge-intensive business services) of what Barcet, Bonamy and Mayère (1987) call functional innovation (the emergence of a new function, see Section 2.2 below). The ideas behind this innovation may stem from the interface (that is, direct exchanges with the client, expression of the client's needs), but they originate more generally from what we call the 'abstract need', that is the 'diffuse' background noise emitted by the environment, which arises out of complexity and uncertainty and is not linked to any particular client (Gallouj, 1994c). As the environment and the client's needs are monitored and listened to, new needs emerge, which must be satisfied. Anticipatory innovation consists of collecting and accumulating new knowledge and expertise relevant to the 'problem' or anticipated need stemming from technological, economic, social or institutional change. Faced with particularly novel problems, that is problems for which there is little available expertise, national consultants will have to draw on foreign experience or try to identify similar situations. In some cases, they may carry out research which creates genuinely new expertise. In this way, information technology has given rise to experts in computer consultancy, computer law, etc. Similarly, ecological and environmental concerns, European construction, the introduction of the Euro and the opening up of the former Eastern bloc have given rise to many 'new fields of expertise' shared by different types of service providers operating in accordance with their favored point of entry (technical, commercial, legal, political, etc.). These new fields of expertise, which have constituted innovations for those who anticipated the corresponding changes, are the equivalent of 'product' innovations in the field of knowledge-intensive services. However, until an interface has been established with the client, anticipatory innovation will remain potential. Consequently, this requires a marketing and communications drive which, in the field of consultancy, usually takes the form of publications, participation in conferences, etc. As a 'new field of expertise', this form of innovation is particularly difficult to protect. Its appropriation can sometimes be facilitated by the realization of another form of innovation: formalization innovation.

3) Formalization or objectifying innovation denotes a heterogeneous set of mechanisms that helps to sketch in the shadowy contours of the ill-defined phenomenon denoted by the term service, thereby imparting to it a certain degree of tangibility. This tangibility can be obtained by two different types of mechanism, which may be combined:

a) tangible mechanisms, such as the introduction of technical systems into service delivery (what are generally known as process innovations);
b) intangible mechanisms: the introduction of methods, that is of 'scripts' describing the distribution of roles in the 'live theatrical performance' that is staged each and every time a service is delivered; the design and use of toolboxes comprising analytical instruments that shape thinking and behavior (for example, BCG's matrix structures); the establishment of an organization that incorporates the intangible service.

These three forms of innovation may manifest themselves singly or they may combine and interact with each other (see Figure 1.2). Anticipatory innovation is the central element in this interactive system, in that it is very often followed by ad hoc and/or formalization innovations. It must not, however, be reduced to a single particular strategy or a stage in a process whose ultimate outcome is one of the other two forms of innovation. Indeed, in consultancy activities, it is just as often an autonomous and viable form of innovation. It is, as we have already said, a particular form, one adapted to knowledge-intensive business services, of functional innovation as defined by Barcet, Bonamy and Mayère (see Section 2.2 below). Anticipatory and formalization innovation can overlap, as when a new field of expertise is being detected and exploited at the same time as methods and tools are being developed and new services within the same field of expertise are emerging. Moreover, as Figure 1.2 shows, ad hoc innovations can be a source of ideas both for improving methods (formalization innovation) and for new fields of expertise to be identified (anticipatory innovation).

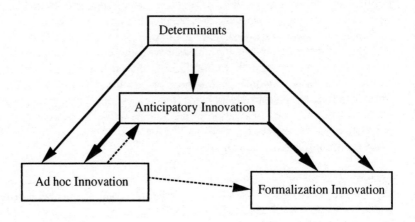

Figure 1.2 The main links between the different forms of innovation in consultancy services

This identification of forms of innovation specific to services is not confined to consultancy activities. Some recent studies (Gadrey et al., 1993, 1995; Sundbo, 1994, 1996; Callon, 1995; Dubuisson, 1995; Claveau et al., 1995; the SI4S European project,[5] 1998; Hamdouch and Samuelides, 2000; Monnoyer, 2002) have also chosen to adopt a Schumpeterian definition of innovation (that is a broad and open one). Sundbo (1993), for example, who is concerned primarily with cleaning services, financial services and the hotel trade, takes the view that innovations in services tend to follow service trajectories (for example, certain sets of ideas on management, banking, etc.) rather than technological trajectories (as defined in evolutionary theory). According to Sundbo, technologies are only one vector of innovation among others. Other studies have also highlighted this formalization trajectory in the field of business catering and associated services (Callon, 1995; Dubuisson, 1995).

2.1.2 The core/peripheral service approach
This approach, developed by marketing specialists (see Eiglier and Langeard, 1987; Jallat, 1992), is applied more particularly to household services, and especially to those that can be readily broken down into various basic service activities.

The relatively simple idea is that these various activities can be divided into two groups:

1. the core or basic service, which satisfies the client's principal needs (what might be termed the 'minimum service', that is the activity without which service delivery cannot take place): the accommodation in a hotel, the meal in a restaurant, transport in the case of an airline, etc.
2. peripheral services, that is all those services that serve to differentiate the 'product' and that are often the source of any competitive advantage (service on individual floors, reception or conference rooms in hotels; in-flight meals and films in an aeroplane; reception and reservation service in a restaurant, etc.).

The notion of service provision as the combination of basic and peripheral services can be used to identify two forms of innovation:

1. radical innovation, which denotes the design and development of a new basic service;
2. the improvement or extension of the service through the addition of new peripheral services.

We will see in the next chapter that this approach to service and innovation can be incorporated into the concept and analysis of services advanced in this book.

2.1.3 Innovation in financial services based on the demand for characteristics

When financial services theorists turn their attention to innovation, their main point of reference is not Barras' model but rather those studies that define new financial products in terms of the demand for characteristics (Hardouin, 1973; Desai and Low, 1987). We regard this theoretical school as part of the service-based approach since its aim is to construct a 'local theory' of innovation that seeks to account solely for innovation in banking and financial services.

From this theoretical perspective, financial products are defined as a finite set of characteristics (for example, liquidity, return and so on). A financial product can therefore be formalized in the following way: $Pi = (c_{i1}... c_{ij}... c_{in})$, in which c_{ij} denotes the 'weight' of the characteristic j in the product i. A financial innovation is produced when the weight of a given characteristic increases (making a financial product more liquid or more profitable, for example) or when a new characteristic that did not previously exist is introduced.

From this same theoretical perspective, Niehans (1983) advances the hypothesis that any financial product can be reduced to a given combination of the following three functions or characteristics: the exchange of present money against future money; the linking of borrowers and lenders; the execution of payments in a client's name. The financial innovation arises when these three functions are combined in any new way.

This approach to innovation in terms of characteristics gives rise here to a local theory of innovation. We shall see in the course of the book how it can be modified and enriched in order to create a more general and integrative approach to innovation.

2.1.4 The commercial innovation school

Like specialists in the financial services industry, students of retailing have sought to develop 'local' theories of innovation adapted to their particular field.[6] In consequence, this section given over to 'services oriented' approaches seeks to give an account of these various theories. The most important of them relate to the dynamic of shop formats, which are conceived of in terms of life cycle. Thus the 'wheel of retailing' model (McNair, 1958) can be summarized as follows:

1. All new forms of retailing appear first in a 'discount' version, that is outlets offer a limited range of goods and services and the main objective is to maximize sales volumes.
2. Their success causes the 'wheel' to revolve as retailers gradually 'trade up' by adding new products and services to the original ranges; this leads in turn to increased operating costs and higher prices.
3. This 'bourgeoisification' of the retail form opens up the market for new, more 'Spartan' entrants (to borrow the terms used by Tarondeau and Xardel, 1992).

Other analyses couched in terms of cycles, which cannot be outlined in any detail here (C. Gallouj, 1997a), have extended the 'wheel of retailing model':

1. Goldman's analyses (Goldman, 1975) distinguish between various possible forms of 'trading up' or ways of causing the wheel to revolve by the degree of innovation in goods or service they introduce into the range;
2. in the 'accordion theory' (Hollander, 1966) the retailing dynamic is characterized by alternation between outlets offering a wide, non-specialized range of products and those with a narrow, specialized product range.

However, the cycle model in its various forms, as well as Barras' reversed cycle model, cannot account adequately for the wide diversity of forms of innovation in the retail sector. These retail cycle models are concerned only with innovation in shop format (i.e. organizational innovation). However, even in this particular case, they are trapped within a binary logic (low/high prices; wide/restricted product range) and fail to take full account of the diversity of new shop formats and of new forms and new channels of distribution.

Nor do these models take account of the following forms or areas of innovation, most of which require detailed investigation if they are to yield up their secrets:

- new methods of selling (mail order, door-to-door selling ...);
- new products and services retailed in stores;
- new products and services designed by the retailer or on his initiative;
- new processes (or new forms of organization and operation) within the same format, whether based on the introduction of new technologies or not (within the same form of retail outlet or within the environment – customers, suppliers, other stores – of the form under consideration).

2.2 The Integrative Approaches

The two studies surveyed in this section share a functional approach to economic activity. A need, that is a function, can be satisfied by consuming a good or a service. From this perspective, there is no need to make a distinction between these two 'products', making it possible to contemplate an integrated analysis.

In order to effect this integration of goods and services, Belleflamme, Houard and Michaux (1986), propose that these two categories should be replaced by the notion of 'vector'. This is an heuristic notion which, in these authors' words, denotes a set of resources and of necessary and sufficient conditions for the preparation and existence of a product.

This heuristic notion is formalized as follows: $V = bP + cS + I$. P denotes the production process, that is all the material resources (deployed) in the preparation of the product (for example, an assembly line in the case of industrial production, back-office computer equipment in the case of service provision). S denotes the the 'servuction' process, that is the set of resources and conditions relating to the differentiation and adaptation of a product to a user's specifications ('consumerization' of a product), while I denotes the entire set of elements in a firm's general organization.

Depending on the value of the coefficients b and c, which represent the relative weights of production and servuction, respectively, any given 'product' will be mainly a 'good' if $b > c$ and mainly a 'service' if $b < c$. Thus depending on the components of the vector that are mobilized, various types of innovation can be identified:

- a new service (or a new good);
- a new or improved process of production (P);
- a new or improved process of servuction (S);

- any combination of the three preceding types.

Barcet, Bonamy, Mayère (1987) also adopt a functional approach to economic activity. They identify three types of innovation that apply to both goods and services:

1. The emergence of new, undifferentiated and abstract functions denoted by the term *functional* innovation. From this point of view, the video recorder can be seen as a functional innovation (recording of pictures and sound), while risk management consultancy can be considered a functional innovation whereby risk is incorporated into management and strategic planning.
2. The process of differentiation from the previous form leads to another type of innovation, namely *specification* innovation in which the functional innovation is given a personalized content (different from that of competitors) and is adapted to various types of clientele. Fast-food restaurants, automated cash machines and telephone/Internet reservation services, in the case of services, and the many developments the automobile has undergone, in the case of manufactures, are just a few examples among a host of others.
3. *Production* innovation, finally, covers what are generally known as process innovations. In many cases, it is based on (back-office) technical systems and aims to reduce the cost of producing the service in question. The introduction of computer equipment to aid decision-making and the development of an expert system in a consultancy company are examples of production innovations.

CONCLUSION

By applying the image of the life cycle to theoretical concerns, we have attempted to identify the main reference points adopted by the various studies of innovation in services. We draw the following lessons from this brief survey:

1. The literature is dominated (in quantitative terms) by studies of technological innovation as applied to services. Whether they confine themselves to examining the impacts of technological innovation on firms or service industries or whether they advance more highly developed theoretical constructions (taxonomies of innovation trajectories, reverse cycle theory), these studies prove incapable of accounting for innovation in services in all its richness.

2. This technologist focus can be reduced by adding to those empirical studies of individual industries that help to highlight particular forms of innovation in services.

3. However, because of the increasing convergence of service and manufacturing activities, it seems desirable to adopt an integrative approach to innovation, one which underestimates neither the importance of technologies nor the possible role of non-technological forms of innovation.

The approach based on competences and (service, technical and process) characteristics that we seek to develop here, and which draws on the work of Lancaster (1966) and Saviotti and Metcalfe (1984), belongs to this integrative school. Firstly, it is concerned with both goods and services. Secondly, it applies both to technological innovation itself and to non-technological forms of innovation. It can be seen as a way of clarifying the functional approach considered above, which has proved to be too general (too 'functional' and insufficiently 'specific'), and thereby making it more operational.

NOTES

1. This life cycle applies not only to innovation in services but also to many other areas of concern to those engaged in the analysis of service industries, such as production, productivity, quality, etc.
2. Since a lack of space precludes a full list of references, we will refrain from citing any individual studies at all.
3. Which would allow ratios of the number of product innovations to process innovations to be calculated subsequently.
4. For more comprehensive analysis of Barras' model, see Gallouj (1998).
5. The SI4S project (Services in Innovation and Innovation in Services) was funded by DG XII of the European Commission as part of the TSER programme. The project ran for two years and brought together 11 research teams from different countries: Germany (DIW, Berlin), Denmark (RUC, Roskilde and DTI, Copenhagen), France (CLERSE-IFRESI, Lille), Great Britain (PREST, Manchester and CENTRIM, Brighton), Greece (CERES, Athens), Italy (CSS, Turin), Norway (STEP, Oslo), Netherlands (TNO, Apeldoorn) and Sweden (NUTEK, Stockholm). It produced a series of reports too numerous to be listed here.
6. For a survey of commercial innovation theories, see C. Gallouj (1997a).

2. An Extended Lancasterian Approach for Goods and Services

INTRODUCTION

In the previous chapter, we saw that most of the studies of innovation in services focus on process technologies or innovations *that produce (more or less) the same result* rather than on new 'products' (or processes that are, in effect, the 'product'). Such studies treat services in the same way as goods. Indeed, neoclassical theory implicitly encourages an approach to technical change that is preoccupied with quantitative variations in the product (and in production factors) but ignores qualitative changes.

Apart from the well-established limitations of such an implicit approach, which reveals that 'things are happening' but is incapable of identifying them in anything other than negative and residual terms ('technical change is everything which, apart from capital and labor, leads to increased output'), other problems arise or are exacerbated when it is applied to services. Firstly, it is very often the case in services that process technologies are sourced from industrial suppliers. Thus it is innovation in another sector that is generally being apprehended by this type of approach. Moreover, Solow's paradox, according to which computers are found everywhere except in productivity statistics, becomes a very serious consideration here.

Thus an explicit approach to innovation and technical change is as necessary in services as in manufacturing activities, if not more so. Some of the attempts that draw on Schumpeter's work in order to develop such an approach were outlined in the previous chapter (functional approaches and those based on the notion of core and peripheral services). Our aim in this chapter is to develop these approaches and make them more operational, taking as our starting point Lancaster's notion of the product as adapted by Saviotti and Metcalfe (1984; see also Saviotti, 1996).

Does a product-based approach mean that process innovations or technologies are to be disregarded? We would answer in the negative. It is true that the distinction between these two categories is more problematic in the case of services than in that of goods. Consequently, any approach we formulate will have to take account of this fact.

This chapter begins by outlining the way in which Saviotti and Metcalfe

28

(1984) and Saviotti (1996), drawing on Lancaster's approach but paradoxically from an evolutionary perspective, advance the idea of modelling a product (a 'material' artefact from their point of view) in order to be able to measure technical change. This notion is examined in the light of the principal defining characteristics of services and proposals are drawn up for adapting it to service activities.

1. THE PRODUCT AS A SET OF CHARACTERISTICS

The notion, developed by Saviotti and Metcalfe, of the product (good) as a combination of technical and service characteristics is now familiar in the economics of innovation and technical change. Its main points are outlined here (Section 1.1) and it is then located relative to other similar attempts (Section 1.2).

1.1 The Product as a Combination of Technical and Service Characteristics

In their attempt to develop an 'explicit approach' to technical change, Saviotti and Metcalfe (1984) suggest that a product (a good) should be defined and represented as the conjunction of three sets of characteristics: service characteristics [Y], technical characteristics [X] and process characteristics [Z].

1.1.1 Services characteristics
Service characteristics (Y), which might also be called final or use characteristics, are considered from the user's point of view (from a Lancasterian perspective). In general terms, they are the services, or utility, provided to customers by the good in question. The examples Saviotti and Metcalfe give are very explicit. A car's service characteristics, for example, are its speed, size (number of passengers, luggage capacity), comfort (ventilation, radio) and reliability (safety). The principal characteristics of plastic (PVC) pipes are flow rate, maximum pressure, combustibility, weight, resistance to corrosion and average operational life (Saviotti and Metcalfe, 1984); those of a helicopter are maximum take-off power, maximum speed, size, etc. (Saviotti, 1996).

This notion could be further developed by hierarchising it and identifying the principal and supplementary service characteristics and the externalities, that is the undesirable characteristics associated with the product (in the case of a car, for example, pollution, noise, danger, etc.).

1.1.2 Technical characteristics
The (internal) technical characteristics (X) describe the internal structure of the technology. They represent the scientific and technological knowledge 'embo-

died' in the set of devices used to provide the service characteristics. According to Saviotti (1996, p. 64), they are the only characteristics that can be
modified directly by manufacturers. 'Thus a motor car manufacturer can only
design the engine and the shape of the car body in order to produce a required
speed, *but not produce directly that speed of transport*[1] otherwise this would be
a service provision (that provided by a taxi driver, for example) rather than a
manufactured good. Thus a car's technical characteristics denote its engine,
transmission, braking and suspension systems, and so on, while those of
plastic pipes include their physical, mechanical, thermal, electrical and chemical properties. A helicopter's technical characteristics include its rotor diame-
ter, power, type and number of engines, the materials it is made of, their
resistance and mechanical properties, and so on.

1.1.3 Process characteristics

The process characteristics (Z), finally, equate to the methods used to produce
the good in question and to the technologies and modes of organization deployed (the materials used, the means used to process them, the forms of
energy, the organization of the process, the competences mobilized, etc.).
Thus in the case of a car, the assembly line is a process characteristic. Although Saviotti and Metcalfe mention and define them, process characteristics
rapidly disappear from their analysis.[2] Indeed, in the case of goods, Saviotti
and Metcalfe (1984) take the view that 'the separability of product and process
technology is not complete but is a reasonable approximation in many situations'. Ultimately, the notion of the product they adopt incorporates only
technical and service characteristics (cf. Figure 2.1).

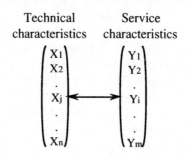

Figure 2.1 The product as defined by Saviotti and Metcalfe
Source: Saviotti and Metcalfe (1984).

1.2 Similar Approaches

In ascribing this notion of the product solely to the studies of Saviotti and
Metcalfe, we are undoubtedly acquiescing in the myth of origins (or even the

myth of paternity) that M. Callon (1994) denounces in his investigation of scientific discoveries and technological innovation. In fact, other authors have adopted a similar approach, in some cases with the same aim of measuring technical change.

1.2.1 A structural-functional approach to measuring techno-logy

We can cite, among others, Kenneth Knight's study (Knight, 1985) of the evolution of information technology. Knight advocates a structural-functional approach to measuring technology (Figure 2.2).

$$
F_n = \begin{pmatrix} F_{n1} \\ F_{n2} \\ F_{n3} \\ F_{n4} \end{pmatrix}
$$

F_{n1} = computing power (operations per second)

F_{n2} = the cost of the computing equipment (seconds per dollar of equipment cost)

F_{n3} = computing reliability (mean number of operations between failures)

F_{n4} = communication costs (seconds per dollar of communication cost)

Figure 2.2 A functional representation of a computer
Source: Knight (1985).

A given computer (n), for example, can be defined, according to Knight, as the conjunction of a functional description or model and a structural description or model:

1. *The functional description* denotes the vector F_n of the computer's per-formance in a set of functions (or tasks) that it has to perform. This re-presentation combines levels of service performance (utility) and costs. In this respect, it departs from the theoretical coherence of Lancaster's formalization (Lancaster, 1966), which is maintained in Saviotti and Metcalfe's approach. Indeed, these latter authors separate service characte-ristics from what they call the *economic environment* which, in the case of a car, for example, comprises the purchase price, maintenance costs, the price of petrol, etc.
2. *The structural model* denotes the description (in various levels of detail) of the components of the technical system. It is the equivalent of a 'produc-

tion manual'.

1.2.2 The product as a combination of functions and technologies

Another study that can be cited is that of H. Desmoutier (1992), which defines a product as 'a combination of functions and technologies'. Thus Desmoutier describes a watch as a combination of four possible *functions* (control, counting, display, energy) and four possible *technologies* (mechanics, electricity, electronics, radio) (see Figure 2.3).

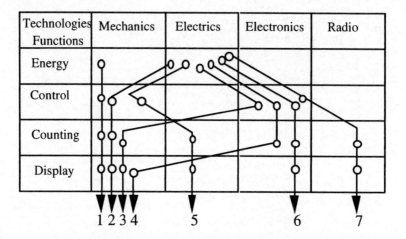

Figure 2.3 The various forms of watch
Source: Desmoutier (1992).

Form 5, for example, represents a watch whose energy, counting and display functions are all carried out by electrical technologies, while the control function is mechanical. The term 'functions' here denotes not service characteristics (or functions) in the sense adopted by Lancaster and Saviotti and Metcalfe, but rather technological sub-systems that correspond more to Saviotti and Metcalfe's definition of technical characteristics. Thus the term 'technologies' does not denote technical characteristics (in the previous sense) but rather broad disciplinary fields or scientific and technological paradigms.

Desmoutier identifies five types of technical innovations (which deserve more evocative names):

1. innovation in a sub-system (which according to him is the most important source of rupture), which involves using a different technology (for example, shifting from mechanical to electronic counting) in order to carry out a function, that is 'operate' a sub-system;

2. innovation in the manufacture of a sub-system (this is a process innovation that involves a change in the process used to produce a sub-system);
3. a change of system architecture, which involves linking the sub-systems in different ways;
4. the use of a new product-assembly technology;
5. a change in the number or nature of a product's functions – in the case of a watch, for example, water resistance, alarm, tachometer and stop-watch functions, illumination, etc.

We will discuss the forms of innovation in greater detail in the next chapter. We will confine ourselves here to noting Desmoutier's judgment (Desmoutier 1992, pp. 17–18) on the last type of innovation:

> In our view, this is the least interesting case since it is not linked to the technologies deployed except in the sense that it is the choice of a particular technology that makes it possible to change the number or nature of functions. For example, once watches began to have digital displays and in-built microprocessors, it became much easier to add functions (calendars or telephone numbers, measurement of heart rate or temperature, etc.).

We beg to differ. Assumed technological easiness should not tempt us to underplay the importance of this form of innovation. Desmoutier's argument seems to us to be based on a 'technology push' approach to innovation. To an even greater extent with services than with goods, it is important to reintroduce need and demand into the equation. As we shall see, these two points of view (the technology and demand perspectives) are very closely linked in Saviotti and Metcalfe's approach.

1.2.3 A Lancasterian approach for technological cluster definition

Zimmerman (1995) also adopts a Lancasterian approach to the product. He draws on Saviotti and Metcalfe's analysis in order to provide the formal framework for the notion of 'technological cluster', which is said to result 'from a bursting of the sectoral boundaries constraining the deployment of technologies, which opens up a multiplicity of possible development paths by creating the potential for new technological combinations capable of extending the range of applications' (p. 1266).

In order to construct this formal model (which we do not intend to develop here), Zimmerman adopts the following three spaces as means of describing any industrial activity (Figure 2.4):

1. a basic technologies space T, which encompasses the industrial know-how used in the production of goods;

2. a product or intrinsic performance space P, which encompasses a product's 'objective' qualities considered independently of the user's point of view (for example, the various chemical, electrical and mechanical properties of a carbon fibre);
3. a use characteristics space C, which encompasses a product's potential characteristics from the user's point of view (thereby marking a return to a Lancasterian perspective). It constitutes the end stage of the process whereby a 'universal product' is transformed into a product adapted to a specific need.

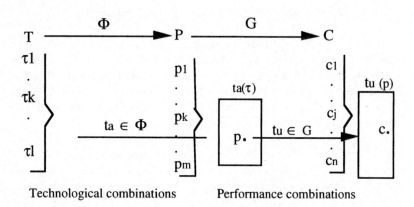

Technological combinations   Performance combinations

Figure 2.4 The general technology cluster model
Source: Zimmerman (1995).

This model does not differ fundamentally from that of Saviotti and Metcalfe, the only variation being the division of the technical characteristics vector or space into the basic technologies and intrinsic performance spaces. The differences that do exist lie more in the analysis of the linkages between these spaces and in the emphasis placed on the combinatory nature of these linkages. The three spaces are linked by two forms of relation:

1. a relation Φ between T and P, which produces performances. It encompasses the whole range of possible combinations of basic technologies that can be put together to produce specific performances. This relation is produced through the mediation of so-called *architectonic technologies* (t_a);
2. a relation G between P and C, which produces use characteristics. It encompasses the whole range of possible performance combinations that

can be put together to provide solutions for clients' needs. It is what Zimmerman calls *utilization technologies* (t_u) that make it possible to meet certain user needs by combining performances.

These utilization technologies are not necessarily the responsibility of the manufacturer of the product in question. According to Zimmerman, they can take various forms: user's handbooks, training and, more generally, the use of service activities, which suggests to him that these utilization technologies 'are the cause of one aspect of the rapidly growing importance of intangible elements in industrial activities, which are often too hastily interpreted as the 'tertiarization' of the economy' (p. 1272).

The fact that it takes account of certain service activities is the main reason why we have dwelt on this study here. However, services cannot be reduced to utilization technologies alone, which serve merely to provide 'downstream support' for an industrial good and are therefore subordinate to it. In fact, some services (notably knowledge-intensive services such as consultancy) can play a role at many other points in this model (on this point see Gallouj, 2002a, 2002b). In their role as providers of support (in some cases, very active and autonomous ones) for manufacturers or service providers, they are able to intervene at all levels of the model: at the level of utilization technologies, certainly, but also at those of the architectonic and basic technologies and of intrinsic performance as well. Moreover, and this is the hypothesis that underlies the present book, they can themselves be modelled along very similar lines, albeit with a few adjustments.

1.2.4 Similar approaches applied to services
A number of approaches of this nature applied directly to services were mentioned in Chapter 1, namely theories of financial innovation couched in terms of demand characteristics and those based on the distinction between core and peripheral services. These theories are in fact analyses of the determinants of innovation and take account only of the service characteristics vector. In this respect, they are close to Lancaster's original analysis. More broadly, mention can also be made here of the numerous attempts that have been made to apply the hedonic prices method[3] not only to goods but also to services, such as air transport, accommodation rental, etc. (Triplett, 1986).

1.3 Conclusion

To conclude this point, our use of Saviotti and Metcalfe's model as the main starting point for our own investigation can be justified in the following terms.

1. This model constitutes an attempt to extend the structural/functional

approach beyond a particular technology (computers or watches) so that it can be applied to any tangible good (artefact).

2.   It gives the product greater depth than theories of financial innovation and the various applications of hedonic methods. It is no longer reduced to its service characteristics, as it is in Lancaster's approach. The introduction of technical characteristics allows us to delve deeper into the 'black box' of innovative processes.

3.   It has a solid theoretical grounding. This model is not an ad hoc management tool (although it could become one) but is firmly rooted in economic theory.

However, this model, like most of the approaches and analyses outlined above, is given over exclusively to tangible artefacts. The authors give no consideration to its possible application to services. The ultimate implication is that only goods can 'render services'. This is a curious inversion of a problematic homonym (Hatchuel, 1994), with the term service denoting both a sector and a relationship and thereby reinforcing the notion that the (service) relationship exists only in the (service) sector.

If it is accepted, as has been suggested in some studies (Hatchuel, 1994), that the service relationship has long been at the heart of certain industrial processes and, more recently, at the heart of production processes in agriculture (Reboud, 1977; Muller, 1991; Le Roy, 1997), it may well be that such a model will have to be adapted if it is to retain its ability to give an account of certain industrial (or indeed agricultural) goods.

2. THE SPECIFICITIES OF SERVICES

Some experts on services have made considerable efforts in recent years to stress that goods are also defined by the 'services they provide' (Zarifian (1987); Bressand and Nicolaïdis (1988), etc.). However, while goods do indeed provide services, it should not be forgotten that services also provide services. Authors like Bastiat,[4] in the mid-19th century, or Colson,[5] in the 1920s, defined 'all capitalist relations as exchanges of service' (Delaunay and Gadrey, 1992). Our hypothesis is that the absence of technical specifications (in the traditional sense) certainly makes the task more difficult, but does not make it impossible to extend and adapt Saviotti and Metcalfe's approach to services. Before embarking upon this task, let us remind ourselves briefly what the (relative) specificity of services consists of.

Once produced, a good usually acquires an autonomous physical existence. It has a high degree of exteriority relative to the individual who produced it and the person who is going to consume it[6] (the anonymity principle, as neoclassical theory has it). Generally speaking, a service is intangible and does not have the same exteriority. It is identical in substance with those who produce it and with those who consume it (it cannot, therefore, be held in stock). It seldom exists outside of them. It is not a given result, but an act or process. By developing the metaphor of the 'service triangle', Gadrey (1996a) has helped to bring into general use the definition of a service as a set of processing operations [...] carried out by a service provider (B) on behalf of a client (A), in a medium (C) held by A, and intended to bring about a change of state in the medium C, 'but not leading to the production of a good able to *circulate economically* independently of the medium C'. Unlike goods, services do not give rise to the establishment or exchange of ownership rights (Hill, 1997), since no entity, that is 'a thing that has a real existence', as Hill (1997) puts it, is produced. The specific way in which services circulate economically clearly has consequences for innovation appropriation regimes in service industries.

This general definition conceals a certain number of analytical difficulties that will have to be taken into consideration in attempting to adapt Lancaster's approach to goods in order to use it for the analysis of services. Most of the difficulties outlined below are linked. Nevertheless, they are presented separately in order to facilitate the analysis and to allow certain slight differences to be pointed up.

2.1 The Difficulties of Product Standardization

In services, the product and, in consequence, the service characteristics vector $[Y_i]$ are not always fully 'formatted' or codified, that is precisely determined beforehand. However, this is also true in a way of certain tangible products that are made to measure: spectacles, for example, are produced to a whole range of highly personal specifications determined by the nature of the pathology to be corrected, individual morphology, aesthetic requirements, etc.

Each service transaction is unique (that is, it gives rise to a set of different service characteristics $[Y_i]$) in that it is produced in *interaction* with clients, in response to their particular (non-standardizable) problems and in an environment that is always different. Of course, this infinite diversity of possible representations of the 'product', which arises out of the variety of customers, environments, etc., is not to be confused with that particular form of variation known as innovation. The first is random, ephemeral and unintentional. The second is generally intentional (possibly a posteriori.[7] It is sufficiently discernible to reach the visibility threshold, can be isolated and adds to system variety, in Saviotti's sense of the term (Saviotti, 1988). In any event, any attempt to separate out these two phenomena requires that the focus of attention be shifted upstream towards the conditions under which the service is designed.

2.2 A product that manifests itself through its effects over time

In services, the 'product' can manifest itself through its effects over a longer or shorter time period (although this is also true, to a certain extent, of spectacles, which help to maintain or even to improve acuity of vision. In order to take account of this characteristic, Gadrey (1991) suggests that a distinction be made between:

1. a direct or immediate 'product', which equates to the very act of service delivery, that is to the (clearly identifiable) moment at which the service provider acts on the medium of service delivery: a consultation in the case of a doctor or lawyer, a visit to a garage owner, etc. and
2. an indirect or mediate 'product', which expresses the longer-term effects (results) of the service provided: a change in the state of health, legal situation, a vehicle's working order, etc.

Thus the question that now has to be answered is how this mediate output (not just for services, but also for 'durable' or 'semi-durable' tangible goods) might be incorporated into Saviotti and Metcalfe's model.

2.3 The Question of the Service Relationship

One of the fundamental characteristics of service activities, particularly 'knowledge-intensive' ones, is client participation (in various forms) in the production of the service.

Various concepts have been developed in order to account for this client involvement. These concepts, which are sometimes used as synonyms, are summarized in Table 2.1. In reality, they denote different aspects of the same phenomenon, and can be differentiated from each other by their theoretical substance.

Thus the notion of *interface* denotes the point at which client and service provider meet. In many cases, the interface is a physical place, such as a service counter, restaurant or office. However, the contact between client and service provider can also take place over the telephone or through a computer system or television set. It generally involves meetings between individuals or groups of individuals. However, it may also take the form of an encounter between the client and the service provider's technologies (for example, a bank's ATMs, ticket machines, etc.).

This interface is the site of *interactions* between customer and service provider, in the course of which information and knowledge, emotions, civilities, whether verbal or gestural, are exchanged and acts of 'reparation' (in Goffman's sense, 1968) are performed. This interaction, which concerns various elements, may be more or less intense. It is also an expression of relations of power, domination and mutual influence. The term *coproduction* generally denotes situations in which the interaction (essentially operational in nature) is intense and balanced. According to de Bandt (1996), it is to some extent synonymous with *cooperation.*

Table 2.1 Various ways of expressing customer involvement in the provision of services

Concept	Meaning
Interface	(Physical or virtual) point of contact between customer and service provider (or his technical systems)
Interaction	Exchanges of information, knowledge and civilities, performance of repair/rectification tasks
Coproduction	Extensive and balanced interaction (essentially operational)
Servuction	The process of creating a service by linking up various elements: the customer, the physical medium, contact personnel, the service, the system of internal organisation, other customers
Socially regulated service relationship	Manifestation of new forms of the social regulation of relationships between producers and consumers
Service relationship	'Mode of coordinating the actors on the supply and demand sides' for services or for goods. Operational relationships (coproduction) + social relationships for the control and regulation of action program

The three other terms (servuction, socially regulated service relationship and service relationship) have acquired the status of theoretical concepts. In management sciences, the neologism *servuction* denotes the process of producing a service (Eiglier and Langeard, 1987). The servuction system takes account of the relations between the following elements: the client, the physical medium, the staff in contact with the client, the service itself, the internal organizational system and the other clients. The notion of *socially regulated service relationship* (Gadrey, 1990) was developed as a means of examining services in terms of the social rules governing the relations between the agents involved in service situations. The edited collection referred to in the introduction to this book (de Bandt and Gadrey (eds), 1994) marks an important stage in the clarification and systematization of the notion of the *service relationship* as a 'mode of coordinating the actors on the supply and demand sides', not only for services but for goods as well. According to Gadrey (1994a), this service relationship comprises, on the one hand, operational relations or interactions (coproduction) and, on the other, social relations that control and regulate the action, whether contractually or by convention.

Whatever term is used, (interface, interaction, coproduction, 'servuction', socially regulated service relationship, service relationship), this link between service provider and client is the most important element that has to be added to Saviotti and Metcalfe's notion of the product if it is to embrace services and, more generally, the rise in the real power (or at least awareness) of the service relationship in the economic system as a whole (including the manufacture of industrial goods).

2.4 A Product that Cannot always be Separated from the Process

In the case of goods, the distinction between product and process – analytically useful but sometimes difficult to effect – is generally accepted. The same does not apply to services. This difficulty is illustrated by a number of postal surveys conducted recently in various European countries, which produced contradictory and unreliable results as to the relative importance of the different types of innovation in the various countries (Djellal and Gallouj, 1999). Any attempt to establish clear-cut boundaries between the various types of innovation is fraught with formidable empirical and theoretical problems. In many cases, the 'product' in services is in fact a process: a service package, a set of procedures and protocols or an 'act'. In reality, this designation depends on conventions. If the protagonists believe that the product they are paying for and from which they are benefiting is the immediate act of service delivery, then process and product are virtually one and the same thing.

Our own survey on innovation in services, already referred to in the previous chapter (Djellal and Gallouj, 1998, 2002) confirms the difficulty, in France, of distinguishing product from process. However, although no definitive conclusions can be drawn, examination of the responses to the open-ended question in our questionnaire on the listing and description of concrete examples of innovations suggests that, in the majority of cases, the following analytical distinctions are being used more or less systematically:

•   A new service function (new service characteristics, new service specifications) based on existing processes and systems is considered to be a pro-

duct innovation.
- An existing service function (existing service characteristics, service specifications) drawing on new systems or processes is generally considered to be a process innovation.
- When the service function and corresponding process are both new, the problem of assigning an innovation category is more difficult. However, most of the managers who replied to our questionnaire regarded this as a product innovation. It can therefore be concluded that, in this case, process innovation is being underestimated.

In other words, on the whole, product innovation covers situations in which the process component is unchanged but the functional specifications are new as well as those in which both components (processes and functionalities) are new.

2.5 A 'Product' that Can be Analysed at a Multiplicity of Heterogeneous Levels

This characteristic is, of course, a logical consequence of those outlined above and of the very diversity of services in terms not only of the mediums, or 'targets' (Bancel-Charensol and Jougleux, 1997), of delivery (goods, money, individuals, knowledge, etc.) but also of the operations to which the medium is subjected (repair, management, care, transfer, etc.).

In the case of goods, the level of analysis (that is of representation) is generally considered to be self-evident, the object of analysis being an artefact. With services, things are quite different. Service activities have hazy, unstable boundaries that have to be specified afresh each time. A certain number of questions has to be asked. For example, what is the unit of activity under consideration? Is the object of analysis (or representation) the service provider and client as organizations, groups or isolated individuals? What approach should be adopted in the case of services made up of packages of goods and services?

2.6 The Correspondences between Vectors of Characteristics

Even though they may be very complex, the correspondences between the technical characteristics [X] and service characteristics [Y] of goods are well known. They figure in the handbooks or user manuals that accompany manufactured products. They may be the subject of laboratory experiments. Even though they may not be evident to the user, they are well known to experts. They constitute the very foundation of any attempt to repair a good, the aim being to detect failings in the service characteristics of the good and to trace right back along the correspondence between technical and service characteristics until the faulty technical system is identified.

In the case of services, and particularly those in which the intangible and relational aspects are important, the correspondences between the competences brought to bear by the service provider and the 'product' certainly exist (one simply has to compare the effect on service characteristics [Y] of a competent service provider with that of an incompetent provider), but they are generally much hazier and much more difficult to codify: they are to a large extent tacit and subject to the difficulties caused by informational asymmetry (cf. C. Gallouj, 1997b). For these reasons (and others), it is not always possible to restore a service that has been provided to its proper or former state. In some cases, however, it is possible. Indeed, if the service provided can be regarded as a maintenance or repair service (in Goffman's sense, 1968), then it may be that an inadequate service can be 'repaired' by a second intervention (e.g. by the mechanic to whom one entrusts one's car).

3. SERVICES AS A SET OF CHARACTERISTICS: AN EXTENDED NOTION

In order to take account of the specific characteristics of services, we intend to adopt two different approaches. One involves an attempt to transpose to services the concepts developed solely for analysis of goods, while the other seeks to add new elements to Saviotti and Metcalfe's theoretical framework.

3.1 Extending the Notion of Service Characteristics to Services

As we have already noted, extending the notion of service characteristics to services does not pose any conceptual problems. Just like goods, services provide services (or service characteristics). The difficulty lies in the designation and evaluation of these characteristics. While we undoubtedly have to accept that the extended notion should be implemented more flexibly (by distinguishing between various scenarios, or by dealing individually with particular categories of services), it nevertheless remains a very productive heuristic tool, as we shall see. The question of extending the notion of service characteristics to service activities is one that cannot be addressed in the same way or with the same degree of ease (or difficulty) for all 'products'. In consequence, it is necessary to examine the question differently for different categories of 'products'. Several factors seem to affect the ease with which the service characteristics of service activities can be identified:

1.	the service provider's level of skill or competence (that is, to simplify matters, his or her level of education, the intellectual qualities of the knowledge he/he draws on, etc.);

2. the extent to which the product is standardized, that is the degree of codification and formalization;
3. the nature of the medium of service delivery (knowledge, information, individuals, materials).

For the sake of convenience, we will adopt only the first two criteria, which are of considerable importance to any consideration of innovation; by combining them, it is possible to construct a typology of services that can be used as a basis for discussing the question of extension (see Table 2.2). It should be noted that this typology is similar to that used by Salais and Storper (1993), which also takes as its starting point the product and the producer's skills (see Chapter 6).

This typology is not a typology of service industries but of the 'products' of those industries, even though in some cases a single 'product' is representative of a given industry. In other words, the problem of identifying the service characteristics may be posed in different terms in the same industry or even the same firm, depending on the product under consideration or the concept of the product that is privileged. This typology is based on two general hypotheses:

1. The more standardized the 'product' is, the easier it is to identify or to describe the service characteristics. Indeed, standardized products are characterized by a 'mandate' (in the sense of the term used by Girin, 1994) that is generally precise and whose terms (the processes brought into play and/or the results striven for) can be codified.
2. The higher the skill level is, the more difficult it is to identify the service characteristics.

However, this typology has certain limitations which do not, for all that, undermine the value of the exercise we are seeking to carry out:

1. The skill or competence criterion is sometimes difficult to put into practice. For example, what is the nature of the skill possessed by a great cook? Consequently, the service characteristics of some craft activities may be difficult to identify.
2. The four quadrants highlighted in the table cannot necessarily be associated with four particular modes of designating service characteristics. For example, what we call quasi-goods (those that can be easily formalized) are to be found in both quadrant A (standardized product, high skill level) and quadrant B (standardized product, intermediate or low skill level). Quadrant B also includes a particular category, namely 'packages', that merits specific examination, as well as mass operational or manual services. Quadrant D (non-standardized product, high skill level) is relatively

homogeneous: for the most part, it includes intellectual and professional services. As far as quadrant C is concerned (non-standardized product, intermediate or low skill level), we propose to examine informational and relational services separately from manual and operational services.

Table 2.2 A typology of 'products' by degree of standardization of service provision and service providers' skill level *

	Non-standardized product (custom-made)	Standardized product
High skill level (professional)	**Quadrant D: Intellectual or professional services** Consultancy (by consultants, bankers, insurers, etc.), Health, Education, Research	**Quadrant A: Quasi-goods** Software, Expert systems,Teleuniversity/distance learning, Telemedicine
Intermediate or low skill level	**Quadrant C: Operational or manual services (craftsmen), informational or relational services** Post office (counter services), Cleaning (self-employed individuals/small firms), Caretaking (self-employed individuals/small firms), Taxi services, Traditional restaurants, Home help services for the elderly	**Quadrant B: Quasi-goods + packages + mass operational or manual services** *Services that put technical capacities at users' disposal:* Automatic cash dispensers and ATMs, Self-service franking and postage, Information and customer guidance booths in supermarkets, Automatic car washes, Automatic food and drink dispensing machines, Car rental *Quasi-goods (strict sense):* Insurance policies (as a set of guarantees), Financial products, Package holidays (brought from brochures) *Packages + mass operational or manual services:* Catering (restaurant chains), Large-scale retailing, Hotels (chains), Postal services (delivery rounds), Public transport, Cleaning (large firms)

Notes:* This table contains examples of 'products' and of perceptions and concepts of products and not of individual industries. Consequently, the various products or product concepts falling within the scope of a single industry are to be found in different quadrants.

3.1.1 Quasi-goods and the service characteristics vector

This category, which is found in quadrants A and B, comprises devices and, more specifically, 'capacities' that are placed at users' disposal. Their service characteristics do not seem to be any more difficult to identify than those of an artefact, making it relatively easy to allocate them a service characteristics vector.

This category includes, firstly, the use on a self-service basis of actual goods and equipments. Some examples are automatic cash dispensers and telling machines, self-service franking machines in post offices, ticket machines (train, underground, aeroplane), information and customer guidance points in supermarkets, the interactive booths operated by the French state employment agency and child benefit offices, etc. Thus the service characteristics of an ATM will equate to the various operations it enables users to carry out (deposits, withdrawals, balance enquiries, ordering cheque books, etc.) and to the system's user-friendliness. Those of a database might include elements relating to the nature and quantity of the available data and the mode of access. These devices are nothing more than technical 'capacities' made available to users. The only way in which they differ from traditional manufactured goods is in their ownership regime and modes of use. A manufactured good is owned privately and consumed 'individually', while these devices are used collectively.

Secondly, it includes rental services of any kind (car rental, for example) whose main characteristic is that they make available technical capacities (and the corresponding service characteristics) on a temporary basis.

Thirdly, it also includes quasi-goods in the strict sense of the term, that is services that are defined *or perceived as* relatively well formatted and standardized 'products'. The most obvious examples are financial products, insurance policies (sets of guarantees) and package holidays (sold through brochures). As far as monetary and financial instruments are concerned, Tobin[8], for example, takes the view that the main service characteristics constitute a finite set, some of the principal elements of which are liquidity, divisibility, reversibility, yield, earnings, anticipated projected value, ease of exchange, risk, etc. In the case of insurance, they include all the specifications contained in the policy (and which are often simplified in advertising material). Such a concept of the product is, of course, restrictive, since the service is not confined simply to the 'policy' but includes its execution and management over time. In other words, the service characteristics contained in the policy do not fully describe the service delivered. Any attempt to take account of the service in its entirety would mean adopting a different concept of the product to that considered here. We will examine this less restrictive concept of the product in Section 3.1.3 below.

3.1.2 Operational or manual services

These are services, whether standardized or not, with a low intellectual content (generally delivered by relatively unskilled individuals) that often involve the processing of a material medium (quadrants B and C). The service characteristics of activities such as cleaning, caretaking, fast-food restaurants, staff canteens and the transport of goods and people do not seem to pose any major difficulties either. They are more problematic when the product is not standardized (quadrant C), which is often the case in small craft enterprises. When the product is standardized (quadrant B), the service characteristics are easier to identify since in a way they have already been designated by the service provider himself, standardization being in effect synonymous with the codification of procedures and/or of results.

Thus the service characteristics may well be set out in relatively simple turns in the terms and conditions specified in contracts. In the case of cleaning services, for example, they would include the cleaning of such and such a surface, at such and such a time and at such and such a speed. In his in-depth investigation of ISS, one of the largest contract cleaning companies in the world, Sundbo (1996) notes that:

> Contractualization was – and remains – IIS's most important instrument of production. A contract is concluded with each client. This contract is not a simple legal instrument defining price and responsibilities. The main purpose of each contract is to lay down a production schedule. The contract specifies in detail the various service activities that are to be provided, when and where.

The service characteristics of the use of taxis or public transport (even, to some extent, of aeroplanes, although in this case there is an increase in the technical content and intellectual dimension) can be represented as those of the means of locomotion used (the speed, comfort and safety of the car or bus), to which should be added other characteristics linked in particular to the competences mobilized by the service provider (driver), such as knowledge of the (optimal) journey, driving skills, quality of the relation and of communication, saving of one's own energies, etc.

3.1.3 Informational and relational services

This category embraces, for example, certain aspects of banking, insurance and postal services (quadrant C). The analytical perspective adopted here is different from that used in the case of quasi-goods (see quadrant B). It is not insurance policies as quasi-goods, financial products or the transport and distribution of mail (delivery rounds are highly programmed and their final characteristics are relatively standardized) that are the object of analysis here but rather the service interactions that accompany them. It does not seem impossible to identify the service characteristics of a relationship established at the service counter of a bank, insurance agency or post office. Indeed, this type of organization has marketing departments dedicated to the very task of refining these characteristics. Very crudely, this vector can be said to comprise elements relating to the effectiveness and efficiency of the various components of transactions (depositing money, withdrawing cash, ordering cheque books, etc.) that are concluded under satisfactory conditions (with reasonable speed, civility, etc.). In the case of banking and insurance services, the analysis has to be modified slightly in order to take account of the rise over recent years in the qualificational levels of those providing the services (it is not uncommon in France for graduates of second-stage university courses to be recruited as counter staff). This rise in qualificational levels is reflected in the increasingly important role of the sales and advice services offered by counter staff. Thus banking and insurance services are tending to migrate from quadrant C to quadrant D of Table 2.2.

When it comes to the most complicated configurations of these last two service categories (operational or manual services and informational and relational services), it can be illuminating to construct models of service provision (a procedure known as 'flowcharting' or 'blueprinting', cf. Shostack, 1984; Lovelock, 1992; Kingman-Brundage, 1992). These models are similar to a service production 'manual' (see on this point Section 3.5 below).

3.1.4 Intellectual or professional services

These are generally non-standardized services requiring high qualificational levels on the part of the service providers (health, education/training, consultancy) (quadrant D). It is in this category that the difficulty of extending the notion of service characteristic is greatest. Nevertheless, we will not abandon our attempts to do so, since any such extension has considerable heuristic value that will be of assistance in our investigation of innovation. Several possible expressions of the characteristics vector of intellectual services can be envisaged (our main concern here being with consultancy services).

[Y] is a vector of contractual or conventional objectives to be achieved. The task of approximating the vector [Y] of service characteristics could also be approached in several different ways:

- General (theoretical) definitions of the activity in question could be used as a basis for inferring the general objectives of the activity. In the case of consultancy services, for example, 'their objective is to provide advice and assistance with a view to solving problems and reducing the uncertainty inherent in decision-making' (Greiner and Metzger, 1983).
- The starting point could be a definition of objectives (what are called briefs or remits). Thus the purpose of recruitment consultancy is to

select, on behalf of the client, an individual with certain predefined characteristics and possibly to monitor his or her integration into the firm.

- A third approach would be to draw on some of the terms used in the call for tenders issued by the client, the proposal drawn up by the service provider and the contract concluded between the service provider and the client. It can reasonably be assumed that the principal's involvement in defining the terms of reference may shed light on a remit that seems, a priori, confused or obscure.

[Y] is a vector of characteristics equating to various stages in a process. In general terms, the definitions of the service to be provided can also be used here, this time as a sequence of phases. This is the approach used in the ISO certification procedures adopted by some consultancy companies. For example, consultancy is an activity whose objective is :

- to analyze a problem within a company,
- to put forward a solution and
- to take part in the implementation of that solution.

In more concrete terms, recruitment consultancy is generally defined as a combination of several successive activities:

- analysis of the need,
- selection of a method of approach appropriate to the recruitment profile,
- selection of the most suitable candidate,
- monitoring and integration of the selected candidate.

Each of these phases can be considered as a service characteristic Y_i expected by the client. As we will see, these service characteristics are based on specific methods (technical characteristics X_j).

[Y] is a vector of competence characteristics. Since consultancy can be defined as an activity involving the transfer of knowledge, a vector of service characteristics equating to certain characteristics of the competences of the service providers and the client organization can also be envisaged. These characteristics are undoubtedly a little more difficult to formalize, but formal qualifications, references, etc. provide a possible starting point.

Another way of looking at recruitment consultancy, in which one of the main outputs is the individual recruited, is to consider the new recruit as a set of competences of various kinds and consequently to take into account, for example, his or her experience, education, capacity for adaptation, etc. If this formulation is adopted, it is self-evident that the innovation lies not in the renewal of the service characteristics [Y] thus defined (they are exogenous, determined by the labor market) but in the renewal of the consultants' competences [C], methods and technical systems [X-Z].

3.1.5 Packages
This category encompasses hotels and catering, large-scale retailing, transport and tourism, for example, which can be regarded as packages of goods and services (quadrant B). One of the trickiest problems is the selection of the unit of analysis. If the service is a package of units (whether goods or services), the task of representing it in terms of characteristics (and that of constructing models of innovation) can be considered on two levels.

1. In general terms, the various goods and services included in the package can, by analogy, be regarded as service characteristics in their own right. In other words, they can be defined in terms of their principal function (sleep quality, hygiene, leisure and security for, respectively, the bed, the bathroom, the television and the safe in a hotel room) (cf. Figure 2.11, Section 3.5).
2. More specifically, focusing on each individual good and service in the package, we return to Saviotti and Metcalfe's initial representation in the case of the goods and to our extended representation in the case of each of the services. Thus the provision of a television set in a hotel room can be broken down into technical characteristics [X] and service characteristics [Y].

Innovation can also be considered on two levels:

1. within the system as a whole: for example, when a service characteristic or function (in fact a good or a service) is added or when one service characteristic (the service provided by a colour television) replaces another (the service provided by a black and white television);
2. in each of the sub-systems represented by a service or a good. In the second case (the good), the innovation is not generally produced by the hotel service provider but by other actors. Nevertheless, it influences the 'technological' evolution of the service.

The following two observations will serve to conclude this section on extending the notion of service characteristics to services:

1. The distinction between core and peripheral services can be applied without difficulty to the service characteristics of a service. This makes it possible to identify not only the core and peripheral service characteristics but also externalities, that is associated undesirable characteristics (for

example, queues and contact with 'problem' populations at post office counters).

2. The distinction between immediate and mediate services (see Section 2.2 above) can be translated here into a distinction between direct or immediate service characteristics ('the act of service delivery') and the indirect or mediated service characteristics (the subsequent results, whether expected or not).   From the user's point of view, the final or use characteristics are characteristics relating to the perceived quality or 'qualifications' of the product, as assessed by the user.   What we are dealing with here is either the user's definition (or his or her 'point of view') of the *direct product* (obtained or expected) or his/her definition of the *indirect product* (obtained or expected).   Table 2.3 is an attempt to depict this distinction.   From the heuristic point of view, there is no difficulty in combining these two aspects in the same vectoral representation.

Table 2.3 Taking account of the distinction between direct and indirect product

Product components Time frame of analysis	Product defined by use characteristics	Internal technical characteristics of production process	Competences deployed (both internal and external characteristics)
Immediate service (activity, process) including user's possible activity	Immediate uses (during and on completion of service delivery)	Technical characteristics of the process	Competences deployed by service providers and clients during service provision
Over a period of time *Service + User + Environment + Random events*	Long-term uses, deferred uses, (where applicable)	Relevant aspects of the environment in which the service is consumed	Ability of users to derive long-tem benefit from the service

Source: Gallouj, Gadrey and Ghillebaert (1996, 1999).

3.2 Technical Characteristics, Process Characteristics

The technical characteristics of goods are those *internal* characteristics of tangible systems that *directly* provide a service.   In the case of services, they are both 1) the *tangible* technical characteristics (particularly of information technologies, but also of logistical technologies, chemical products, e.g. in cleaning services, etc.) used to produce the service characteristics, and 2) what we shall call the *intangible* technical characteristics: legal or financial expertise, mathematical instruments (economic and financial modelling, operational research methods), consultants' methods or the (adaptable) standard contracts used by legal advisers, for example.

Daft and Macintosh (1978) propose a thought-provoking typology of technologies, in which they combine two parameters: on the one hand, the variety of tasks involved and, on the other, the degree of precision, clarity and intelligibility of tasks from the point of view of the person delivering the service (Figure 2.5). It should be noted that this distinction is fairly close to that drawn by Girin (1994) between the simplicity or complexity of a commission and its precision or vagueness.

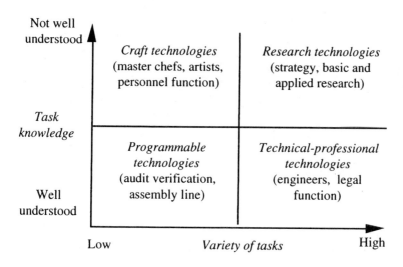

Figure 2.5 Typology of 'technologies'
Source: Daft and MacIntosh (1978).

This typology comprises four types of technologies:

1. *craft technologies* characterized by low variety and intelligibility of tasks. Examples would include the technologies deployed by master chefs, artists or those at work in the 'personnel' function;
2. *technical-professional technologies* characterized by high variety and intelligibility, for example, the technologies deployed by engineers, the legal function;

3. *programmable technologies* (low variety, high intelligibility) such as audit verification procedures, assembly lines;
4. *research technologies* (high variety, low intelligibility); examples might include strategy formulation and basic or applied research.

The technical characteristics of services (with the exception, to some extent, of transactions that make use of self-service equipment, such as ATMs in banks) cannot claim the *interiority* that is a feature of those of tangible systems. One of the major features of service activities is undoubtedly the fact that the 'technologies' involved usually take the form of knowledge and skills embodied in individuals (or teams) or recorded in written form (method manuals, instruction books, etc.) and implemented directly when each transaction occurs, rather than in physical plant or equipment. Section 3.3 below is given over to the question of the distinction between competences and intangible technical characteristics. Similarly, it is difficult to separate technical characteristics from process characteristics. Nevertheless, there is no question of excluding them from the conceptual framework, as Saviotti (1996) decided to do. It is possible to envisage two different ways of getting round the problem of distinguishing between technical and process characteristics:

1. The view can be taken that, in services, they are one and the same thing, in other words that the processes in all their tangible and intangible forms are, as it were, (partial) replacements for internal technical specifications. This amounts to an assumption that, while the distinction between product and process can be considered a reasonable approximation in the case of goods, as Saviotti and Metcalfe (1984) suggest, this is not true of services.
2. The reference to the interface can be used as an instrument of discrimination. Thus the technical characteristics will be those of the (tangible and intangible) front-office technologies (i.e. that part of the organization in direct contact with customers) and the (tangible and intangible) back-office technologies will be described as process characteristics. This solution seems to us more satisfactory than the first one, for several reasons. Firstly, of course, it goes beyond a mere acknowledgement of impotence. Secondly, and more importantly, its discriminatory power is based on the notion of *service relationship* which, as we have already stated, is of fundamental importance to our approach. It is the proximity of the technology in question to the customer that is the basis for the distinction between technical characteristic and process characteristic. These interface or front-office technologies, mobilized by the service provider, by the client or, more generally, by both at the same time, supply certain service characteristics directly to the customer, and in that respect have something in common with the internal technical specifications of goods. Home

banking is undoubtedly the archetypal example of this scenario, in which all the customer has to do is 'press a few buttons' in order to obtain the service he or she requires. ATMs, an insurance salesman's computerized simulator, self-service franking machines and the various methods used by consultants are other examples. On the other hand, the mainframe computers servicing an insurance company or bank or postal sorting systems fall more within the sphere of process characteristics. Despite its pertinence, this solution does not resolve all the difficulties in practice, and particularly not those located on the boundary between front and back-office, especially in the current situation in which some service firms are trying to eliminate that boundary altogether.

For the sake of convenience, however, we shall adopt the first solution in the rest of this book. Whatever approach is adopted, *processes lie at the heart of product analysis*. As we shall see, this finding is of the utmost importance for the study of innovation (in services).

In reality, we should also be able to take account of certain 'organizational' and spatial characteristics. In some cases, indeed, it is organizational characteristics that embody the service, just as tangible technologies constitute the essence of goods. It is necessary, therefore, to include these organizational and spatial characteristics in the vector (X-Z) of technical and process characteristics. One example might be the décor of a restaurant, which produces those service characteristics [Y] linked to 'ambiance' or aesthetics. Similarly, spatial or geographical organization can be regarded, as Moulaert, Martinelli and Djellal (1990) suggest, as a component of the service provision that produces service characteristics (for example, the proximity or accessibility of service establishments).

To summarize, what is termed here a technical characteristic (denoted by the term [X-Z] or henceforth, for simplicity's sake [T]), differs in content from the term used by Saviotti and Metcalfe. It embraces tangible front-office technical characteristics (which are fairly close to technical characteristics [X] in Saviotti and Metcalfe's sense), tangible back-office technical characteristics (which are fairly close to Saviotti and Metcalfe's process characteristics [Z]), intangible back-office or front-office technical characteristics (which do not exist in Saviotti and Metcalfe's framework) and possibly, organizational and spatial characteristics.

3.3 Adding in the Competences Mobilized (by the Service Provider)

For goods as for services, technical characteristics are knowledge, *competences* embodied in tangible (or intangible) systems. However, the provision of a service (i.e. of service or final characteristics) is generally the result of a combination of the following two mechanisms: the utilization of (tangible or intangible) technical characteristics that are themselves based on competences, and the *direct* mobilization of competences (i.e. without any technological mediation). We propose adding to Saviotti and Metcalfe's framework all the competences [C] mobilized by the service provider (cf. Figure 2.6).

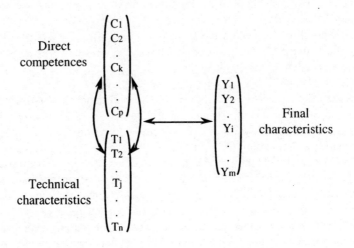

Figure 2.6 A representation of a product or service as a system of characteristics and competences
Source: based on Saviotti and Metcalfe (1984).

A product (good or service) is therefore represented by a set of final (or service) characteristics (Y_i). Each Y_i indicates the 'level' of a characteristic i. These final characteristics are obtained by a certain combination of technical characteristics (T_j), with each Y_i being obtained by a certain subset of the T_j. Similarly, each technical characteristic mobilizes the competences C_k (certain competences may involve the ability to combine different technologies); in certain situations, those same competences may be mobilized directly.

The specific characteristic of service activities (or of some of them at least) is that the provision of the service may take place without a good or set of goods (material artefact) being supplied. Knowledge and competences embedded in individuals may be directly mobilized in order to obtain a certain set of final characteristics. Figure 2.7 constitutes a particular case of Figure 2.6, and depicts the ideal-type configuration of a 'pure', 'intangible' service (whether it be an intellectual service, such as consultancy, or a manual one, such as some aspects of cleaning that merely involve emptying waste-paper baskets or even remedial massage, when the masseur uses only his hands). It also clearly illustrates the following statement by Baumol (1967, p. 416):

> In some cases [mainly manufacturing industries] labor is primarily an instrument – an incidental requisite for the attainment of the final product – while in other fields of endeavor [for example services], for all practical purposes the labor is itself the end product.

In this type of configuration, the ability to provide a service $[Y_i]$, and the quality of that service, depend crucially on the ability to implement and organize the various competences required, which is why, in certain services,[9] the design of organizational systems, and innovation in that area, is extremely important. The strategic importance of the vector $[C_k]$ in the case of 'knowledge-based' services is obvious, since it is the greater ability to mobilize competences that is the main argument in favor of using the external service provider.

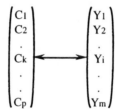

Figure 2.7 The case of a 'pure', 'intangible' service

This question of competences merits separate investigation, a starting point for which is provided by the following two questions:

1. what is the nature of these competences?
2. what distinguishes these competences from intangible technical characteristics?

3.3.1 The nature of the competences
This is not of course the place to carry out an in-depth investigation of the notion of competence. We will confine ourselves here to listing a few general characteristics that will give some idea of the enormous diversity of the components making up vector [C]. Despite this diversity, the various methods for evaluating competences developed and used by specialists in human resource management (the Hay method, for example), and perhaps also ISO norms in the case of consultancy services, suggest that hope of 'measuring' this vector of competences should not be abandoned entirely.

The 'vector' [C] of competences mobilized in service delivery is made up of *individual* competences or those of a small group, that is the team involved in the delivering the service in question. However, some of these are also shared competences, which belong therefore to the organization as a whole.

These competences [C] are derived from various sources: initial education, continuing training, experience and, more generally, interaction. They can be codified, that is they can be reduced to messages that can be diffused at zero cost, but in many cases, and particularly in services, they are also tacit, that is not easily transferable and indissociable from the individual. Whether codified or tacit, these competences can be roughly classified into several types: scientific and technical competences (cognitive competences); internal and external relational competences (depending on whether the relations in question are those within the team or those with the customer or other players in the provision of the service), combinatory[10] or creative (i.e. those that combine technical characteristics into coherent sets and subsets) and operational (or manual) competences.

In many operational or 'manual' services (cleaning, for example), these 'operational' competences occupy a key position. Thus the diagram shown in Figure 2.7 [C] <——> [Y], which establishes correspondences between a vector of competences and a vector of service characteristics, encompasses both pure intellectual services (consultancy, for example) and operational services in which operational competences predominate (cleaning, some services for the elderly). The provision of cleaning services (without the use of sophisticated technical systems) involves the direct mobilization of simple operational competences (use of a broom[11], emptying of waste bins into a refuse sack, etc.) in order to provide certain service characteristics. If, on the other hand, the cleaning service relies on sophisticated tangible technologies (robots, complex chemicals, etc.), we go back to the diagram in Figure 2.6, since there is some increase in the complexity of the vector of competences (competences in the use of technical systems, chemicals, etc.).

3.3.2 Competences and intangible technical characteristics

As we have already stressed, it is important to distinguish the vector of competences from that of intangible technical characteristics. Intangible technical characteristics [T] are (systems of) codified and formalized competences. They are used by the individual (or group), and thus require the mobilization of individual competences [C], but are independent of them. They exist independently of individuals and constitute the various elements that make up organizational memory.

In the case of recruitment consultancy, for example, knowledge of psychology, knowledge of the firm, know-who, etc. are all components of the vector of competences [C], whereas job analysis methods, selection tests, candidates' or clients' files, etc. are intangible technical characteristics that ensure the survival of the consultancy company independently of the individual consultants (who may leave at some time in the future). These intangible technologies can be sold as end products.

In a static model, competences and intangible technical characteristics are linked by a relationship already alluded to above, namely the mobilization of competences in order to bring technical characteristics into play. In a dynamic model (and we shall return to this point when discussing models of innovation in next chapter), another relationship emerges, one that equates to the change of state in certain C_k or combinations of C_k. These competences undergo a socialized process of codification, through which they come to form the organization's 'cognitive maps' (Argyris and Schön, 1978); this formalization shifts them away from the level of individual competence towards that of organizational competence. In this way, they become intangible techniques (T) of which all members of the organization can avail themselves.

3.4 Adding Customer Competences in order to Take Account of the Service Relationship

The customer is absent from both Figure 2.6 and Figure 2.7. However, as has already been noted, the customer's participation, in one way or another, in the production of a service (coproduction, service relationship) is one of the major characteristics of service provision (and is increasingly shared with the production of certain industrial and agricultural goods).

Thus we propose to introduce into our diagrammatic representation a distinction between two types of competence: those of the service provider (column vector $[C_k]$) and those of the client (linear vector $[C'_k]$). The coproduction relationship, therefore, is represented by the combination of the terms of the two vectors (Figure 2.8). Thus demand theory is present not only on the side of the service characteristics (in accordance with Lancaster's analysis) but also on the side of the customer competences mobilized through the service relationship.

$$ \overline{C'_1\ C'_2 .. C'_k .. C'_q} \begin{pmatrix} C_1 \\ C_2 \\ . \\ C_k \\ . \\ . \\ C_p \end{pmatrix} \longleftrightarrow \begin{pmatrix} Y_1 \\ Y_2 \\ . \\ Y_i \\ . \\ . \\ Y_m \end{pmatrix} $$

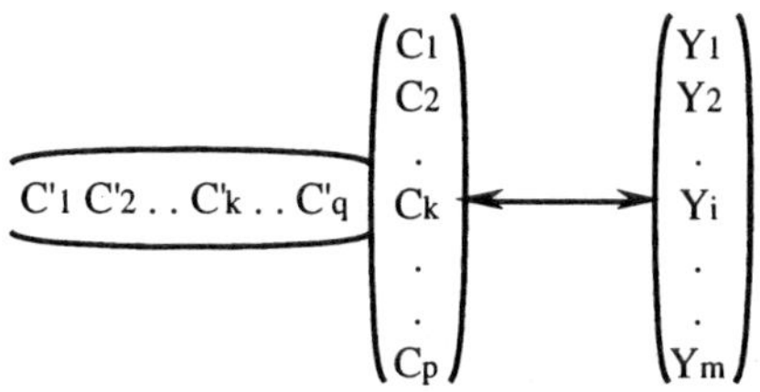

Figure 2.8 The case of a 'pure' service (including coproduction relationship)

There are several reasons for taking account of this client/provider interface (Gadrey and Gallouj, 1998). Firstly, it may itself be the subject of innovations (organizational changes, interface management methods, etc.); secondly, it is the 'laboratory' where a form of innovation often neglected in economic analysis, ad hoc innovation (cf. Chapter 1 and 3), is initiated; finally, the quality of the client's (individual or firm)[12] competences (C'_1 C'_2....C'_k) is one criterion for the success of innovations and technology transfer (in the broadest sense). In this respect, it may be useful to make a distinction within the vector [C'_k] between the technological competences of the client firm (i.e. the areas of knowledge in which it has expertise) and its capacity to absorb and assimilate new competences.

3.5 The General Formulation and an Investigation of some Specific Applications

3.5.1 The general formulation of the product
Figure 2.9 depicts the most general possible representation of the product, whether it be a good or a service. The various scenarios and specific configurations considered previously are encompassed by this general formulation.

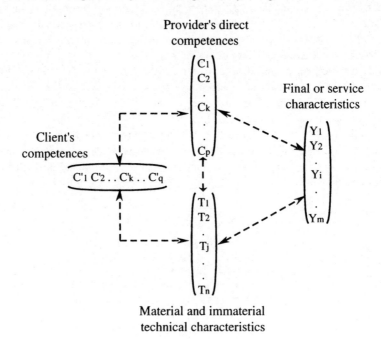

Provider's direct
competences

Client's
competences

Final or service
characteristics

Material and immaterial
technical characteristics

Figure 2.9 The most general form

This formulation of the product can be read as follows. In the most general configuration, the service characteristics are obtained by mobilizing simultaneously (internal and external)[13] competences and (tangible and intangible) technical characteristics.

Various scenarios can be envisaged, in particular the following:

1. Saviotti and Metcalfe's initial configuration [T] <----> [Y], in which the final characteristics are obtained through a certain combination of technical characteristics;
2. the 'pure' service configuration, in which (internal and external) competences are directly mobilized in order to produce the service characteristics;
3. the self-service type of configuration, represented by the system $\{[C'_k], [T_j], [Y_i]\}$, through which consumers make direct use of their own knowledge and competences in order to provide themselves with a service. The animating principle in this configuration is the provision of technical capacities to consumers. It involves putting customers themselves to work in various ways within the providing organization: self-service situations (large retail outlets, fast-food restaurants, self-service banking, etc.), hire of various items of equipment (vehicles, for example), etc. In general, the competences mobilized in self-service situations (those of customers) are (or tend to be) less tacit or more 'simple' than in other cases. What happens, in effect, is that relatively simple competences are mobilized in order to produce pre-programmed, formatted services or service characteristics.

3.5.2 Some specific applications

As a heuristic tool, this general representation of the 'product' can be applied without too much difficulty to the most complex of the service situations we have previously considered (Section 3.1).

Consultancy. It is, for example, entirely consistent, with the classic definition of consultancy drawn up by Greiner and Metzger (1983) (our parentheses and emphases). According to these authors, consultancy consists of:

services provided to organizations by *specially trained and qualified personnel* (C), who objectively and independently help *the client organization* (C') to *identify* (Y_1) problems, *analyze* them (Y_2), *recommend solutions* (Y_3) for the problems and, if requested, help them *to implement those solutions* (Y_4).

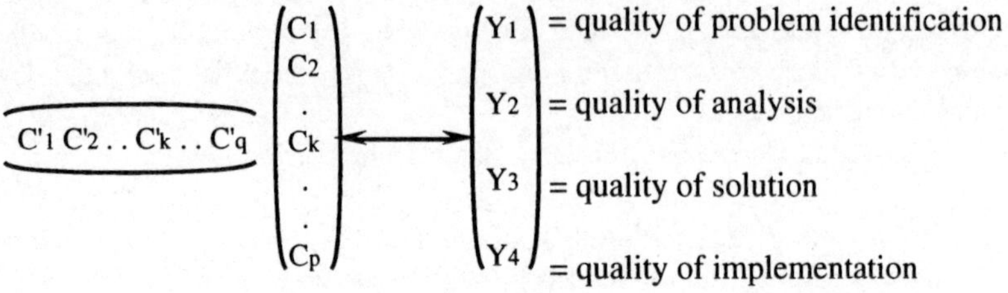

$$\overline{C'_1\ C'_2\ ..\ C'_k\ ..\ C'_q}\quad \begin{pmatrix}C_1\\C_2\\.\\C_k\\.\\.\\C_p\end{pmatrix}\longleftrightarrow\begin{pmatrix}Y_1\\Y_2\\Y_3\\Y_4\end{pmatrix}$$

Y_1 = quality of problem identification

Y_2 = quality of analysis

Y_3 = quality of solution

Y_4 = quality of implementation

Figure 2.10 A possible representation of the provision of consultancy services

This general diagram (Figure 2.10), to which the vector [T] of technical characteristics should be added, is a flexible one. It covers the following specific configurations:

- [C]<---->[Y] illustrates a relation of the subcontracting type, in which the customer plays little part. He confines himself to setting up and monitoring the service provision.
- [C'][C]<---->[Y] represents a coproduction relation, in which the customer participates actively in the provision of the service.
- [C][C']<---->[Y] illustrates a coproduction relation in which the balance of power tends to favor the customer. In this case, the service provider symbolized by the vector of competences [C], which is no longer 'at the centre' of the representation, will be regarded as carrying out an essentially maieutic or Socratic activity, his task being to help the client himself to define the nature of his problems and to develop his own solutions.
- [C'][C]<---->[Y]
  [T]
  introduces the use of technologies, particularly, intangible ones: methods.

Insurance services. As already noted (see Section 3.1 above), the provision of insurance services can be considered from at least two different analytical points of view.

1. The simplest is that of the quasi-good, in which each insurance policy sold can be defined in terms of its entire set of specifications, that is the guarantees it contains (set of service characteristics);
2. The second, more complex and more realistic perspective is that of the process of service provision as a whole, that is the sale of the contract and the whole set of potential transactions that sale may trigger, such as the payment of compensation (or the provision of repair services) in the event of loss or damage.

These two analytical perspectives are combined in the general representation depicted in Figure 2.9.

The vector [Y] represents, firstly, the specifications of the insurance policy (quasi-good), in the sense of the term used in theories of financial innovation. The service characteristics of the repair services (approved repairers, etc.) provided in the event of the risk being realized, or even the guarantees on time limits, etc., should also appear here. It is not difficult to understand (and we will return to this point) why a service characteristic corresponding to a 'guarantee on time limits' cannot be added without improvements to both the competences [C] and the technical characteristics [T] (tangible and intangible technical characteristics, process and organizational characteristics).

[T] equates to the back-office or front-office computer systems used when policies are registered, claims are settled, etc. The back-office systems are more akin to process characteristics [Z], while the front-office systems are analogous to technical characteristics in the strict sense of the term [X].

[C'][C] – the relationship between customer and service provider – is very episodic and rudimentary in the case of mass market insurance services (which fosters the view that insurance policies are quasi-goods), involving just the taking out of a policy (purchase), the payment of premiums and possibly the payment of compensation in the event of loss or damage. It has to be recognized, nevertheless, that insurance brokers are engaged in essentially 'relational' activities. These relationships become genuine coproduction relationships in the case of customized policies (particularly those produced for large companies).

Packages. In the case of services of the 'package' type, such as those provided by hotels, adoption of the simplifying hypothesis advanced in Section 3.1.5 above, whereby each good or service in the package can be reduced to its main function (or service characteristic) gives rise to the (incomplete) representation depicted in Figure 2.11, which is constructed on the basis of the analysis in Wind et al., 1992 (see next Chapter).

In order not to overload the next figure, we have not attempted to link the various characteristics in any systematic way. Nevertheless, by way of illustration, it can be said that the 'security' service characteristic brings into play in particular the competences of the security personnel and the following 'technical' characteristics: safe, video surveillance, smoke alarm, etc.

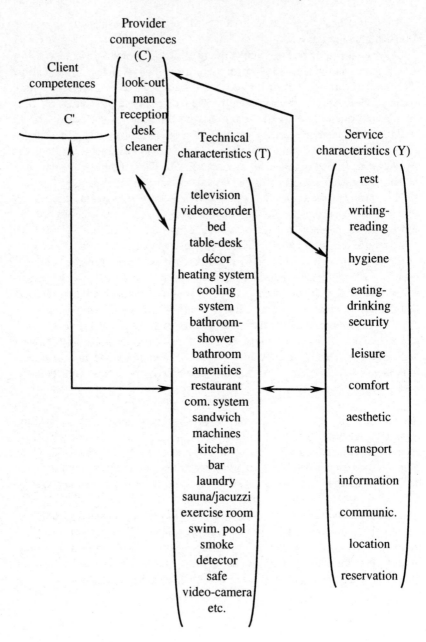

Figure 2.11 Service provision in hotels

(Non-knowledge-intensive) services. As has already been noted, in the general case of (non-knowledge-intensive) services, attempts to construct this extended Lancasterian approach to services can also draw on the closest thing to a services 'production manual', namely blueprints or flow charts of service provision (an example is provided in Figure 2.12). It should be pointed out, however, that these blueprints are concerned more with technical and process characteristics than with final characteristics. L. Shostack (1981, 1984) has undoubtedly made the greatest contribution to knowledge of these concepts and instruments, whose value she defends in normative terms. However, other authors, including Lovelock (1992) and Kingman-Brundage (1992), have also helped to develop this type of construction, both empirically and theoretically.

J. Kingman-Brundage (1992) makes a distinction between two types of blueprints of service provision: a *'concept blueprint'*, which provides a general overview of the service, showing the way in which each function or department fits into the overall service, and a *'detailed blueprint'*, which describes the service in detail.

The blueprint is task-oriented, that is it represents the basic acts performed by those involved in the process of service provision. However, it also describes both a process (a set of actions or tasks performed with the aim of obtaining [Y], that is the desired service characteristics) and a structure [T] (physical installations, organizational structures, computer systems, etc.). In the general theoretical blueprint, the structure is represented by a vertical axis on which are shown the service firm's internal management functions, support functions and the interaction with the client. Various lines of 'demarcation' or interaction are plotted between the various elements of the structure (a client interaction line, a 'visibility' line separating what is traditionally called the front-office from the back-office, an internal interaction line, etc.). The process is represented by a horizontal axis on which are shown the various successive basic actions performed by those involved in providing the service.

Such a blueprint can have many functions involving different departments in the service firm. It is a tool that enables the customer to 'picture' the service he is being offered, in the same way as the future owner of a house under construction might consult the architect's plans. In its simplified versions, therefore, the blueprint can be used as a communication and marketing tool. It is also a tool that enables the service provider to enhance his understanding of the service he provides and to control quality more effectively. Thus staff training can be based on the blueprint, particularly when new services are being launched. In a way that is, paradoxically, both Taylorist and non-Taylorist, it defines each individual's role in the process at the same time as enabling each individual's function to be located within the system as a whole. Finally, it is a tool for improving the service provided (incremental innovation). Incremental improvements cannot be identified when an ill-defined service is delivered informally. Thus the blueprint provides development managers engaged in implementing such improvements with the reference points they need. The blueprint can also be considered as a sort of prototype.

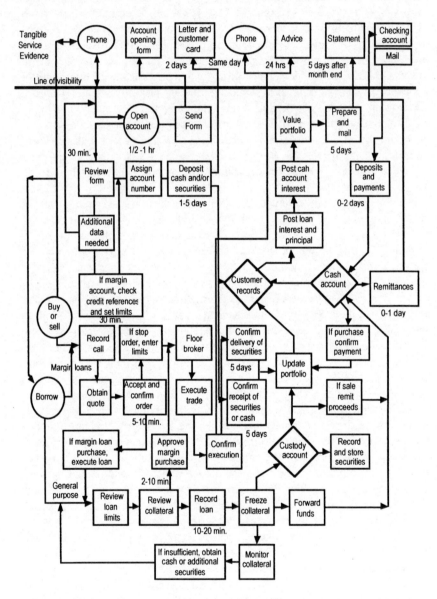

Figure 2.12 The blueprint of a discount brokerage service
Source: Shostack (1984).

CONCLUSION

We bring this chapter to a close with a statement of the following six conclusions.

Conclusion 1: Our basic idea is that the absence of technical specifications in the usual sense of the term does not prohibit (although in some cases it may make more complex) the use of a Lancasterian approach to services. Indeed, what are technical characteristics (in the traditional sense) if they are not technological knowledge embodied in an artefact? What is there to prevent the characteristics associated with competences embodied in individuals or in methods (intangible technologies) from playing this role in the case of services?

Conclusion 2: In a way, the extended notion of the product we have just put forward satisfies the 'nomenclature' hypothesis posed by neo-classical theory. Establishing conventions for the designation of service characteristics should make it easier to define and differentiate 'service products'. On the other hand, the hypotheses that there is no interaction between production and consumption and that the product is 'anonymous' are most certainly called into question by our general approach. Indeed, the linkage between customer and service provider (particularly tacit) competences vectors symbolizes this interaction, while at the same time releasing the product from its anonymity and showing it to be heavily dependent both on those who produce it and on those who consume it, as well as on the various uses to which it is put (consumption environment).

Conclusion 3: This approach highlights the distinction (which is so important in services) between undertakings to make available resources (which here bring into play competences [C] and technical and process characteristics [T]) and undertakings to produce results (which relate to service characteristics [Y]).

Conclusion 4: The approach outlined here can be applied to both goods and (external and internal) services. This conclusion is grounded in the following five statements:

1. our approach is an adapted version of a formalization originally developed by Saviotti and Metcalfe and applied to goods;
2. goods produce lasting effects, which are services;
3. 'the service model' plays a part in the production of many goods. This long-established fact is new only in the sense that researchers have recently become aware of it... (Hatchuel, 1994);

4. despite the homogenizing role played by technical specifications ([X] in the strict sense), goods themselves are always different from each other in one way or another. That this is so is not a new idea. Chamberlin expressed it in the following terms as long ago as 1953 (Chamberlin, 1953, p. 114):

    > It is of the utmost importance at the outset to realize that there is literally no such thing as a given product. Products are actually the most volatile things in the economic system – much more so than prices. To begin with, almost every 'product' has a variable element, at least in the circumstances surrounding its sale: convenience of location, peculiarities of shop environment, personalities, service, methods of doing business, etc.

5. the service characteristics independent of internal technical specifications are, increasingly, essential components of many goods. To use Saviotti and Metcalfe's example, cars are increasingly being designed as hybrid products, in which pure service characteristics play a not insignificant role (cf. Figure 2.13): for example, the addition of assistance contracts (Y_{m+1}) or the extension of guarantee periods (Y_{m+2}). These elements serve to enrich the vector of service characteristics $[Y_i]$. However, their implementation depends on new technical characteristics $[T']$ and new competences $[C]$ that are extrinsic to the car as an artefact. Moreover, they involve the client $[C']$ to a greater extent.[14] By the same token, the scope for innovation is extended, as we shall see.

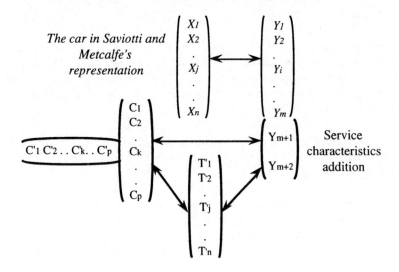

Figure 2.13 The car as a good-service hybrid

Conclusion 5: However, this approach does not allow us to apply the following two propositions derived from Saviotti and Metcalfe's representation to services:

- Proposition 1: two goods with the same technical characteristics necessarily have the same service characteristics. They are *two identical goods*. To use a biological analogy, two goods with the same genotype could be said to have the same phenotype.
- Proposition 2: two goods can have the same service characteristics without having the same technical characteristics. In this case, we are dealing with two competing technologies.

Proposition 1 is refuted in the case of services. In other words, two services with the same technical (and competence) characteristics (same genotype) do not necessarily have the same service characteristics (phenotype). This is due to several factors: 1) the variations produced by the involvement of customers (and of their environment) in service provision; 2) the nature of the technologies (and competences) mobilized in services, which are even more tacit and idiosyncratic than in the case of goods. In the case of services, proposition 2 should be formulated as follows: two services with the same service characteristics rarely have the same technical and competence characteristics. The reasons for this are those put forward in the critique of proposition 1.

Conclusion 6: The general approach outlined above could provide a stimulating basis for revealing the multiplicity of different modes of innovation in services from a neo-Schumpeterian perspective. In an attempt to define the service relation, Gadrey (1994a) warns against a possible confusion between 'the intensification of service relations' (or closeness) and improvement of the service provided. While closeness is often intended to improve the service as well, the reverse is not true.

> There are other ways for a service firm to provide a service adjudged to be superior than to establish closer relations with its clients: adapting the technical, spatial or architectural framework of service delivery, providing technical tools for use on a self-service basis (...), diversifying the services and solutions offered to customers, greater professionalism, reducing malfunctions and mistakes, etc.

All the arguments advanced in this quotation can be interpreted in terms of our general approach to the 'product':

1. 'the intensification of service relations (that is the forging of stronger

links with clients)' equates to the relationship [C']<---->[C] that links customers' competences with those of service providers;

2. 'adapting the technical, spatial or architectural framework of service delivery' has its counterpart in the improvement of the technical characteristics [T], that is – as already noted – both the technical characteristics [X] and the process characteristics [Z] in Saviotti and Metcalfe's sense of the term;

3. 'providing technical tools for use on a self-service basis' describes the relation [C']<---->[T]<---->[Y] between client competences, technical characteristics and service characteristics;

4. 'diversifying the services and solutions offered to customers' concerns service characteristics [Y] primarily, but also affects the system as a whole;

5. 'greater professionalism' equates to the evolution of competences [C];

6. 'reducing malfunctions and errors' has its counterpart in the reduction of external service characteristics (externalities).

In sum, innovation may arise out of the (positive or negative) 'dynamic' of the vectors of characteristics: [T] in its various forms, [C], [Y], [C'] or any combination of these various vectors. We turn in the next chapter to a more systematic examination of the various innovation models that may result from our approach based on characteristics vectors.

NOTES

1. The emphasis is ours.
2. There is no reference at all to them in Saviotti's most recent publication on this topic (1996).
3. This method is based on a notion of the product as a set of quality characteristics or levels. It consists of a multiple regression analysis that seeks to evaluate the prices associated with these various quality characteristics (cf. Griliches, 1961; Triplett, 1986).
4. Bastiat, F. (1851), *Harmonies économiques*, Paris: Guillaumin, 2nd edition.
5. Colson C. (1924), *Cours d'économie politique*, Paris: Gauthier-Villars et Alcan.
6. Unless it is a good custom-made for someone and not readily transferable to anyone else (e.g. spectacles, machine tools, customized software, etc.).
7. This is the case, for example, with what in consultancy activities we call ad hoc innovations (see Chapters 1 and 3).
8. Unpublished manuscript on monetary theory, Chapter 2, 'Properties of Assets', cited in Greenbaum and Haywood (1971).
9. Those described in a recent book by Jacques de Bandt (1995) as 'informational services'.
10. What Henderson and Clark (1990) call architectural competences.
11. Although in this case, the broom might be considered a technology falling within the scope of the vector [T].
12. This applies to business services, as well as to certain household services (health, education, etc).
13. These are, respectively, 1) competences embodied in those employees of the providing company engaged in service delivery and 2) competences of the individual customer or of members of the client organization.

14. The analysis could be made even more complex if it were assumed that a car's use (or service) characteristics are heavily dependent on other service characteristics (which might be described as external use characteristics): those of petrol stations, of various categories of motor engineers, or repairers, etc.

3. Models of Innovation derived from a Characteristics-Based Approach

INTRODUCTION

If the approach to the product (good or service) outlined in the previous chapter is accepted, innovation can be defined as any change affecting one or more terms of one or more vectors of characteristics (of whatever kind – technical, service or competence). These changes are brought about by a range of basic mechanisms: evolution or variation, disappearance, appearance, association, dissociation or formatting (in the etymological sense of giving shape to or imposing a format on an ill-defined element). They may be 'programmed', that is intentional, the product of R&D, design and innovation activity, or 'emergent', that is the fruit of natural learning mechanisms.

In this book, innovation is seen not as an outcome but rather as a process. Thus our concern is not so much with 'forms' of innovation as with 'modes' or 'models' of innovation that *describe the particular dynamics of characteristics* (those listed in the opening paragraph). The notion of the 'product' advanced here has the advantage, as we have already noted, of not excluding processes (and thus analysis of innovation processes). Nevertheless, the models of innovation outlined here are not articulated around the problematic dichotomy of product and process innovation. The representation adopted here has a further advantage: it breaks with the distinction between radical and non-radical innovations by introducing different modes of product improvement (learning, or the addition of characteristics).

Drawing on the characteristics-based approach and the empirical material at our disposal, we will attempt, firstly, to identify the main models of innovation at work not only in service activities but also in manufacturing and, secondly, to examine the possible links between these various models.

1. SIX MODELS OF INNOVATION BASED ON A DYNAMIC OF CHARACTERISTICS

Saviotti and Metcalfe (1984) identify five types of technological change:
1. change in the absolute values of X_j;

2. change in the weightings of X_j;
3. change in the topography $(X_j) \longleftrightarrow (Y_i)$;
4. change in the weightings of Y_i;
5. change in the absolute values of Y_i.

For our part, we are concerned here not solely with technological changes but with innovation in a broader sense, in all its tangible and intangible aspects. The notion of the product we have adopted provides the basis for such a broader approach to innovation. Thus six models of innovation can be identified: radical innovation, ameliorative innovation, incremental innovation, ad hoc innovation, recombinative innovation and objectifying or formalization innovation (the first two reflect a distinction traditionally made in the economics of innovation).[1]

These various models of innovation are not always unconnected. They are linked to each other in various ways that need to be clarified (see Section 2.1 below). The terminologies used to denote these models can give rise to ambiguity, since they contain both judgements on the degree of novelty or originality (the extent of innovation) and indications as to the procedure leading to the design (or emergence) of the innovation. For us, the most important thing is that these various models highlight the existence of different dynamics of characteristics. In other words, our models of innovation describe the emergence and evolution (that is, the 'life') of characteristics. These various forms of 'action' on the characteristics of a product are summarized in Table 3.1 and then examined in greater detail.

Table 3.1 The various models of innovation and the dynamic of characteristics

Innovation models	*Nature of the 'action' on the characteristics*
Radical	- Narrow definition: creation of a new set of characteristics {[C'*], [C*], [T*], [Y*]} - Broad definition: creation of a new set of characteristics {[C'*], [C*], [T*]} even though [Y] remains unchanged
Ameliorative	Increase in the weight (quality) of characteristics
'Incremental'	Addition (or elimination) of characteristics
Ad hoc	Production of new competences [C]; codification and formalization of [C], that is the transformation of [C] into [T] (intangible technical characteristics)
Recombinative	Combining or splitting of groups of characteristics
Formalization	Formatting and standardization of characteristics

1.1 Radical Innovation

What is involved here is the creation of a totally new product, that is a new set of characteristics and competences $\{[C'^*], [C^*], [T^*]^2, [Y^*]\}$. This new set and the set $\{[C'], [C], [T], [Y]\}$ are separate from each other. In other words, the new product's final and technical characteristics $[T^*], [Y^*]$ are different from those of an old product; new competences $[C^*]$ are introduced that did not exist in the old products. It should be noted that the competences $[C']$ are also renewed, since the more radical the innovation is, the more necessary it is to teach the client to adopt and use it. This is a 'competence destroying' mode of innovation, to use the expression coined by Tushman and Anderson (1986).

This definition is the narrowest and most exacting. In many cases, the term 'radical innovation' is also applied to those innovations that replace all the $\{[C'], [C], [T]\}$, that is the 'internal structure' or its equivalent, even if it leaves the service characteristics $[Y]$ unchanged (to a certain extent), at least in absolute terms (it is rare for the 'levels' not to change at all). The transition from horse-drawn carriages to motor vehicles was a radical innovation, even though to a certain extent the service characteristics remained the same, that is individuals were still transported with certain degrees of comfort, safety and speed...

The design and marketing by insurance companies of care and assistance products (Europ Assistance, for example) may, for example, be seen as a radical innovation that has changed the entire system. Companies offering these products are no longer selling life insurance, savings or damage insurance products but are actually providing services. The technologies used are different (alarm, monitoring, communications and transport systems, social networks, specific commercial networks) and the service characteristics are different: it is no longer a case of making a money payment when a specified event has taken place, but rather of providing a more or less complex service (housing, health care, transport, etc.). The service provider's competence vector, and to a certain extent that of the client as well, are also modified of course.

In insurance itself, radical innovations might include, for example, policies offering cover for totally new risks: the emergence of new vehicles requiring insurance (electric vehicles) or the identification or, more precisely, the social construction of new events to be insured against (therapeutic risk).

In the sphere of legal consultancy, a radical innovation would be, for example, the identification of and entry into a new area of expertise (by various means, including the accumulation and exploitation of expertise and the perfection of new methods). Examples might include, in their time, patent law and the law on information technologies, space, environmental protection, etc.

The cleaning industry has also seen a radical innovation, described as 'computer cleaning'; the term denotes not the use of IT in the provision of cleaning services, but rather the cleaning of computer systems. This new service, which constitutes an entry into an unusual area of activity for cleaning companies (strategic materials), has required a multiplicity of changes that amount to the development of a new set of characteristics and competences: recruitment and training of technicians (professionals of a good level, with adequate communication skills), changes in working hours (the service is provided during office hours) and the development by the company's technical department not only of a trolley suited to this kind of cleaning service but also of special chemicals, techniques for spraying air and sucking up dust, cleaning methods (scripts), etc.

1.2 Ameliorative Innovation

Product 'improvement' or enhancement can take a multiplicity of different forms. As we will see, other models of innovation share the objective of product 'improvement'. This applies, for example, to incremental, ad hoc and formalization innovation. The model we describe as 'ameliorative innovation' is based on a narrow definition of improvement, which does not in any way change the structure of the system {[C'], [C], [T], [Y]} but involves simply an increase in the value or weight (or quality) of certain service characteristics $[Y_i]$. This rise in the quality of the service characteristics can be produced either directly, by improving certain competences C_p, or by improving certain technical characteristics T_j. This is a 'competence enhancing' form of innovation, to use Tushman and Anderson's term (1986), which is a result more of the learning effects that normally accompany any activity ('joint product learning process', in the words of D. Foray, 1994) than of innovation in the strict sense of the term. Nevertheless, this type of innovation cannot be ignored: the extent and cumulative nature of its effect on overall productivity are widely recognized.

In the insurance industry, for example, learning effects have led to the more rapid payment of compensation in the event of loss or damage.

In our view the studies of Desai and Low (1987), which are well known in financial economics, offer an illustration of this ameliorative model of innovation (although learning phenomena play no role in them). These authors are concerned with financial assets and define them in terms of two characteristics, namely access (liquidity) (L) and return (yield) (R). The diagram thus constituted (Figure 3.1) makes it possible to locate and describe existing assets.

Since reference assets A and B are characterized by a low return and high liquidity and a higher return and low liquidity respectively, Desai and Low consider the development of asset C as a 'trivial innovation', since the distance between A and C in terms of characteristics, as measured by the angle

(OA, OC), is small. On the other hand, asset D is an 'important innovation', since it fills an 'empty space' between the two reference assets.

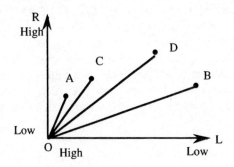

Figure 3.1 Representation of financial products in a diagram of characteristics
Source: After Desai and Low (1987).

1.3 'Incremental' Innovation

This mode of innovation also describes an improvement to the product. In this case, however, the improvement takes a different form, since it involves the addition (and possibly also the elimination) of characteristics. Thus in our approach, *incremental* innovation is understood in its original meaning of innovation produced through the addition of *increments* rather than in the broader sense of the term generally used in economic theory, which encompasses the various modes of innovation (including ameliorative innovation) that cannot be classed as radical innovations. Indeed, one of the advantages of the characteristics-based approach is that it enables us to make precisely this distinction. Thus in the case of incremental innovation, the general structure of the system {[C'], [C], [T], [Y]} remains the same, but the system is changed marginally through the addition of new elements to the vector of technical characteristics [T] and/or to the vector of service characteristics [Y] or through the substitution of elements.

This may involve, for example, the addition of one or two new characteristics to a certain type of product, either by directly mobilizing certain competences or by adding new technical characteristics. It may also involve the improvement of certain final characteristics (increasing the weight, the value or the quality of certain Y_i), or a reduction in production costs by adding or changing certain technical characteristics T_j. Thus it can be seen that ameliorative and incremental innovations, whose great importance in practice is widely recognized, can take various forms and may or *may not* be based on technical advances in the usual sense of the term. Figure 3.2 offers a pictorial representation of the difference between incremental and ameliorative innovation.

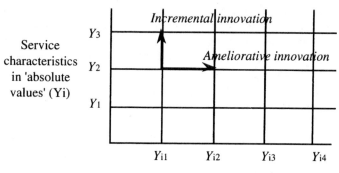

Figure 3.2 The distinction between incremental and ameliorative innovation*
Note: *Considered solely from the point of view of service characteristics, for simplicity's sake.

It is undoubtedly difficult, however, to mark out the boundary between the ameliorative and incremental modes of innovation, that is to distinguish the point at which a new characteristic is added from that at which a simple improvement is made. If we turn again to the example of the settlement of an insurance claim, how can an improvement in the time taken to pay compensation be distinguished from the addition of a guarantee on settlement times? It is often the desire to formalize the improvement as a new specification that makes the difference: the transition from one mode to the other can, therefore, be interpreted as a social construction or convention.

Another way of distinguishing these two similar modes of innovation is to remember that ameliorative innovation takes place continuously (learning effects), while incremental innovation is discontinuous (that is, it proceeds bit by bit).

Another problem with the determination of boundaries can be mentioned at this point. Incremental innovation can be seen as a particular case of recombinative innovation, which we will examine below.

In the insurance industry (cf. Gadrey and Gallouj, 1994), incremental innovations are commonplace. The basic form of the contract remains unchanged, but certain specifications or options can be added or taken away. Thus there are always opportunities to introduce new guarantees, to diversify the product by grafting a range of options on to the same stem.

Comparable examples can be found in the cleaning industry, where optional service characteristics can be added on to or taken away from the basic service (frequency of vacuum cleaning, washing office floors or simply dusting) (Sundbo, 1996). As the firm evolves, new service characteristics (or modules) are added to the basic service.

Checkout packing services in supermarkets and the introduction by car-hire companies of computer-aided route selection services can be regarded as incremental innovations. There are plentiful examples of this type in the hotel and air transport industries, among others.

It should be noted, finally, that product reliability agreements, indeed any kind of guarantee on goods and, more generally, what the management literature calls 'services around goods' (Furrer, 1997), may also fall within the scope of this incremental model.

As far as this incremental innovation model and the previous one (the ameliorative innovation model) are concerned, this line of argument can be pushed even further. Firstly, the distinction between the improvement and the addition of core or supplementary characteristics, already alluded to above, can be introduced.

Secondly, the distinction drawn by Baily and Gordon (1988) between 'proportional' innovations, which increase the quantity and/or the quality of the service characteristics (that is the product's performance, for example, a computer's power, processing speed or memory) in proportion[3] to the cost of the resources deployed, and 'non-proportional'[4] innovations, which increase performance by more than the cost of the resources used, may prove to be useful from this point of view. Thus if it is assumed that the cost of production can be reduced to the cost of the technical and process characteristics, a proportional innovation can be said to be one that changes the service characteristics[5] by the same 'proportion' as the technical and process characteristics, while a 'non-proportional' innovation, conversely, would be one that changes them by a disproportionately greater amount.

These two situations are depicted in Figure 3.3 below, in which C (Q, β_0) is, in a given technological context β_0, the cost function associated with the production of a given good defined by the quantity of technological characteristics or functions it incorporates (Q). The shift from A to B is equivalent to a 'non-proportional' innovation (more service characteristics Q_1 for less cost C_1), while that from A to G denotes a 'proportional' innovation (the cost increases 'at the same time' as the quantity of service characteristics).

'Non-proportional' innovations seem to be particularly common in services. Easingwood (1986), for example, makes a distinction between change and innovation in the 'software' dimension (what we call service characteristics [Y]) and change and innovation in the 'hardware' dimension (what we call technical characteristics in the strict sense [X] and process characteristics [Z]). The originality of most new services lies in the intangible 'software' dimension, while the 'hardware' dimension remains unchanged. For example, an airline might introduce a ticket with new conditions attached to it (a software change). However, this new product will be supplied by means of the same aeroplanes, the same crews, the same reservation systems, etc. In other words, 'software' innovations will tend to proliferate in services. This excessive development of new characteristics (what biologists call hypertely) may, in some cases, cause difficulties for firms and their customers, particularly with the learning process, and consequently discourage customers and employees alike.

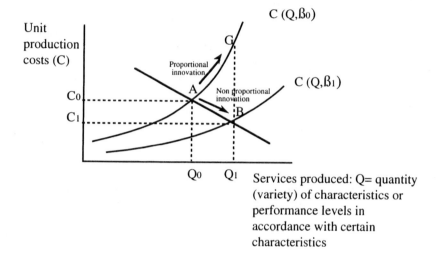

Figure 3.3 'Proportional' and 'non-proportional' innovation
Source: After Baily and Gordon (1988).

1.4 Ad hoc Innovation

Ad hoc innovation (which was mentioned in Chapter 1 and will be re-examined here from the point of view of the dynamic of characteristics) can be defined in general terms as the interactive (social) construction of a solution to a particular problem posed by a given client. It is a very important form of innovation in consultancy services[6], where the available knowledge and experience accumulated over time are harnessed and put to work synergistically in order to create fresh solutions and new knowledge that changes the client's situation in a positive and original way. Mention can be made, by way of example, of the many new legal arrangements that can be accommodated in the gaps in the system, or the development by various categories of consultants of especially novel strategies that give their customers a certain competitive advantage.

It is at the client/provider interface that this form of innovation is mainly produced. In fact, ad hoc innovations are often produced jointly by the service provider and the client. They usually appear during the normal process of delivering the service and are frequently not recognized as innovations until after the service has been provided. Thus they are a form of 'non-programmed' innovation (Zaltman et al., 1973) that might be described as 'emergent'.

The service characteristics $[Y_i]$ (output) of an ad hoc innovation can be seen as an original solution, or a set of original solutions, of an organizational, strategic, legal, fiscal, social or human nature that emerges in response to a (partially new) problem. From the point of view of the service provider, an ad hoc innovation helps to produce new knowledge and competences that have to be codified and formalized in order that they might be re-used in different circumstances. There is thus a significant change in the vector of competences $[Ck]$, and particularly in the intangible elements of the technical characteristics $[Tj]$. This a posteriori codification and formalization of certain elements of a given solution in order that it may be partially and indirectly reproduced is what distinguishes ad hoc innovation from the ad hoc nature of many service transactions.

In particular, the existence of this interface helps to limit the reproducibility of an ad hoc innovation in its original form. However, the knowledge, the experience (whether codifiable or not) and the tacit, idiosyncratic techniques that emerge from practical experience and the methods used to produce and transfer them can be reproduced. Ad hoc innovations are profitable, even if they are not reproducible, since they are based on an informational and cognitive input that can be transferred in part to other ad hoc situations.

What is generally known as customized innovation can be included in both incremental and ad hoc modes of innovation. In the case of the insurance industry, for example[7], 'adaptive customized (or tailor-made)' innovations, in which a standard contract is tailored to suit a particular client (or often a whole market segment) by changing the rates or introducing certain additional clauses, could be included in incremental category. On the other hand, 'fully customized (or tailor-made)' innovations, in which a genuinely new contract is drawn up for a specific client (often a large company), and 'cover for special risks', in which insurance is provided against a risk that might affect very small populations (for which no statistics are available) would be included in the ad hoc category, since the ad hoc element is much more significant.

Ad hoc innovations are often said to be invisible, since it is difficult to specify their service characteristics. It is equally difficult to pin down consultancy itself, since its boundaries are not easily defined, but nobody would conclude from this that it does not exist. Ad hoc innovation represents a definite change of state compared with the routine provision of consultancy services, and finds concrete expression in attempts to formalize the experience acquired. The difference between ad hoc innovation and the change inherent in the provision of all consultancy services is that it marks a non-random, permanent change of state that is mediated through the codification of the experience acquired and, in many cases, through an expansion of a firm's organizational memory. This clearly sets it apart from the random changes that take place in the configurations of consultancy service provision (as a result of variations in the environment, in clients, etc.).

1.5 Recombinative innovation

As the name suggests, recombinative innovation (Foray 1993)[8], or what Henderson and Clark (1990) call architectural innovation, relies on the basic principles of combining or splitting final and technical characteristics. This form of action on a product's characteristics leads to the relatively routine production of innovations within the framework of a given technological trajectory or technological and cognitive base. This mode of innovation is based on the systematic re-use or 'recycling' of existing 'components' or characteristics, which does not preclude the creation, in some cases, of radically new 'products' (requiring specific competences, design work and a certain degree of creativity). Incremental innovation, that is innovation based on the addition of characteristics, can be regarded as a form of recombinative innovation, particularly when the characteristics added have their origins in pre-existing products. There are two other possible forms[9] which, in the field of services, have been particularly highlighted by Bressand and Nicolaïdis (1988). The first involves the creation of a new product by combining the characteristics of two or more existing products (Figure 3.4), while the second involves the creation of new products by splitting up an existing product, separating out various characteristics and turning certain elements into autonomous products (Figure 3.5).

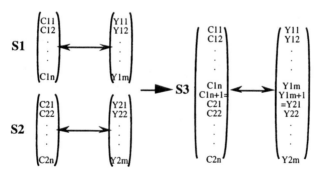

Figure 3.4 A new service (S3) produced by recombining the characteristics of two existing services (S1 and S2)

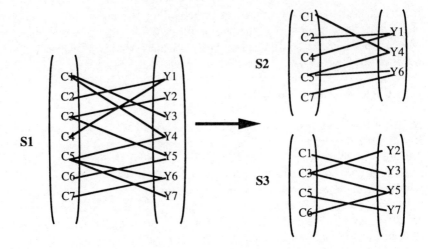

Figure 3.5 Two autonomous new services (S2 and S3) produced by splitting up the characteristics of an existing service (S1)

This twin notion of recombining and splitting, or bundling and unbundling, is deliberately oversimplified: the new system is regarded simply as the sum of the two old ones or as the product of fragmentation. In reality, recombination and fragmentation techniques should also be brought into play (together with the corresponding technical characteristics) (cf. Bressand and Nicolaïdis, 1988). According to Henderson and Clark, architectural innovations 'destroy the utility of a firm's architectural knowledge, but preserve the utility of its knowledge of the product's individual components'. Thus, as Bressand and Nicolaïdis emphasize, the processes of bundling and unbundling should not be reduced to a simple engineering exercise, involving the mere assembly of spare parts.

There are numerous illustrations of this model. Broadly speaking, a recruitment service provides the service characteristics inherent in four types of sequential activities: the analysis of the client organization's needs, the choice of a method of approach (direct, through advertisements, etc.), the selection of candidates, their monitoring and assistance in integrating them into the firm. In accordance with the principle of architectural innovation, consultancy companies have split up this generic service in such a way as to provide perhaps only that set of service characteristics specific to one or more phases of the combination outlined above. Recombinative innovation can go further by creating a totally new product through a combination of existing technical characteristics and elements, since the mere fact of combining certain characteristics in different ways or adding certain others might be sufficient to make possible totally new modes of use.[10] It should also be pointed out that recombinative innovation may also manifest itself through the implementation of a new technology, such as the use of a new medium (e.g. CD-ROM) in order to provide an information service.

According to Bressand and Nicolaïdis (1988), charter air services emerged from this process of fragmenting or splitting up an air travel service made up of a combination of different elements: the travel itself, baggage handling, catering and reservations. The emergence of fast-food restaurants, brokerage and publishing (proliferation of photocopying companies) can be interpreted in the same way. The launch of the 'Formule 1' hotel chain in France is also a product of 'unbundling', with the provision of hotel services being reduced to its basic service characteristics or, in other words, all the supplementary service characteristics being eliminated. Thus the 'Formule 1' concept is based on a minimum level of service, without a restaurant (only breakfast is provided), no en-suite bathroom facilities, etc. Outside of the brief periods when the reception desk is manned, guests check themselves in and out.

Thus innovation can be produced either by adding services or by what might be called a 'decline in service', that is the elimination of services. The theories of innovation in retailing alluded to in Chapter 1 ('wheel of retailing theory', 'accordion theory') are based on this dialectic between 'trading up' (that is, the addition of services) and 'trading down' (decline in service).

Conversely, examples of innovation based on the recombination of existing elements are provided by the recovery services originally conceived by Europe Assistance (thus the recombination model can lead to radical innovations, as defined above). The concept of 'club' as devised by Club Med or the fitness centres' invented by Viatrop are further examples. Moreover, transport services can be combined in the same package with a hotel reservation service, car hire, etc., leading ultimately to a comprehensive tourist service. Similarly, 'teleshopping' and mail order services combine retailing, transport and informational services. The French firm J.C. Decaux combines various activities that previously existed independently: the manufacture of bus shelters, cleaning and maintenance services for them, advertising services, information services, city maps, etc.

The management sciences literature (Wind et al., 1992) provides a good example of what, in our view, can be seen as an implementation of the recombinative model with the aim of producing a new kind of hotel service (see Table 3.2). The approach to the design of the new service is based on the definition of a set of service characteristics. A total of 50 characteristics accompanied by between two and eight levels of weighting as the case may be (167 levels in all) are used to represent the hotel 'product' in the general sense of the term. These 50 characteristics are divided into seven broad categories: 1. External factors; 2. Rooms; 3. Food-related services; 4. Lounge facilities; 5. Services; 6. Leisure activities; 7. Safety and security factors.

Table 3.2 The technical and service characteristics of a hotel product

1 Ext. Factor	2. Rooms	3. Food	4. Lounge
Building Shape	Entertainment	Restaurant in hotel	Atmosphere
L-shaped w/landscape	Color TV	None (coffe shop next	*Quiet bar/lounge*
Outdoor courtyard	Color TV w/movies at $5	door)	Lively, popular bar/lounge
Landscaping	Color TV w/30 ch. cable	*Restaurant/lounge*	Type of people
Minimal	*Color TV w/HBO,*	*combo, limited menu*	Hotel guests and friends
Moderate	*movies, etc.*	Coffee shop, full menu	only
Elaborate	Color TV w/free movies	Full-service restaurant,	*Open to public-general*
Pool type	Entertainment/Rental	full menu	*appeal*
No pool	*None*	Coffee shop/full menu	Open to public-many
Rectangular shape	Rental Cassettes/in-room	and good restaurant	singles
Free form shape	Atari	Restaurant nearby	Lounge nearby
Indoor/outdoor	Rental Cassettes/	None	*None*
Pool location	stereo cassette	Coffee shop	Lounge/bar nearby
In courtyard	playing in-room	Fast food	Lounge/bar
Not in courtyard	Rental Movies/	Fast food or coffee	w/entertainment nearby
Corridor/View	in-room BetaMax	shop and moderate	
Outside access/	Size	restaurant	
restricted view/	Small (standard)	*Fast food or coffee*	
Enclosed access/	*Slightly larger (1foot)*	*shop and good restaurant*	
unrestricted view/	Much larger (2,5 feet)	Free continental	
balcony or window	Small suite (2 rooms)	None	
Hotel size	Large suite (2 rooms)	Continental included in	
Small (125 rooms, 2	Quality of decor	room rate	
stories)	Budget motel decor	Room service	
Large (600 rooms, 12	Old Holiday Inn decor	*None*	
stories)	New Holiday Inn decor	Phone-in order/guest to	
	New Hilton decor	pick up	
	New Hyatt decor	Room service, limited	
	Heating and Cooling	menu	
	Wall unit/full control	Room service, full menu	
	Wall unit/soundproof/full	Store	
	control	*No food in store*	
	Central Hor C (seasonal)	Snack items	
	Central H or C/full control	Snacks, refrigerated items,	
	Size of Bath	wine, beer, liquor	
	Standard Bath	Above items and gourment	
	Slightly larger/sink	food items	
	separate	Vending service	
	Larger bath w/ larger tub	None	
	Very large/tub for 2	Soft drink machine only	
	Sink location	Soft drink and snack	
	In bath only	machines	
	In separate area	*Soft drink, snack, and*	
	In bath and separate	*sandwich machines*	
	Bathroom features	Above and microwave	
	None	available	
	Shower Massage	In-room kitchen facilities	
	Whirlpool (Jacuzzi)	None	
	Steam bath	*Coffee maker only*	
	Amenities	Coffee maker and	
	Small bar soap	refrigerator	
	Large soap/shampoo/	Cooking facilities in room	
	shoeshine		
	Large soap/bath		
	gel/shower cap/sewing kit		
	Above items + toothp.,		
	deodorant, mouthwash		

Source: Wind, Green, Shifflet and Scarbrough (1992).

5. Services	6. Leisure	7. Security
Reservations	Sauna	Security guard
Call hotel directly 800 reservation	None	None
number	*Yes*	11 a.m. to 7 p.m.
Check-in	Whirlpool/jacuzzi	*7 p.m. to 7 a.m.*
Standard	None	24 hours
Pre-credit	Outdoor	Smoke detector
clearance	*Indoor*	None
Machine in lobby	Exercise room	*In rooms and throughout hotel*
Check-out	None	Sprinkler system
At front desk	*Basic facility w/weights*	None
Bill under door/leave key	Facility w/Nautilus equipment	Lobby and hallways only
Key to front desk/bill by mail	Racquet ball courts	Lobby/hallways/rooms
Machine in lobby	*None*	24-hour video camera
Limo to airport	Yes	*None*
None	Tennis courts	Parking/hallway/public areas
Yes	*None*	Alarm button
Bellman	Yes	*None*
None	Game room /Entertainment	Button in room, rings desk
Yes	*None*	
Message service	Electric games/pinball	
Note at front desk	Electric games/pinball/ping pong	
Light on phone	Above+movie theater, bowling	
Light on phone and message under	Children's playroom/playground	
door	*None*	
Recorded message	Playground only	
Cleanliness/upkeep/management skill	Playroom only	
Budget motor level	Playground and playroom	
Holiday Inn Level	Pool extras	
Nonconvention	*None*	
Hyatt level	Pool w/slides	
Convention Hyatt level	Pool w/slides and equipment	
Fine Hotel level		
Laundry/Valet		
None		
Client drop off and pick up		
Self-service		
Valet pick up and drop off		
Special Services (concierge)		
None		
Information on restaurants,		
theaters, etc.		
Arrangements and reservation		
Travel problem resolution		
Secretarial services		
None		
Xerox machine		
Xerox machine and typist		
Car maintenance		
None		
Take car to service		
Gas on premises/bill to room		
Car rental/		
Airline reservations		
None		
Car rental facility		
Airline reservations		
Car rental and airline reservations		

Table 3.2 provides a more comprehensive overview of the set of technical and service characteristics that go to make up a hotel 'product'. This table of characteristics can be seen as defining a 'technological regime' for the hotel trade. Statistical techniques applied to marketing make it possible to design a product suited to a given target population by combining the appropriate characteristics in an optimal way. In the present case, the combination adopted is depicted in italics in the table. This combination can be regarded as a particular 'technological trajectory', a particular way of appropriating the hotel trade's technological regime.

This example provides a good illustration of the recombinative innovation model. The starting point is an allegedly exhaustive list of a hotel's characteristics (each bearing several performance levels) which are combined or recombined in such a way as to satisfy a new or potential need.

Recombinative innovation has now become a fundamental mode of creating innovations. As innovations become increasingly 'systemic', some authors have suggested that it constitutes a new model of innovation (Foray, 1993) that operates particularly in the informational and biotechnology industries. As we shall see, it also lies at the heart of the innovation and R&D mechanisms in services.

The rise to prominence of this model of innovation can be interpreted in various ways:

1. it relies on a fundamental mechanism of scientific phenomena identified by the philosophers of antiquity, namely the combination of knowledge;
2. it is easy to put into practice because it draws on what exists. Faced with a new problem, the first response will be to mobilize the most accessible knowledge, methods and technologies: those that have already been mastered or that can be easily acquired;
3. cognitive leaps are unlikely and costly. As a result, firm's cognitive advances tend to be based on current knowledge;
4. in the case of services, implementation of this model is made even more frequent and easy by 'the less important role played by material inertia and constraints' (Bressand and Nicolaïdis, 1988).

This model has certain fundamental implications, particularly for services:

1. The capacity for innovation depends on the ability to explore and mobilize an extended set of knowledge and techniques. This has major implications for the role of the social forms of the flow and appropriation of information and knowledge (cf. on this point Foray, 1993)[11] and for the modes of innovation organization within firms. Although this point cannot be developed here, the specificity of the position of service firms should be noted.

The organizational innovation dimension is particularly strong in services, whereas there is relatively little research or innovation relating to components or materials[12] that draws upon the natural and life sciences. The main disciplines involved are the social sciences, computer science and sometimes mathematics (in banking and insurance, for example) and new disciplines located on the boundary between the social sciences and the 'hard' sciences, such as linguistics, cognitive sciences and operational research methods.

These are forms of knowledge and 'technologies' that largely elude intellectual property systems. This facilitates access to new knowledge and considerably strengthens the role of imitation in the innovation dynamic.

We are also dealing here with areas in which there is generally no clear distinction between basic research, on the one hand, and applied research and development, on the other (Gadrey et al. 1993). In manufacturing, this distinction is justified by the fact that basic research relates to components and materials, whereas the emphasis in applied research and development tends to be on architecture and assembly. In services, most innovation is 'architectural' in nature, with a very heavy emphasis on the design and development of organizational formats. However, the evolution of the computer industry towards 'object-oriented development' means it may be possible in future to envisage a clearer distinction between basic research on the relevant 'objects' (the components and materials of an 'informational industry') and the design and development of 'service products' that combine these various components in innovative ways.

2. The second implication of the recombinative innovation model is the need to design a modular architecture for products and systems. Indeed, implementation of this mode of innovation requires that the 'product' be broken down into clearly identified and defined elements – in other words, the characteristics of the service and of the way in which it is obtained have to be rigorously specified. Thus what has to be done is to reformulate the existing activities, to formalize them to a greater extent and to define 'standardized' services. Referring back to the general representation shown in Figure 2.9 (Chapter 2), this means defining the service characteristics $[Y_i]$ more precisely and, in some cases, attaching greater importance to the technical characteristics $[T_j]$. This is the issue at stake in the next innovation model, namely the objectifying or formalization model of innovation (cf. Section 1.6 below).

3. The third implication of the recombinative model is located at industry level. Clusters of innovations emerging from different service industries are combined in such a way as to constitute systems. What we are dealing

with is a group of initially independent services that then forge links with each other and thus develop into a system. Examples of this process would include the systems that tend to develop around supermarkets, insurance, banking, consultancy services, etc., or even those that are beginning to emerge around the various forms of transport, catering services, hotels, tourism, leisure services, etc. (Gallouj, 1994b).

4. More generally, as soon as the question of (re)combination is raised, questions should also be asked about what it is that is being combined: knowledge, characteristics (which ones?), goods and services, human resources or institutions. This amounts to a shift away from analysis of cognitive processes towards notions of networks and local innovation systems. For example, when it comes to the organization of R&D processes in services, new combinations of competences or characteristics may mean new combinations of individuals (particularly when expertise is highly tacit). This observation helps to explain the trend towards the establishment of flexible project groups to manage innovation in service firms.

The recombinative model of innovation can shed new light on certain characteristics generally attributed to innovation and research in the service sector.

1. The unspectacular nature of product innovation. Defined in terms of 'the routine use of a technological base', the recombinative model operates not through ruptures but rather through the continuous and cumulative production of knowledge.

2. The difficulty of evaluating R&D. Traditional measures developed by national and international institutions are in fact based on criteria of novelty which are not relevant within the framework of the recombinative model.

2. The low cost of innovation. If research or innovation rarely requires substantial investment, this is perhaps due to the process of recombination and the 'systematic re-utilization' of components to enable major resource savings.

4. The relative lack of research in the classical sense: the production of new knowledge. The recombinative model produces and also demands more in terms of 'architectural knowledge' (as in engineering) than of knowledge of the components themselves.

5. No prototype perfection. Innovation consists of assembling existing components which have been proven in practice.

6. The difficulty of protecting innovations which can be imitated relatively easily. If the validity of the recombinative model is accepted, the important thing is not so much to protect innovation and impede imitation as to facilitate recombinations.

1.6 Formalization Innovation

The various models of innovation outlined above are based on qualitative or quantitative variation in technical or service characteristics or competences (creation, addition, elimination, improvement, bundling, unbundling). There is a final model in which it is not quantity or quality that varies, but rather the 'visibility' and the degree of standardization of the various characteristics. This model, which we will call the formalization model, consists of putting the service characteristics 'into order', specifying them, making them less hazy, making them concrete, giving them a shape. The underlying aim of this activity, therefore, is to produce signs or markings, what are known in the sociology of innovation (Latour and Woolgar, 1988; Callon, 1989) as 'inscriptions', to make 'investments in forms' (Thévenot, 1986; Eymard-Duvernay, 1986,1989), in other words to undertake operations that enable the good in question to acquire 'generality (objectivity) through the establishment of equivalencies'. This objective is often achieved by putting in place technical characteristics, whether tangible (equipment, software, etc.) or intangible (for example, methods, organization, toolboxes).

This formalization model also constitutes an attempt to clarify the correspondences between these technical characteristics and the service characteristics.

Putting the service characteristics 'into order' frequently involves the transformation of a general function into sub-functions or service characteristics. This general process makes it clear why this formalization model often precedes the recombination model.

In many services, this formalization model constitutes a genuine 'natural trajectory', in the sense of the term adopted by Nelson and Winter, although we cannot speak of industrialization, as A. Mayère (1994) does, for example, in the case of professional services.

The formalization model readily lends itself to biological analogies. It can be compared to a process of cellular division and differentiation based on a single original cell. In the initial stage of this process, competences and functions/characteristics are relatively undifferentiated and tacit (contained within the original cell), while by the third and final stage functions and services are clearly differentiated and articulated (Figure 3.6).

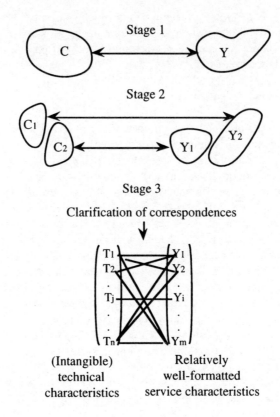

Figure 3.6 The formalization model and the analogy of cell differentiation

There are plenty of examples of this model. They are found in the cleaning industry, where Sundbo (1996) highlights the growing importance of what he calls modularization. They are also found in the fast-food industry (cf. the organization of work at McDonald's, analysed by Levitt, 1972) or in business catering (Callon, 1995; Dubuisson, 1995). Legal consultancy also provides examples. The service known as 'legal audit', for example, has always been provided by consultants more or less automatically and always informally. The formalization process consisted of finding a name for the service and establishing (following the model of financial auditing) reference points or methodological markers by which it could be defined. In this case, as in the other, the various elements can be said to have 'existed' implicitly beforehand: they are rendered explicit through a process of social construction. It should be noted that this process of formalization innovation was followed by implementation of the recombination model, in which the general legal audit is broken down into a number of specific audits: contract audits, patent audits, etc., all of them 'products' that can be given an independent existence and be sold as such. The same can be said of all the examples cited in the case of recombinative innovation, to the extent that they had to be formalized before-hand (charter flights, recovery services, etc.).

The modernization of some public services in France has also followed this trajectory. As C. Delfini (1997) notes, the employment service (ANPE) is the public service that has undergone the most radical modernization. The emergence of mass unemployment provided the impetus for a rationalization of the service with the twofold objective of defining more precisely the range of services on offer and establishing the routine use of new technologies as a medium for the delivery of those services (distance services, self-service).

The ultimate configuration of this formalization model is the one that leads to the production of a real object that can be reduced to Saviotti and Metcalfe's original representation. This is the case, for example, with the development of expert systems. The substitution of automatic cash dispensers and telling machines for over-the-counter transactions in banks (that is the replacement of the human capacities formerly made available to customers with technical capacities placed at their disposal) falls within the scope of this model (Figure 3.7).

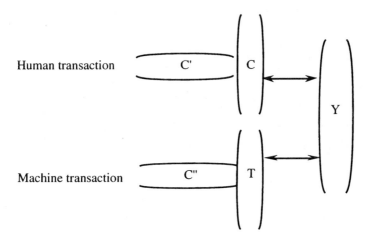

Figure 3.7 A formalization model of banking transactions (provision of human capacities versus provision of technical capacities)

If it is assumed that the service characteristics provided (Y_i) are identical (which is debatable), we are dealing here with a special example of 'pure substitution', since competence characteristics on the customer's and service provider's sides ((C') and (C) respectively) are being replaced by technical characteristics on the provider's side (T) and new types of competences on the customer's side (C'').

In reality, if the service characteristics Y are not identical in both cases, the 'pure substitution' hypothesis can be withdrawn. In fact, transactions mediated through human beings can have greater variety and flexibility than those mediated through machines. On the other hand, machine transactions facilitate access. An analysis couched in terms of production worlds (see Chapter 6) should help provide a more balanced view of the meaning of this evolution.

1.7 An Attempt at Statistical Analysis of these Different Models of Innovation

In our survey on innovation in services (Djellal and Gallouj, 1998, 2002),[13] we attempted to test the existence and scale of some of these models in quantitative terms. In order to achieve this objective, we tried to evaluate the importance of various statements likely to characterize the new service products introduced by firms between 1992 and 1997.
The following statements were evaluated:

1. New service products are tailor-made (to meet clients' particular needs) and are not standardized.
2. New service products are produced by combining elements from existing products/services.
3. New service products are produced by splitting up existing products/services ('dissociation' or 'unbundling').
4. New service products are created by the firm in close cooperation with the client, which limits the extent to which they can be reproduced.
5. The new service product is the result of adding a supplementary or peripheral service to an existing service.
6. The originality of the service product lies more in the mode of delivery to the client than in its basic function or content.

To some extent, these statements describe, respectively:

1. tailor-made innovation,
2. associative innovation,
3. dissociative innovation,
4. ad hoc innovation,
5. incremental innovation,
6. formalization or objectifying innovation (at least, in some of its forms).

Table 3.3 Different modes of service product innovation (%)*

Questionnaire statement	Mode of innovation	Unimp./not very important	Imp./very important
Tailor-made	Tailor-made	24.1	57.9
Combining elements	Associative	25.9	51.7
Splitting up elements	Dissociative	70.2	11.8
Close cooperation...	Ad hoc	44.7	27.6
Adding service	Incremental	25.4	51.7
Delivery mode changed	Formalization	53.1	25.0

Note: * Shares of firms to have introduced service product innovation which regard each of the modalities as unimportant/not very important or important/very important (n = 228).

The modes of innovation most often considered important or very important in describing the new or improved service products introduced between 1992 and 1997 are: tailor-made innovations, combination of existing service products and the addition of supplementary or peripheral services to an existing service (cf. Table 3.3).

The other modes of innovation summarized in the following statements: 'new service products are created in close cooperation with the client, which limits the extent to which they can be reproduced', 'new service products are produced by splitting up existing products' and 'the originality of the service product lies more in the mode of delivery to the client than in its basic function or content' are relatively less frequently regarded as important or very important. They do, however, exist as not insignificant modes of innovation.

To conclude, the survey can be said to confirm the existence of the different models of innovation, which is in itself a valuable finding. As far as the judgements on the relative importance of the various models are concerned, they should be treated with considerable caution. It is likely, indeed, that certain types of innovation are more important than the figures suggest. For example, ad hoc innovation cannot be easily captured by a statement of the kind required in a postal survey, precisely because of its ad hoc nature. There is very considerable room for manoeuvre in interpreting a concept that is not sanctioned by usage. It is likely, therefore, that some respondents compared the definition of this type of innovation with their own implicit (and rigidified) notion of service product innovation and then rejected the statement corresponding to ad hoc innovation. Moreover, it is possible that a certain amount of ad hoc innovation is included in the tailor-made category, which is very similar (and more familiar) and which also, it should be noted, has the highest score: 58 per cent of firms consider it to be an important or very important mode of service product innovation. As far as formalization or objectifying innovation is concerned, it should be noted that the approach adopted here was a restricted one, namely that of the modes of service delivery.

2. WHAT ARE THE POSSIBLE LINKAGES BETWEEN THESE VARIOUS MODELS?

Our concern here is with the way in which these various models might be linked within a firm or service industry. We begin by addressing the question in a general way, irrespective of the industry or product under consideration. We will then attempt to identify any possible tropism between models of innovation and types of service. Finally, we will examine the linkages between some of these models over the long term in a few service industries.

2.1 The Possible Theoretical Linkages

Whatever the industry in question, these various models are not unconnected to each other. A certain number of bilateral relations can be identified. As we shall see, the principles linking these different models are very diverse. For simplicity's sake, they can be reduced to two general principles which may combine with each other and which incorporate a certain number of heterogeneous basic principles.

- The first general principle (P) is static. It denotes some possible overlap in the contents of certain models. One model may thus be the particular case of another (P_1). It may be differentiated from the other only by social construction or convention (P_2). Two models may be implemented simultaneously and merge with each other (P_3). Two models may overlap but without merging (P_4).
- The second general principle (Q) is dynamic. It describes the various modes of *relationships in time* between the various models of innovation. Thus one model may sustain another (determine it) (Q_1). One model may precede another (Q_2). One model may be the result of another one being repeated (Q_3).

In more concrete terms, but without for all that any claim to exhaustiveness, the following relations can be identified (summarized in Table 3.4):

1. The repeated implementation of the incremental innovation model (addition or substitution of characteristics) may lead, over time, to a radical innovation (Q_3). Such a result is unlikely to be produced by repeated implementation of the ameliorative model (which does not add characteristics but merely increases their 'level' or quality). To put it another way, a

continuous increase in a car's top speed, level of comfort and safety will not lead to a radical innovation, unlike the repeated addition of technical (and service) characteristics, which could conceivably end in the creation of a vehicle that no longer had anything to do with the current vehicle (an amphibious vehicle that could also fly, for example).

2. As already noted, the boundary between the ameliorative model and the incremental model can in some cases be regarded as a social construction (P_2). Intentionality can transform an ameliorative innovation, the mechanical product of learning processes, into an incremental innovation.

3. As we have seen, ad hoc innovation involves an a posteriori process of codification and formalization (transformation of elements of [C] into intangible elements of [T]) which, to some extent, falls within the scope of the formalization model. It may also feed into the various other models, serving as a source of ideas for improvements or the addition of characteristics, refinement of methods, etc. (Q_1).

4. The ad hoc and incremental innovation models both cover some aspects of what is generally called tailor-made innovation (P_4). In the case of insurance, already mentioned above, it will be remembered that 'adaptive tailor-made innovation' (the adaptation to a particular client of a standard product through the addition of specific guarantees) has much in common with the incremental model, while 'fully tailor-made innovation' (creation of a specific policy for a large firm) has much in common with the ad hoc model.

5. The formalization model often precedes the incremental and recombinative models (Q_2). This model contributes to the formatting of characteristics, which opens the way for processes of recombination, addition and substitution.

6. The incremental model can be seen as a borderline case of the recombinative model (P_1), particularly when the objective is to add a service characteristic that exists in another product. Furthermore, the repeated addition of characteristics may contribute to the development of hypertely (or saturation) which might in turn hasten the fragmentation of the service in question (recombinative model) (Q_3).

7. The formalization model may lie at the heart of radical innovation, since the new system of characteristics produced by a radical innovation can immediately be the object of a certain degree of formatting (P_3).

8. The radical model may be followed by any of the other models (Q_2), whether the aim is:
   - to add one or more new characteristics, for example with a view to differentiating and adapting a product to a particular model (incremental and ad hoc model);
   - to raise the quality of some of the existing characteristics (ameliorative model);

- to format or improve the existing formatting of a radical innovation (formalization model), or
- to fragment a radical innovation into sub-categories (recombinative model).
9. The ameliorative model may succeed any of the other models (Q_2).

Table 3.4 Some possible links between innovation models*

2nd model	Rad.	Am.	Incr.	Ad	Rec.	Tail.	Form.
1st model							
Radical		Q_2	Q_2	Q_2	Q_2	Q_2	P_3, Q_2
Ameliorative			P_2				
Incremental	Q_3	Q_2, P_2			P_1, Q_3	P_4	
Ad hoc	Q_1	Q_1, Q_2	Q_1		Q_1	P_4	Q_1, P_4
Recombinative		Q_2					
Tailor-made		Q_2	P_4	P_4			
Formalization	P_3	Q_2	Q_2	P_4	Q_2		

Note:
*P_1: the first model is a particular case of the second
P_2: the two models are differentiated from each other by social construction or convention
P_3: the two models are implemented simultaneously and merge
P_4: two models may overlap
Q_1: the first model sustains (determines) the second
Q_2: the first model precedes the second
Q_3: repetition of the first model leads to the second

2.2 What Innovation Models in What Service Sectors?

Our objective here is to answer the following question: are there particular tropisms between these innovation models and certain types of service or certain service industries or functions? The general answer to this question runs as follows: these models can manifest themselves in virtually all service industries or functions (albeit to varying degrees). Differences are also to be found within the same firm or industry depending on the type of service being provided. The radical innovation model can be implemented in more or less any service industry or function and at any point in time. In so far as it is based on learning processes, the ameliorative model is also universal.

The ad hoc model is frequently encountered in consultancy activities, where it seems to represent the minimal form of innovation. However, it is also found in other activities that would seem, on the face of it, to be less 'intellectual', such as neighbourhood services, repair services (garages), etc. The incremental model is characteristic of those services in which the service characteristics can be readily expressed. These include mass informational services (financial and insurance services, for example), mass operational services (catering, transport, cleaning) and services made up of packages of goods and services. When the service characteristics vector is more of a 'black box' (intellectual and professional services), the incremental model manifests itself in its most general form, namely the recombinative model, since in this case the characteristics vector can be reduced to a vector of more general functions or subsets of characteristics. The recombinative model is universal. Like the previous model, however, it is generally all the commoner the better formatted the product characteristics already are.

The formalization model is a quasi-natural trajectory in all service activities. It is a model that also has cultural and structural specificities: the culture of the English-speaking world and large firms are particularly sensitive to it.

Once again, we can draw on the data gathered in the postal survey already referred to (Djellal and Gallouj, 1998, 2002) in an attempt to quantify the various qualitative hypotheses outlined above (Table 3.5).

Table 3.5 Modes of service product innovation by type of service activity (%)*

Modes of innovation		Financial Services	Consulting	Operational Services	Hotels-catering retailing	Total
Tailor-made	a*	31.6	21.6	14.3	38.1	24.1
	b	39.5	62.2	66.7	52.0	57.9
Associative	a	13.2	27.0	28.6	38.1	25.9
	b	65.8	51.3	47.6	33.3	51.7
Dissociative	a	73.7	70.9	57.1	71.4	70.2
	b	18.4	10.1	14.3	9.5	11.8
Ad hoc	a	55.3	40.5	38.1	61.9	44.7
	b	23.7	33.1	19.0	4.8	27.6
Incremental	a	18.4	26.3	33.3	23.8	25.4
	b	65.8	48.0	42.9	61.9	51.7
Formalization	a	42.1	60.1	23.8	52.4	53.1
	b	36.8	18.2	47.6	28.6	25.0
	N	38	148	21	21	228

Note: *a = unimportant or not very important, b = important or very important, N = number of firms.

The 'tailor-made and non-standardized' mode of innovation is most often cited as an important or very important mode in consultancy and operational services. This similarity between two types of service which, on the face of

96 *Innovation in the Service Economy*

it, seem to be completely different, represents a paradox which merits consideration. We are not, in fact, dealing with the same type of tailor-made innovation in each case. Indeed, in the case of operational services, the tailor-made
nature of innovation stems from the combination of standardized modules,
while in consultancy, the type of tailor-made innovation is less clearly defined. If we use the distinction established by Girin (1994), we can say that, in
the first case, it is a simple activity (which is easy to describe) and whose
mandate is clear (the result is easy to assess), while in the second case (consultancy) the activities are more complex (difficult to describe) and their mandates
are more confused and difficult to define.

However, there are variations within the consultancy field. Proportionally
speaking, more management, advertising and legal consultancies attach importance to this mode of innovation than the others, that is information technology consultancies, market research and recruitment consultancies.

The largest share of firms citing associative innovation as an important or
very important mode of innovation is in financial services. However, it must
be noted that this mode is also relatively important in all the other fields, with
the exception of retailing.

Innovation through the addition of supplementary service functions (or incremental innovation), which is a particular form of associative innovation,
plays a particularly important role in financial services, hotel, catering and
retailing.

Dissociation is a mode regarded as unimportant or not very important in all
the industries.

As already noted, the 'coproduced and not highly reproducible' mode of service product innovation (which provides indicators of the existence of what we
have called ad hoc innovation) is regarded as important or very important by a
relatively small share of firms in our sample, regardless of activity. However,
this mode of innovation is relatively more important in consultancy and financial services.

The importance of the mode of innovation summarized in the statement
that 'the originality of the service product lies more in the mode of delivery
than in its basic function or content' varies more according to the type of
service. It is regarded as an unimportant or not very important mode by 60
per cent of the consultancy firms and 52 per cent of the hotel/catering/retailing
firms surveyed and as an important or very important mode by 50 per cent of
the operational services firms (cleaning, transport, etc.). In financial services,
it is regarded as unimportant/not very important or important/very important
by equal shares of firms.

In the financial services industry, the 'tailor-made' (39.5 per cent), 'associative' (65.8 per cent), 'additive' (65.8 per cent) and 'change in mode of delivery'
(36.8 per cent) forms of innovation are considered to be important or very

important more frequently than the 'dissociative' and 'ad hoc' (low reproducibility and high level of coproduction) modes.

In consultancy, the main forms of innovation (regarded as important or very important) are the 'tailor-made' and 'associative' modes. These modes, along with 'change in the mode of delivery', also predominate in operational services. Finally, in hotel/catering/retailing, the main form of innovation is the 'additive' mode, followed by the 'tailor-made' mode. Once again, however, it should be noted that the results must be assessed in the light of the limits imposed by the size of our samples and of the difficulty of including new analytical and theoretical categories in questionnaires.

2.3 The Long-term Structuring of Innovation Models in Certain Service Industries

2.3.1 Industrialization versus service-orientation

One widespread view of the general model of innovation and change in services (including highly relational and information and knowledge intensive services such as consultancy) draws on the notion of *industrialization*. Despite its prevalence, this is a particularly imprecise and polysemous notion. As Gadrey suggests (1994c), it can be assumed that, in general terms, 'the notion of industrialization denotes a process in the course of which an organizational category not belonging to the *industrial world* tends increasingly to resemble that world, at least in certain respects considered significant'. Examination of the operating principles that characterize the industrial world (particularly in terms of work organization) provides a good starting point for considering various complementary facets of industrialization.

Thus according to Gadrey (1994c), if the industrial world is defined in terms of the *production of material or tangible goods*, then industrialization denotes a process of development towards the production of tangible goods to the detriment of the provision of intangible services. If the industrial world is defined by reference to *a certain mode of production* (the form of work organization and type of technologies that dominated heavy industry in the post-war period), then industrialization denotes the tendency to implement that mode of production in service firms and organizations. Finally, if the industrial world can be defined by reference to *methods of management and productivity measurement,* then industrialization can be apprehended as the 'use of 'industrial' criteria to evaluate performance'.

A possible (vectoral) representation of such a process of industrialization in services (with industrialization understood as the production of tangible goods) is shown in Figure 3.8.

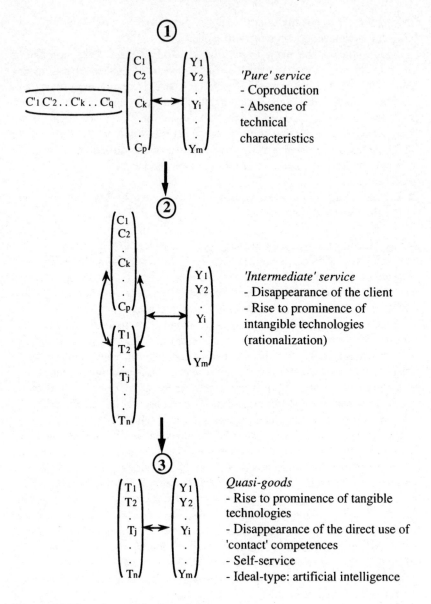

Figure 3.8 The process of industrialization in services in terms of the dynamic of characteristics

The initial stage is the 'pure' service phase, in which the service characteristics are produced solely by mobilizing competences – those of the service provider combined with the client's (coproduction). The industrialization process manifests itself firstly in phase 2 through the gradual disappearance of the client (the weakening and then the disappearance of the coproduction relationship) and the introduction of intangible technologies. This process leads to the production of a service that can be likened to a quasi-good, characterized by the increasing use of tangible technologies and self-service and the elimination of the direct use of 'contact' competences (phase 3).

This process would lead eventually to the universal application of Saviotti and Metcalfe's initial representation, namely the formatting of the technical characteristics T and of the service characteristics Y and the elimination of the client's competence characteristics C'. The ideal type of this process is the use on a self-service basis of a technical system or an expert system.

In the field of the law and of legal services, Auer-Bernet (1986), for example, provides a fairly impressive list of the possible uses of legal expert systems:

> Search for precedents, aid in the drafting of legislation, teaching, search for arguments and strategies, planning of commercial transactions, extraction of relevant facts, simulation of consequences of legislative reform, help in decision-making with suggested decision or verification that a discretionary administrative decision is consistent with previous decisions.

In this particular case, however, these expert systems are usually used not to sell a final quasi-good but rather to enhance the efficiency of the process whereby a service that is not yet a quasi-good is produced.

This trend towards *industrial rationalization* (to use Gadrey's expression) is demonstrably at work in certain operational service activities. It is long established in fast-food restaurants. And in a study of the leading international cleaning firm, Sundbo (1996) describes the following process of development:

- *Phase 1* (1960s and 70s): the industrialization principle is dominant. The firm develops a Taylorist mode of production organization, in which the services offered are highly standardized and contractualized. The back-office and 'production' dominate.

- *Phase 2* (1980s): the service relationship becomes the dominant principle. The key element in the firm's activities is the interface (importance of employees in direct contact with customers). It is from here (that is from listening to clients) that innovation is produced. The marketing department and function become increasingly powerful.

- *Phase 3* (1990s): the modularization principle prevails. Modularization is a combination or reconciliation of the previous two principles, that is the standardization principle of the first phase and the service relation principle of the second phase. It allows the firm to dominate the process of developing new services and not to remain in thrall to the innovations emerging from the interface. The process of standardization and industrialization continues, leading eventually to the creation of standarized modules that can be combined in such a way as to meet the specific needs of particular clients. What we are dealing with here, in effect, is mass customization.

In many services, however, the development process is not so simple. There is a contradictory dialectic between two trends, both of which are sources, sites and consequences of innovation:

1. a process of industrialization (formalization model), characterized by rationalization, formalization, action on [T] (technical and process characteristics) and the introduction of technical methods and resources;

2. an inverse process of increasing customization and individualization, which manifests itself particularly through the ad hoc and incremental models (which are also encountered in manufacturing industries).

Taking Gadrey's analysis (Gadrey, 1994a) and our own investigations as starting points, we will now consider this dialectic in terms of the dynamic of characteristics and the corresponding models of innovation in several service industries.

2.3.2 The general model of change and innovation in large-scale retailing

Adopting a long-term perspective, it can be seen that, starting in the 1940s and 50s in the USA and in the 1970s in France, supermarkets followed a natural technological trajectory characterized by increasing mechanization and the exploitation of economies of scale based on two fundamental innovations: self-service and the development of chains. For a long time, the innovation model at work was the one we denote by the term formalization innovation. In essence, it revolved around the product vector [T] (introduction of Fordist logistical systems, incorporation of service provision into a new organizational structure) and a strengthening of the relationship [C'][T][Y] (self-service relationship). On the other hand, it had little impact on the service characteristics [Y] except through the addition, in some cases, of the qualities of proximity and accessibility and, on another level (the domestic world), by destroying the network of domestic relations that characterized the world of the small shopkeeper.

For some years now in the USA and more recently in France, innovation in large-scale retailing has gone in two different directions, both of them at odds with the previous one (which has not been abandoned, however) (Gadrey, 1994a):

1. the addition of 'new services' or new service relations, which equate to new functions or sets of new service characteristics that are a product of two different strategies (which sometimes merge), one focused on supplementing the basic service and the other on conquering new markets. The results include, for example, information and guidance booths, help with packing bags at checkouts, crèches, home deliveries, the development of financial and insurance services, the opening of travel agencies and petrol stations and the proliferation of departments offering individualized services;
2. the improvement of the 'social relations' of service through the introduction of loyalty cards, credit cards, the granting of advantages to loyal customers, etc.

In other words, the natural technological trajectory that is still at work has been overlaid by what can best be described as a service trajectory.

If the new services can be likened to a new service characteristic (a new group of service characteristics), as was assumed in Section 3.1.5, then the model at work here can be said to be the incremental innovation model (addition of service characteristics) or, more generally, the recombinative model in its 'associative' variant, resulting in the incorporation of different services such as banking and transport functions, etc.

2.3.3 The general model of change and innovation in banking

To some extent, the evolution of 'products' and 'services' or of production systems in banking can be described along the lines proposed by Barras, whose reverse life cycle model, as already noted, is made up of:

1. an initial phase of incremental innovations linked to the computerization of back-office functions;
2. a second phase of radical process innovations arising out of the computerization of front-office functions;
3. a third phase characterized by the introduction of new service products.

In terms of our model, phase I falls within the scope of an ameliorative model of innovation based on learning and brought into play through the relation [C]<--->[T] (service provider's competences<--->technical characteristics). Phase II falls within the scope of a formalization model of innovation based on the installation of devices (automatic cash dispensers, ATMs) that partially replace human transactions and can be used on a self-service basis. The relationship at work here is [C']<--->[T]<--->[Y] (customer's competen-

ces, technical characteristics, service characteristics). Phase III is the final
stage in the formalization innovation process, with the service being provided
in the home by means of a technological system ($[X]<\text{---}> [Y]$ in its initial
version, that of Saviotti and Metcalfe).

However valuable it may be, this analysis suffers from a significant technologist bias, as we saw in Chapter 1. Indeed, from a characteristics-based
perspective, Barras' model can be said to consider innovation from a single
point of view, namely the vector of process characteristics [Z] or the vector of
technical characteristics [X] (in the strict sense of the term); as we have already
noted, the distinction between the two is difficult to make. Taking as its
starting point a service defined as the set $\{[Z], [X], [Y]\}$, the 'reverse product
cycle' theory considers the following dynamic, which corresponds to the three
phases of the cycle:

1. $\{[Z'], [X'], [Y]\}$: the introduction of new process characteristics (linked to
    the introduction of mainframes in banks, for example), which gives rise
    to new technical characteristics (computerization of the back office) but
    no real change in final characteristics: [Y] is not altered (even if its cost
    falls);
2. $\{Z''], [X''], [Y'']\}$: the introduction of new process characteristics (mini-
    computers), which gives rise to new sets of technical characteristics
    (ATMs in banks) and a certain improvement in the service characteristics
    (improved quality of service);
3. $\{[Z'''], [X'''], [Y''']\}$: the introduction of new process characteristics (net-
    work technologies), which gives rise to new technical characteristics
    (home banking) and a multiplicity of new service characteristics.

It is interesting, therefore, to introduce a different perspective, not that of
the 'products' but that of the service relations associated with the various
phases of the cycle. Gadrey (1994a) defines this model of change in the
following terms: 'a dialectical relationship between the reduction of simple
operational interactions and the intensification of complex service relations'.
This means that the model of change, which from Barras' perspective is dominated by the formalization model, is characterized in reality by the increasing
prominence of the ad hoc and incremental modes, which finds concrete expression in the introduction of non-standardized, more complex, individualized,
interactive services (sales and consultancy services).

2.3.4 The general model of change and innovation in consul-
tancy services

The industrialization argument has also been applied to the most knowledge-
intensive and relational services. Bounfour (1989) and Mayère (1994) take the

view that the industrialization process is already under way in consultancy services, particularly in the large consultancy companies in the English-speaking world, and that it is likely to continue and spread to all consultancy activities. This process of industrialization is said to be mediated essentially through the proliferation and standardization of methods. This would suggest that what we have called the formalization model is pre-eminent.

Apart from the fact that there are significant differences depending on the type of consultancy, size of firm and national origin, the industrialization thesis itself is questionable. Gadrey (1994c) sees the problem as originating in the confusion between '*industrial rationalization*' or industrialization, the objective of which is to supply quasi-goods by standardizing professional work and achieving significant and measurable productivity gains, and '*professional rationalization*', the aim of which is to normalize cases as far as possible, to produce problem-solving procedures, scripts and methods. In terms of our 'vectoral' approach, professional rationalization is reflected in a process whereby competences [C] are transformed into intangible technical characteristics [T] (some of which define the client's role in service delivery, that is the linkage between the customers' competences [C'] and those of the service providers [C]). For all that, it does not signify the standardization (formatting) of the outcome [Y]. Industrial rationalization, for its part, is based on intangible and tangible technical characteristics [T] and is intended to standardize this outcome [Y] to some extent.

There is no doubt that some of the methods (that is, some of the stages of the process) used by consultants have been standardized; however, this does not mean that consultancy firms now provide quasi-goods. A process of 'professional rationalization' (the rationalization of intellectual work) is at work, rather than one of industrialization. This professional rationalization reduces uncertainties, releases energies and opens up 'access to areas of greater complexity' (Gadrey, 1994c).

This standardization-complexification dialectic indicates that the formalization model is operating in tandem with the ad hoc (and tailor-made) models.

By way of conclusion to this section, we would like to suggest that the general model of change and innovation in many public services is not significantly different and can be best approached in terms of a dialectic between objectification or formalization and 'increased service provision'. Thus in the French child benefit offices and the public employment service, the generalization of social problems has contributed to the emergence of the twin dynamic of objectification or formalization (particularly through the use of technical systems) and specific treatment (made-to-measure, support/back-up, service relation).

CONCLUSION

As we have just demonstrated, an approach to products couched in terms of (service, technical and process) characteristics and competences provides a fruitful starting point for the study of innovation in services. Such an approach is sufficiently flexible to encompass both goods and services, without ignoring any of the possible specificities of service activities in respect of innovation. Various modes of innovation are revealed (radical, ameliorative, incremental or additive, ad hoc, recombinative and formalization innovation) and interpreted within the framework of a dynamic of characteristics.

In the next chapter, we will retain the same framework in order to examine, in a more concrete way, the conditions under which innovation is produced: its sources and determinants, its modes of organization (actors, process) and its modes of appropriation.

NOTES

1. The findings presented here are based on a study carried out in collaboration with O. Weinstein (Gallouj and Weinstein, 1997).
2. The reader is reminded that, for simplicity's sake, we use the vector [T] of technical characteristics (in the broad sense) to denote tangible technical characteristics ([X] in Saviotti and Metcalfe's model), intangible technical characteristics (service 'technologies', methods, etc.) and process characteristics ([Z] in Saviotti and Metcalfe's model).
3. This may be measurable in some cases, but would tend to be expressed as an order of magnitude in others.
4. The term 'proportional' that Baily and Gordon use to describe this form of innovation is ambiguous: what they are really talking about is innovations with increasing or decreasing costs.
5. Baily and Gordon call them technological functions, but they are in fact synonymous with service characteristics (which may possibly be embodied in technical characteristics).
6. The following observations on ad hoc innovation relate largely to this area of activity. However, the same applies to most 'informational services, as defined by De Bandt (1995), and to other services involving a high level of interaction between provider and client.
7. A typology of innovation in insurance industries is provided in Chapter 1 (Table 1.5).
8. As early as 1912, Schumpeter defined innovation as a new combination of existing knowledge: 'To produce other things or the same things by a different method, means to combine these materials and forces differently... Development in our sense is then defined by the carrying out of new combinations' (Schumpeter, 1934, pp. 65–66).
9. However, a distinction should be made between combinations of characteristics and combinations of modules (which is one of the technical forms in which architectural innovation commonly manifests itself).
10. This is the basis of 'multimedia' systems.
11. Some service providers, notably consultancy firms, play an essential role as diffusers of 'elements' or as the medium through which they are combined (cf. Gallouj 1994b, 2002a; Djellal, 1995; Bessant and Rush, 1995).
12. Except in those services such as transport and telecommunications that are highly capital-intensive.
13. Cf. Chapter 1, Section 1.4.

4. The Organization of Innovation and the Characteristics-Based Approach

INTRODUCTION

This chapter addresses the following question: how are the various ways of organizing innovation in service firms to be interpreted in the light of an approach to innovation couched in terms of the dynamic of characteristics and of competences? Some aspects of this question were examined in the previous chapter, which focused more on modes or processes than on outcomes or forms of innovation. Our aim here is to go into the question more closely by establishing what a characteristics-based approach might tell us about the various aspects of the organization of innovation in service firms – its determinants, the actors involved, the processes that unfold and the possibilities of protecting it.

It is not our aim (allowing for exceptions) to undertake the excessively complex and doubtless futile task of investigating the links between these various aspects of the organization of innovation and all six models of innovation outlined in the previous chapter (the radical, ameliorative, incremental, ad hoc, recombinative and formalization models). After all, depending on the circumstances, each of these models or, to be precise, the innovations to which they give rise, may result from different sources or determinants. Each model may bring into play different actors (individuals, project groups, departments, etc.), different, more or less formalized processes, and so on. It would be pointless, therefore, to seek to establish systematic unilateral relations between our different models of innovation and the various elements in their organization. Consequently, our enquiries will concentrate for the most part on the approach based on characteristics and competences.

Three major points are examined in this chapter. The first is the way in which a characteristics-based approach reveals the various possible sources of innovation. This question is also considered in terms of a concept of the firm as a 'chain of linked competences'. Such an approach to the firm seems to be consistent with our concept of the product in terms of characteristics and competences and with the models of innovation derived from it. The second point is the organization of innovation in service firms, that is the main actors mobilized within firms and the characteristics of the processes brought into play. Several general models of the organization of innovation are highlighted and their (quantitative) significance estimated by a statistical exercise based on a postal survey. The third and final point concerns the implications of a characteristics-based approach for the diffusion and protection of innovation in services.

1. THE SOURCES AND DETERMINANTS OF INNOVATION

This question will be considered from two different points of view. First, it will be examined from the perspective of a characteristics-based approach. The unit of analysis will then be changed and the question approached in terms of a definition of the firm as a 'chain of linked competences' (Guilhon and Gianfaldoni, 1990; Guilhon, 1992).

1.1 The Sources and Determinants of Innovation from the Perspective of a Characteristics-Based Approach to the Product

The general formalization of the 'product' adopted here is an heuristic tool that allows us to uncover the main possible sources and determinants of innovation (Figure 4.1).

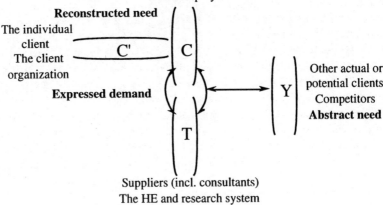

Figure 4.1 *The possible sources of innovation as revealed by a characteristics-based approach to the product*

Each term or vector in the diagram denotes a certain number (though not an exhaustive list) of possible (direct or indirect) sources of innovation or ideas for innovations.

1. The client's competences [C'] represent the possible contribution of the individual client (the individual or limited group with whom the service provider interfaces) and, more generally, of the client organization as a whole.

2. The service provider's competences [C] represent the role of the service provider's employees (in the first instance, those employees in direct contact with the client and, more generally, the organization as a whole) as a source of innovation. [C] can also be said indirectly to symbolize the education and research systems that have helped to create the competences and to take account of the use of external consultants, particularly in the transfer of competences, or even of the informal networks of managers and professionals within which various types of information circulate. The interface between [C] and [C'], the service provider's competences and those of his client, plays a very important role. It is a locus for the exchange of information and ideas and for the expression and (re)construction of demand. In some cases (for example, in the ad hoc innovation model), it is this interface that is the site of the innovation process and which acts, as it were, as a 'flexible laboratory'.

3. The technical and process characteristics [T][1] illustrate another potential source of innovation, namely the providers of tangible 'technologies' (technical systems), intangible technologies (methods, modes of organization) and other supplies. These providers may be internal (R&D department, functional departments, project groups, and so on) or external, including consultants. Thus the role of consultants as a source of innovation is located at the level of both the vector [C] of competences and the vector [T] of technical and process characteristics, which represent the transfer of various elements, such as competences, methods and technical systems, that are frequently complementary but sometimes independent of each other. The education and research systems, located upstream of the innovation process itself, could also be included here.

4. Finally, the service characteristics [Y] take account of the role of other actual or potential clients (that is, the whole of the market, or need) and of competitors, that is all the actors who are generally the responsibility of the marketing function. The distinction introduced here between this source of innovation (represented by [Y]) and the sources represented by [C'] (the client's competences) and by [C'][C] (the interface) is the same as that made elsewhere (Gallouj, 1994c) between:

    *   *abstract need*, that is the 'diffuse' background noise emitted by the environment (clients, competitors) and arising out of complexity and

uncertainty but not linked to any particular client,

- *expressed demand*, that is the way in which a need detected by a service provider in a given client organization is expressed by that client, and
- *reconstructed need*, that is the redefinition or reconstruction of expressed demand by client and service provider working together. In intellectual services, in particular, the problem to be solved is not always objective, and may even 'be waiting to be discovered'. It is also a social construction that does not exist outside of the balance of power between those articulating it (mutual influences, powers of persuasion). Thus if the balance of power favors the service provider, innovation in consultancy can operate in accordance with the 'garbage can' principle, with individual innovations becoming 'solutions in search of a problem'.

In the postal survey we conducted (Djellal and Gallouj, 1998, 2001, cf. also Tether and Hipp, 2000), we also examined the question of the relative importance of the main sources of innovation or ideas for innovations. Table 4.1 shows the share of firms that consider the various sources of information as unimportant/of little importance or important/very important.

Table 4.1 The main sources of information, knowledge and competences for innovation (%)*

Sources	Unimp./not very important	Imp./very important
Sales force and contact personnels	10.4	66.7
Other staffs in the firm	33.3	26.2
Parent company	31.9	17.6
Subsidiaries	35.1	10.7
Competitors	26.2	31.2
Clients	5.4	76
IT equipments and systems suppliers	41.6	24.7
Other suppliers	52.3	16.1
IT consultants	58.4	12.9
Other consultants	49.8	16.5
Univ. and other educ. and research instit.	71.3	9
Public organizations (e.g. ANVAR)	68.8	6.4
Fairs, exhib., conf., meetings, journals	42.3	23.3
Informal networks of executives...	35.1	31.2

Note: * Shares of innovative firms over the period 1992-1997 regarding the different sources as unimportant/not very important or important/very important. Remaining percentages for each line regard the response in the middle of the scale. (n=279).

The main sources of information, knowledge and competences on products, processes, organization and external relationship are, in descending order: clients (for 76 per cent of the innovating firms in our sample), the sales force and contact personnel (66.7 per cent), competitors (31.2 per cent), informal networks of executives and professionals (31.2 per cent).

'Other staff in the firm', 'suppliers of information technology equipments and systems', 'fairs, exhibitions, conferences, meetings, newspapers and journals' also play a role, but to a lesser extent (respectively, 26.2 per cent; 24.7 per cent and 23.3 per cent of the innovative firms in our sample).

The sources of information which are least often cited as important or very important are 'other suppliers' (16.1 per cent), 'information technology consultants' (12.9 per cent), 'other consultants' (16.5 per cent), 'universities' (9 per cent) and 'public organizations' (6.4 per cent).

The fact that clients and sales forces play an important role as sources of information in relational activities is not surprising. Nor is the fact that competitors and informal networks, and to a lesser extent fairs, conferences, journals, etc. play an important role in activities where protection is difficult and imitation a quasi-natural law.

Other results, some of which seem paradoxical, also warrant particular attention:

- the relatively minor involvement of suppliers of materials as sources of information, which argues in favor of non-technologist approaches to innovation in services;
- the minor involvement of different types of consultants as a source of information, whilst one of their main missions is precisely to supply information. This finding contradicts the idea of a model of coproduced innovation (i.e. coproduced by consultants);
- the negligible role of public organizations (ANVAR [French state technology transfer agency], ARIST [French regional scientific and technical information agency], CCI [Chambers of Commerce], etc.) and universities as sources of information; result, which has been confirmed several times by surveys in manufacturing.

On a more theoretical level, the characteristics-based concept of the product can be said to reconcile the 'science-push' and 'demand-pull' approaches to innovation: science, symbolized by the vectors [C] and/or [T], and the demand for service characteristics, symbolized by the vector [Y], constitute the two facets of the product (good or service). In reality, as we have seen, demand also manifests itself at another site, namely the interface [C'][C]. Innovation can take one of these two points of entry, or both at the same time.

It should be noted, however, that the science-push determinant goes beyond the physical sciences to encompass progress in the human and social sciences as well (cf., in the case of insurance services, Table 4.2, where the human and social sciences are shown in italics). In other words, the vectors [T] and [C] include not only techniques in the strict sense of the term and the competences associated with them but also service techniques (legal, financial, commercial techniques, for example) and the corresponding competences.

Table 4.2 The principal fields of knowledge deployed in a large insurance company (according to an internal study)

Fields of knowledge deployed	Property insurance	Life insurance	Retirement savings scheme
Pure and applied mathematics	X	X	X
Statistics	X	X	X
Modelling	X	X	X
Information technology	X	X	X
Automation-robotics	X	X	X
Physics	X		
Chemistry	X	X	
Cosmology	X		
Life sciences		X	
Ethnology	X	X	X
Geography	X	X	
Economics and management	X	X	X
Law and politics	X	X	X
Sociology	X	X	X
Cindynics (science of danger)	X		
Demography-epidemiology		X	X
Linguistics	X	X	X

1.2 The Firm as a 'Chain of Linked Competences'

If the firm rather than the product is adopted as the unit of analysis, the subset {[C'], [C],]T]}, which includes the client's and service provider's competences and the technical and process characteristics, can be seen as an expression, at a given moment, of the notion of the firm as a 'chain of linked competences' (Guilhon and Gianfaldoni, 1990; Guilhon, 1992), that is as the linkage of a knowledge base to an experience base.

Such an approach to the firm is consistent with the notion of the product as a system of characteristics and competences and, as we shall see, with the six models of innovation already identified. It provides some clues as to the sources of innovation and, more generally, its organization (to anticipate the second part of the chapter).

1.2.1 An approach to the firm consistent with our approach to the product

As already suggested, a firm can be regarded as a system for the production and management of competences that links two elements whose relative importance varies depending on the firm in question. These two elements are a knowledge base and an experience base (Guilhon and Gianfaldoni, 1990; Guilhon, 1992) (cf. Figure 4.2).

1. *The knowledge base* (in the sense of the term used by Dosi, 1988) consists of a stock of various forms of knowledge (tacit, codified, embodied, disembodied...) relating to the organization's various activities (production, marketing, etc.) that the firm taps into when it needs to find a new solution for a problem. This stock is fed by the various flows of knowledge the firm creates or acquires: R&D, technology monitoring, staff transfers, technological progress made by suppliers, etc.
2. The *experience base* consists of four generic categories of competences:
    a) competences in the *use* of theoretical knowledge (managerial as well as technical knowledge) derived from the knowledge base;
    b) competences arising out of the *performance* of tasks ('learning by doing') at all levels and in all functions of the firm;
    c) *organizational* competences (which in some cases can be described as methodological competences), i.e. competences in the establishment of routines and organizational learning processes;
    d) competences in the *management of information* derived from markets (management of the producer/client interface).

The following observations can be made in respect of this experience base.

1. As regards the *use* competences, account has to be taken of the combinatory or architectural competences which, as we will see, play a role in both the experience base and the knowledge base, providing the linkage between the recombinative model or its variants, on the one hand, and the two bases, on the other. The form of learning at work here might be described as 'learning by learning'.
2. The *management information* competences (which relate to *management of the producer/client interface* and of knowledge derived from markets) and the *organizational* competences are not separate sets. Indeed, interface management involves both informational and organizational aspects. Methods are nothing other than intangible techniques or organizational models for the gathering and processing of information with a view to solving a problem.

A firm's experience base is fed by its knowledge base. Conversely, a firm taps into its knowledge base when it is confronted with problems requiring a more theoretical approach and the production of new solutions, feeding into it material (inputs) derived from experience.

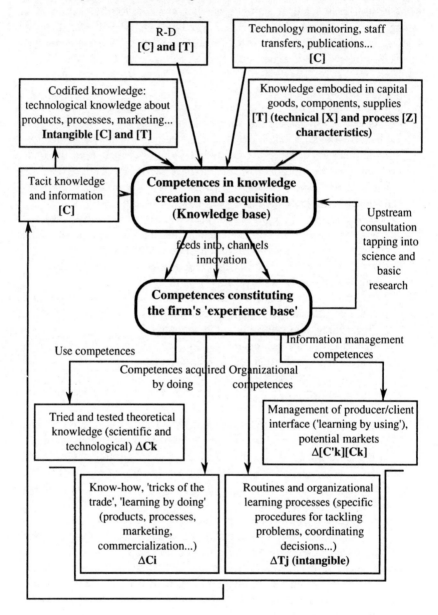

Figure 4.2 A graphical representation of the chain of competences*
Source: After Guilhon (1992).
Note: *The various vectors or elements of our extended Lancasterian approach appear in bold.

The various constituent elements of these knowledge and experience bases fall perfectly within the scope of the system of competences and characteristics {[C'], [C],]T]} representing the structural components of the product, that is its cognitive and technical specifications. Figure 4.2 is an attempt to indicate the sets of competences or characteristics mobilized in the various cases considered.

In sum, we can say that the knowledge base is enriched by (internally produced or externally acquired) technical characteristics and competences that are new in absolute terms (at least for the firm in question), whereas the experience base tends rather to increase the 'weight' or' value' of these characteristics or competences (which is what the symbol Δ is intended to represent in Figure 4.2). We are dealing here with two different generic modes of innovation, which are examined in greater detail in the following section.

1.2.2 A concept of the firm consistent with our models of innovation

The notion of the firm as a chain of competences located within a socio-technical network (Callon, 1991) is consistent with our various models of innovation (Figure 4.3). Guilhon and Gianfaldoni (1990) link the knowledge base to radical innovations and the experience base to incremental innovations. Our notion of the product as sets of characteristics and competences, together with the greater diversity and differentiation we have introduced into the innovation models, enables us to refine the analysis still further.

The knowledge base is the source of radical innovations, since it is the site at which new knowledge is amassed. The knowledge base is the locus for the accumulation of various items of new knowledge – whether tacit, codified, embodied in equipment, etc. – that is new systems {[C], [X],]Z]} that are unconnected with those already stored in the base.

In our view, the recombinative model and the incremental model (in the specific sense attributed to it here, that is the addition of characteristics) can also be linked to this competence base in certain circumstances, for example, when the recombination of competences or characteristics leads to radically new knowledge or 'products' (which is not uncommon in certain high-tech industries, such as IT, electronics, biotechnology, genetic engineering) or when the competences or characteristics added are newly created or acquired competences.

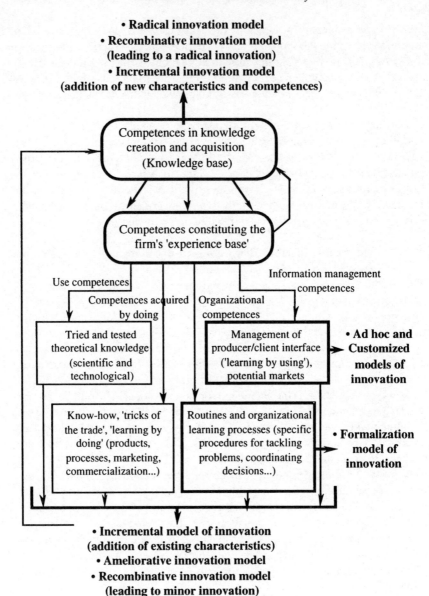

• **Radical innovation model**
• **Recombinative innovation model**
(leading to a radical innovation)
• **Incremental innovation model**
(addition of new characteristics and competences)

Competences in knowledge
creation and acquisition
(Knowledge base)

Competences constituting the
firm's 'experience base'

Use competences

Information management
competences

Competences acquired
by doing

Organizational
competences

Tried and tested
theoretical knowledge
(scientific and
technological)

Management of
producer/client interface
('learning by using'),
potential markets

• **Ad hoc and**
Customized
models of
innovation

Know-how, 'tricks of
the trade', 'learning by
doing' (products,
processes, marketing,
commercialization...)

Routines and organizational
learning processes (specific
procedures for tackling
problems, coordinating
decisions...)

• **Formalization**
model of
innovation

• **Incremental model of innovation**
(addition of existing characteristics)
• **Ameliorative innovation model**
• **Recombinative innovation model**
(leading to minor innovation)

Figure 4.3 The linkage between competence chains and models of innovation

According to Guilhon and Gianfaldoni (1990) and Guilhon (1992), the experience base, for its part, is the source of incremental innovations (in the
usual sense of the term, that is gradual, or non-radical innovations).   Given

the differentiation we have introduced into this category (see Chapter 3), this incremental mode of innovation encompasses a number of different cases.

1. The experience base is the source of ameliorative and incremental innovations. In the second case, however, in contrast to the incremental model linked to the knowledge base, innovation involves the addition of competences and characteristics already stored in the knowledge base.
2. It is also, it seems to us, a source of ad hoc innovations mediated through the information and interface management competences.
3. It is also a source of formalization innovations mediated through the organizational competences (production of organizational learning routines and, more generally, specific procedures for tackling problems and coordinating decisions).
4. Finally, it is a source of combinatory innovations (at least in those variants of this model of innovation that do not significantly modify the system of characteristics and competences).

2. THE ORGANIZATION OF INNOVATION

In this section, we draw on, and enrich, a typology of the modes of innovation organization in service firms advanced by Barcet, Bonamy and Mayère (1987) (see also a similar approach developed in Sundbo, 1992 and Sundbo and Gallouj, 2000). This typology encompasses not only the actors and processes involved in innovation but also the types of innovation strategy (plans and resources deployed in order to produce innovations) adopted by the firms in question.

Barcet, Bonamy and Mayère identify three models of innovation in services (the professionals in partnership model, the managerial model and the industrial model), which we will attempt to interpret within the framework of a dynamic of competences and characteristics. A further three models will be added: the neo-industrial model (obtained by differentiating the industrial model), the entrepreneurial model and the artisanal or craft model.

2.1 The Professionals in Partnership Model

This is the model that seems characteristic of medium-sized firms that supply services with a high 'grey matter' content and sell not service 'products' exactly but rather competences and problem-solving capabilities in particular areas of expertise (for example, consultancy, research and engineering companies).

In this model, there are no formalized innovation structures. 'Research' is, above all, individual, informal and pragmatic. Extending the analysis developed by Horne and Martin (1985), we could also describe this model as the 'bottom-bottom' or 'top-top' model. In this respect, the professionals in partnership model has a number of advantages: it is flexible and capable of rapid response to market signals and of synergistically combining the individual thoughts of its members. However, depending on its individual make-up, it also has a number of disadvantages, including the risk of the innovation process remaining unfinished, the absence of a 'corporate plan' and the risk of a 'brain drain' linked to turnover among the 'professionals in partnership'.

2.2 The Managerial Model of Innovation Organization

This model is encountered in large international audit and consultancy networks. It reflects the existence of an R&D/innovation policy, strategy or function within the firm but the absence of an R&D department. In this model, there is no permanent innovation/R&D department. Research and, more precisely, the search for ideas is 'everybody's business', but development, which is a longer process, is the business of ad hoc project teams. The favored approach here is one in which a 'product' is designed to be as reproducible as possible. It does not, however, equate to the industrialization of services. As already noted, it is the *professional rationalization* principle that is at work here rather than the *industrial rationalization* principle.

In this model, innovation policy is supplemented by two important actions: the accumulation of knowledge (Gallouj, 1990, 1995), with a view to ensuring its reproducibility and the socialization of individual knowledge, and quality control, which is not only a means of assessing compliance with service standards but also an indicator of changes in the nature of customer demand.

These first two models of innovation organization (the managerial and professionals in partnership models) are also drawn from Sundbo (1992), where they are denoted by the terms 'top strategical organizations' and 'collective professionals'.

• To oversimplify somewhat, we can say that the main lever of innovation in managerial firms is the vector [T] of technical characteristics, particularly in its intangible forms (methods, etc.). The vector of competences [C] is also an important lever as a result of training, recruitment, 'up or out' strategies and strategies for tapping into external sources of accumulated expertise, such as databases, links with universities and research centres, etc. (On these various issues, see Gallouj, 1990). All the models of innovation can be implemented here, but the formalization model plays an important role.

In an earlier study (Gallouj, 1995) of the consultancy industry, we showed that the formalization model (for example, the design of a method or of a formatted service product) can fall within the scope of the standard model of industrial R&D (that is, it can be more or less formalized) since, in theory at least, R&D, production and sales can all be dissociated from each other. The genesis of ideas can be formalized to some extent by means of internal procedures for gathering the ideas and dissatisfactions articulated by consultants and clients (by setting up user groups, for example). Moreover, with the increasing 'tangibility' that is characteristic of the formalization model, certain forms of experimentation become possible.

• In the professionals in partnership model, the main source of innovation is expertise, that is the set of individual competences [C]. The interface [C'][C] is an important site for innovation. Although it is not the only one at work, the ad hoc mode of innovation plays an important role here.

Analysis of the various phases of the innovation process in such a model (cf. Gallouj, 1990, 1995) reveals that the production, marketing and R&D-innovation phases can merge or occur simultaneously. The client's problem (in the concrete, actual sense), whether it be corrective, progressive or creative (to use the terminology employed by Kubr, 1988), is the starting point for the production process in which the client is an active participant. The important point here is that this production process, which also becomes an innovation process while still in progress or retrospectively, concludes with a formalization stage (transformation of [C] into [T]) that takes place outside the client organization. The aim of this phase is to review the problem and the innovative solution, to formalize them, to modify them, to reappropriate certain elements and to store or record them in the consultancy firm's 'read-only memory' (whether the storage medium be paper, computer systems, audiovisual equipment, etc.).

Ad hoc innovation is produced at the interface and depends on the nature and constituent parts of that interface, particularly in the case of consultancy. Thus interfaces of the 'sparring' type, which are characterized by coproduction, as opposed to those of the 'jobbing' type, which are characterized by subcontracting (Gadrey et al., 1992; Gadrey and Gallouj, 1998), are the ones most favorable to the realization and success of this form of innovation, since they help to improve understanding and acceptance (legitimacy) of the innovation. Moreover, problems of a strategic nature, which are potential sources of innovation, are usually dealt with at an interface of the sparring type: they tend not to be subcontracted. However, it should not be inferred from this that only 'creative problems', where a totally new situation has to be created, can produce ad hoc innovations. 'Corrective problems', in which the consultant is called upon to act as a therapist, and 'progressive problems', in which he or she is expected to improve a given situation that is feared to be deteriorating, can also give rise to such innovations. Furthermore, the opportunities for ad hoc innovation seem to increase with the size of the service provider and of the client organization, that is as the possible interfaces multiply both quantitatively and qualitatively. Finally, the actual realization of an ad hoc innovation also depends on the quality of the professionals in the client organization who are active at the interface (vector $[C'_k]$).

2.3 The Industrial Model of Innovation Organization

According to Barcet, Bonamy and Mayère (1987), this model is less frequent in services. It is, however, encountered in large firms that specialize in the standardized production of operational services, dealing with materials as well as information. Examples of this are large firms specializing in mass information processing, large-scale contract cleaning and telesurveillance. This is a replica of the traditional industrial R&D model, which clearly separates the R&D department from production. In this type of firm, the production and delivery of services are separated. It is therefore possible to envisage a research and innovation department responsible for improving the 'products' to be delivered or developing new 'products'.

The industrial model, as defined above, seems to us to be ambiguous. Indeed, it takes as its reference point the old industrial model and fails to take account of the fact that it has changed a great deal. The new industrial model, in which the old standardization principle has given way to the flexibility principle, far more clearly describes the way service activities actually operate, since they are often, by definition, interactive. We propose that this model should be divided into a traditional or Fordist industrial model and a neo-industrial model.

2.4 The Traditional Industrial or Fordist Model

This model is defined as above. It is rare in services and is becoming increasingly rare in manufacturing itself. It is encountered in large operational services firms. The main lever of innovation is the vector of technical and process characteristics [T]. There may be specialized innovation departments that maintain linear relationships (but no true feedback) with the other departments (linear model of innovation). There are often technical production departments and IT departments.

2.5 The Neo-industrial Model

Firms run according to the traditional industrial model are tending to move towards a neo-industrial model. This new model reflects certain developments taking place in mass informational services, which have traditionally functioned according to the Fordist model but which are today exposed to fierce competition (banks, insurance companies, postal services). In this model, innovation is produced from multiple sources (actors) which interact (these are unavoidable 'technical' interactions, whatever their effectiveness or quality may be). In the case of an insurance company, these sources might include, for example, the IT department, the different technical product departments and possibly a 'think tank' resembling a genuine R&D department. Project groups involving members of different departments are favored and tend to proliferate with varying degrees of success. In this model, the main levers of innovation are the competences [C], the technical and process characteristics [T] and the service characteristics [Y], the respective producers of which interact with each other.

Two different forms of this neo-industrial model can be identified: one in which the interactions between the technical and process characteristics [T] and the service characteristics [Y] are in disequilibrium, and another in which those interactions are in equilibrium.

In the first case, the service characteristics [Y] change much more rapidly than the technical and process characteristics [T]. To some extent, new service characteristics proliferate while technical and process characteristics remain unchanged. The incremental model of innovation, in which characteristics are added, plays a very important role here. Some management sciences specialists (Easingwood, 1986) have examined the perverse effects of such a model, which destroys learning sequences not only in the client organization but in the service provider as well.

In the second case, some members of the organization are responsible for producing technical and process characteristics [T] and others for producing service characteristics [Y]. There is a division of labor and, to some extent, a balance of power, which does not mean there are no conflicts. All the modes of innovation can be considered within this configuration.

Figure 4.4, which portrays a neo-industrial model in which the technical and process characteristics and the service characteristics interact in equilibrium with each other, describes the process whereby new insurance policies are produced in a major French company. It can encompass the incremental, recombinative and formalization models. There is a genuine division of labor between those who produce the service characteristics [Y] and those who produce the technical characteristics [T]. The former include the departments in charge of the various categories of products (life insurance, property insurance, corporate insurance) and the marketing department, while the second include, in particular, the various parts of the IT department.

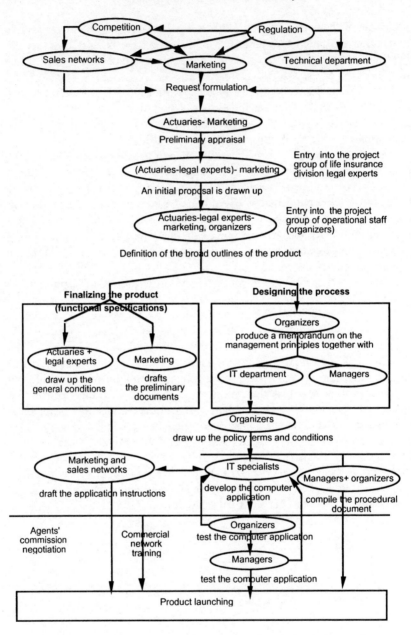

Figure 4.4 The stages in the development of a new life insurance product
Source: Gadrey and Gallouj (1994).

The innovation process can be described in the following terms (cf. Figure
4.4). The idea for a new insurance policy, which can come from a number of
different sources (competitors, loss adjusters, sales networks, marketing, tech-

nical departments, etc.) is taken up by a project group made up, initially, of actuaries and marketing specialists, joined subsequently by legal experts. A first draft of a solution is drawn up, laying down the functional specifications, that is, in essence, an initial formulation of the service characteristics [Y]. The 'organizers' then join the group and take part in the process leading to a broad definition of the product (functional specifications [Y], process specifications [T]).

Two parallel processes then get under way. One involves finalizing the product's formal specifications [Y]; the main participants here are the actuaries and legal experts, who draw up the general conditions, and the marketing specialists, who draft the initial documents and then the application instructions. The other involves the design of the process [T] that will support the 'product', which brings into play organizers, managers and IT specialists.

2.6 The Entrepreneurial Model

In this model, service firms are set up on the basis of a radical innovation. These small firms have no R&D department and their main activity is selling the initial radical innovation. The models of innovation that such firms draw on, namely, incremental and ad hoc innovation models, can be used to improve this initial innovation. The emergence of IT services, repair services, etc., can be interpreted in these terms. Many of the service firms founded by university researchers also fall within the scope of this entrepreneurial model (cf. the studies by Mustar, 1993, 1994).

2.7 The Craft Model

This is the innovation model at work in small firms involved in operational services (contract cleaning, caretaking and security, hotel and catering, etc.). These firms have no innovation strategy, nor do they have a R&D or IT department. However, innovation does occur through the ameliorative model and the associated learning processes. It affects the 'level' or 'weight' of the characteristics or competences rather than their absolute value.

Table 4.3 summarizes the main characteristics of the various models of innovation organization outlined above.

Table 4.3 The various models of innovation organization

Modes of innovation organization	Definition	Main lever of innovation, representative model of innovation	Type of firms or industries
Professionals in partnership	No specialized innov. structures Innovation is individual, infor- mal, pragmatic - Top-top model	[C], [C'][C] Ad hoc model	Medium-sized firms providing intellectual services
Managerial	- Innovation policy or function, but no department - Project groups - Strategies for accumulating knowledge	Intangible elements of [T] (methods) and [C] Formalization model	Networked service firms originating in the English- speaking world (auditors, consultants)
Traditional industrial (Fordist)	- Existence of specialist innovation department	Tangible and process elements of [T]	Large firms providing operational services
Neo-industrial	- Multiple, interacting sources of innov. (interactive model)	[C], [T] and [Y] produced through interaction	Mass informational services (banking, insurance)
Entrepreneurial	- Establishment of a service firm on the basis of a radical innovation, no R&D department	Improvement of the original radical innovation	Small high-tech services, operational services, firms set up by researchers
Craft	- No innovation strategy or department	Ameliorative model (learning)	Small operational services firms

3. AN ATTEMPT TO EVALUATE STATISTICALLY THE IMPORTANCE OF THE MODELS

These various modes of innovation organization emerged from in-depth empirical investigations of a qualitative nature. As a result, they are complex notions that do not lend themselves readily to quantification. Nevertheless, it is not impossible statistically to verify the existence and importance of these models. We have already attempted such an exercise (Djellal and Gallouj, 1998, 2001), taking as our starting points an analysis of the main actors involved in innovation and a simplified definition of the various modes of innovation.

3.1 The Actors Involved in Innovation in Services

The qualitative empirical studies which we have carried out on a number of service industries (Gallouj, 1994; C. and F. Gallouj 1996) have enabled us to highlight different modes of organization of the innovation activity. These different modes are not antinomic: some of them can coexist within the same firm. They can be informal processes: where individual effort plays the main role (1), or involving a significant amount of teamwork (2). This activity can be carried out by an R&D department in the traditional sense of the term (3), or by another type of innovation department (specializing in designing new services without being an R&D department) (4). The marketing department (5), IT department (6) or other departments, examples of which we will give at the end of this section (7) can also play a key role. Finally, it can be the work of organized project groups, involving members from several departments (8).

The aim here is to try and quantify the relative importance of each of these different modes of innovation organization. Table 4.4 shows the share of innovative firms which regard each of the modes of organization as unimportant or not very important or important or very important.

From this table, we can see that flexible modes of organization (that is temporary formal or informal 'structures') are far more frequently cited as being important or very important than the others. These can consist of informal individual activity (44.8 per cent), informal team activity (56.6 per cent) and (formal) project groups involving members of different departments (41.6 per cent).

The survey unambiguously confirms that innovation is more rarely organized along the lines of specialized departments, whether they are R&D departments, or (less traditional) innovation departments. Indeed, more than 80 per cent of the innovative firms consider the R&D department to be an unimportant or not very important modality of innovation organization. Nearly 72 per cent of them apply the same judgement to innovation departments.

IT and marketing departments are evaluated in similar terms. This is not surprising, if we bear in mind the importance of the balance between market and science (the 'science push' and 'demand pull' determinants) in innovation. However, this evaluation is (paradoxically) ambiguous. Indeed, in both cases, the share of firms to consider that these two departments play no role or an unimportant role is larger than the share which considers them to play an important or very important role. But, at the same time, the proportion of firms which considers them to play an important or very important role is far from negligible (a third of firms).

In the case of the IT department, this result should go some way towards reconsidering the place of IT in innovation in service.

Nevertheless, in both cases, this ambiguity could stem from the over-representation of small firms in our sample (which do not have an IT department or a marketing department).

Other departments can intervene in innovation, particularly the following departments and instances (the first two being the most frequently cited): sales department, top management, 'telecommunication', 'technical', 'operational', 'administrative', 'creativity', 'human resources', 'design', 'scanning', 'logistics', 'development', 'quality', 'research' and 'products and advice' departments (the latter cited by a hotel firm). But the share of firms which accord them importance is relatively small (17.2 per cent).

Table 4.4 Different modes of innovation organization in service firms (%) (n=279)

The modalities of innovation organization	Unimportant or not very important	Important or very important
Informal individual process	31.2	44.8
Informal team work	19.3	56.6
R-D department	81.4	6.8
Innovation department	71.7	12.5
Marketing department	46.9	33.0
IT department	48.7	32.3
Other departments	50.5	17.2
Project groups across departments	42.6	41.6

3.2 From Actors to Models of Innovation Organization

The combination of the different instances of innovation envisaged above, allows the existence of the first four general innovation organization models (see Section 2) to be statistically verified, taking account not only of the main innovation actors and processes, but also of types of general innovation strategies implemented by service firms.

To this end, we propose simplified definitions of each of the models:

1. *The professionals in partnership model (in the strict sense)* describes firms which consider only the informal individual process to be an important/very important innovation modality.
2. *The professionals in partnership model (in the wide sense)* describes firms for which:
   - the individual informal process is important/very important;
   - or the individual informal process and the informal team process are important/very important;
   - (all the other instances are unimportant or not very important).
3. *The managerial model* is that in which:
   - the project group is important/very important;
   - or the project group and informal team process are important/very important;
   - or the project group and the informal individual process are important/very important;
   - or the project group and the informal individual and the informal team processes are important/very important;
   - (all the others are unimportant or not very important).
4. *The traditional industrial model (in the strict sense)* describes firms for which all the instances are unimportant or not very important, with the exception of the R&D or innovation department, which are important or very important.
5. *The traditional industrial model (in the wide sense)* corresponds to firms for which all the instances are unimportant or not very important, with the exception of the R and D or innovation departments, or the IT department.
6. *The neo-industrial model* describes the mode of innovation organization corresponding to firms for which, regardless of the degree of importance of the other instances, at least three formal structures (one of which being a 'project group involving members of several departments') are important or very important.

To summarize the definitions we have just proposed, the central elements for establishing a quantified evaluation of the innovation models are the following:

- the 'individual' element for the professional partnership model;
- the existence of formal project groups for the managerial model;
- the existence of specialized innovation departments for the industrial model;
- the existence of organized interaction for the neo-industrial model. Project groups involving members of several departments can be regarded, in

this case, as indicators of this interaction, provided that importance is accorded to other formal structures.

Table 4.5 and 4.6 summarize the principal statistical results established on the basis of these definitions. These quantitative results can have no claim to statistical representativeness because of the relatively small sample sizes (particularly in Table 4.6). Nevertheless, they merit consideration because they are reasonably consistent with the results of many qualitative studies (based on the in-depth interview methodology).

Table 4.5 The models of innovation organization

Model	N	(%)
Professionals in partnership (in the strict sense)	26	9.3
Professionals in partnership (in the wide sense)	58	20.8
Managerial	36	12.9
Industrial traditional (in the strict sense)	0	0
Industrial traditional (in the wide sense)	6	2.15
Neoindustrial	60	21.5

Note: * Numbers and shares of the innovative firms in our sample functioning according to the different models, n=279).

Table 4.6 The models of innovation organization according to service industry (share of firms from different industries in different innovation models).

Types of serv. Innov. model	Financial Serv.		Consul-tancy		Operat. Serv.		Hotels-cat. retailing		Total	
	n	%	n	%	n	%	n	%	n	%
P. partnership (strict sense)	2	7.7	24	92.3	0	0	0	0	26	100
P. partnership (wide sense)	3	5.2	53	91.4	1	1.7	1	1.7	58	100
Managerial	4	11.1	27	75	3	8.3	2	5.5	36	100
Industrial trad. (strict sense)	0	0	0	0	0	0	0	0	0	
Industrial trad. (wide sense)	1	16.7	4	66.6	0	0	1	16.7	6	100
Neoindustrial	23	38.4	20	33.3	9	15	8	13.3	60	100

Our analysis suggests that just under one tenth of the innovative firms in our sample (n = 279) belong to the professionals in partnership model in the strict sense; and that a little over a fifth belong to the professionals in partnership model in the wide sense (Table 4.5). In both cases, more than 90 per cent of the firms described by these models are consultancy firms (table 4.6). The few financial services belonging to this model are brokers who, as an intermediary service, can be regarded as a particular category of consultancy.

The managerial model also mainly describes consultancy firms: 13 per cent of the innovative firms in our sample conform to this model's definition, and 75 per cent of them are consultancy firms.

No firms in our sample seem to conform to the traditional industrial model. If the definition is relaxed by introducing IT departments, 2.15 per cent of the firms in our sample (one bank, two IT service firms, one recruitment consultant, a market research office, one firm from the retailing field) seem to conform to a traditional industrial model in the wide sense.

Finally, a little over a fifth of the firms in our sample conform to our definition of the neo-industrial model. The largest share of firms belonging to this model were financial services firms, but significant shares of the other industries also conformed to this model, including consultancy firms, particularly in the following fields: IT consultancy, market research (ten and six firms, respectively) which, together, represented 27 per cent of the firms functioning according to the neo-industrial model.

4. DIFFUSING AND PROTECTING INNOVATION

The notion of the product as a set of characteristics and competences also serves to reveal the ways in which innovations might 'leak' out and the consequent difficulties in appropriating and protecting them.

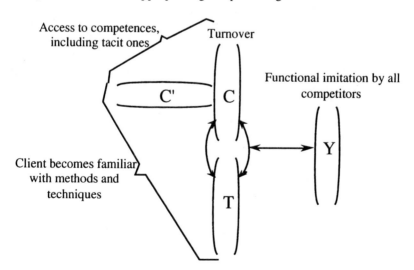

Figure 4.5 The product as a set of characteristics and possible sources of leakage

Figure 4.5 shows some of the ways in which innovations might 'leak' away; they are linked to the various sets of characteristics and reveal potential 'imitators' or groups of imitators.

1. The vector of service characteristics [Y] is linked to possible functional imitation by all actual or potential competitors (including clients). The service characteristics are indeed highly visible and 'volatile', which makes them easy to imitate. The most convincing examples are to be found in financial and personal insurance services. The specifications of an insurance policy or of a financial product are in the public domain. They are the object of firms' marketing and advertising policies (advertising leaflets, etc.).
2. The relationship [C'][T] symbolizes the client's capacity for learning and appropriating the service provider's methods and techniques as client and service provider interact with each other (possibly even in a self-service situation).
3. The interface [C'][C] represents access for the client to the service provider's competences, including to some extent the tacit competences that are memorized in the course of the service relationship ('learning by interacting').
4. The vector [C], finally, illustrates the possibility of knowledge leaking out as a result of labor turnover.

The first source of leakage is particularly characteristic of mass-market personal services, while the other three are characteristic of knowledge-intensive services (particularly business consultancy).

However, while it is difficult to afford innovation in services legal protection, the following points should be noted.

*   The characteristics [C] and [T] may have a strong tacit and idiosyncratic element, which from this point of view constitutes a natural mode of appropriation (at least with regard to external imitators).
*   More generally, the knowledge produced at the interface is shaped in such a way as to adapt it to the 'topology of a multidimensional socio-economic space' (Antonelli, 1995). It is localized knowledge that eludes the mechanical universe of information and knowledge as a (non-excludable and non-rival) transparent and transferable public good.[2] The information and knowledge arising out of innovations produced at the interface (interactional mode of innovation, cf. Gallouj, 2002a) is knowledge adapted to the client's socio-economic problem. As a result, it becomes a quasi-private good (and therefore excludable and rival). It has a significant local and idiosyncratic content, which limits its transferability and facilitates its appropriation by the client. On the other hand, raw, non-localized (generic) information can be regarded as a public good, which the

service provider has at his disposal and can transfer elsewhere without damaging the interests of previous clients.

- Management of this interface, that is the combining or juxtaposing of $[C'_k]$ and $[C_k]$, may offer a solution to the problem of protection. Whether voluntarily, in order to ensure customer loyalty, or involuntarily, because of differences in levels of expertise, service providers can 'lock in' their customers, creating cognitive dependencies and complementarities unfavorable to the client or the system. This notion of 'lock-in' is understood here in a broad sense. Thus, for example, a legal consultant could put together a legal and fiscal arrangement of such complexity that only he or she can fully fathom its intricacies. This problem is more familiar, if not more frequent, when tangible technical systems or software are involved (IT consultancy, for example). Methodological 'lock-ins' (those involving intangible techniques) are also common. However, it should be noted that such 'lock-ins' can, conversely, work in favor of the client himself, when it is the service provider who is subordinated to the client, that is when the balance of cognitive and technological power favors the latter.
- The technical characteristics [T] may be the object of certain forms of protection. In the insurance and financial services industries, for example, where service characteristics are particularly volatile, attempts at appropriation could concentrate on the technical and process characteristics, which are less directly accessible to imitators.
- The question of protection can also be posed in different ways depending on the model of innovation in question. As we have already stressed, the ad hoc innovation model is beset by particularly awkward problems of appropriation because of the important role played by the interface, while the formalization model, which is driven by the codification principle, facilitates imitation at the same time as it lends itself to certain forms of protection. The recombinative and incremental models, for their part, pose the question of innovation in terms of the free circulation of knowledge rather than of appropriation for private purposes.

CONCLUSION

As this chapter has shown, our concept of the product in terms of characteristics and competences enables us to incorporate, with some degree of coherence, a number of questions relating to the organization of innovation in service firms as well as in manufacturing firms.

Drawing on this concept of the product, therefore, we have been able to identify the sources or determinants of innovation, the difficulties involved in appropriating it and the various models of innovation organization.

The concept of the firm adopted here, that is the firm as a linked chain of knowledge, as opposed to the firm as a production function or a nexus of contracts, is essentially evolutionary in nature. In the next chapter, we will attempt to demonstrate how far our concept of the product and the models of innovation that flow from it also fall within the scope of evolutionary theory and, over and above that simple observation, how far they might enrich that theory.

NOTES

1. The reader is reminded that, in order to simplify matters, the vector [T] is used to denote both the technical characteristics [X] and the process characteristics [Z].
2. For a recent survey of economic analyses devoted to the nature of information and knowledge, see Petit (1998).

5. Models of Innovation and Evolutionary Theory

INTRODUCTION

In Chapter 2, we extended Saviotti and Metcalfe's Lancasterian approach to the product to services, suggesting in particular that account should be taken of the service relationship (coproduction relationship). Drawing on this extended approach, we were able in Chapter 3 to identify a number of models of innovation (the radical, incremental, ad hoc, ameliorative, recombinative and formalization models), whose various mechanisms and modes of organization were investigated in Chapter 4.

Our aim in this chapter is to examine how far the analyses and models of innovation presented in previous chapters can be said to belong to the evolutionary tradition and to what extent they might help to enrich or advance that tradition.

This chapter begins by examining the evolutionary nature of our concept of the product and of the models of innovation derived from it (Section 1). Attempts to apply evolutionary concepts and methodologies to services are not in themselves anything new. The main points were discussed in Chapter 1, in particular the attempt by Soete and Miozzo (1990) to construct a sectoral taxonomy of the forms of technical change adapted to services. The main weakness of the various analyses outlined in that chapter is that they focus almost exclusively on tangible process technologies. As we shall see here (Section 2), it is possible, by adopting an approach to services couched in terms of functions or characteristics, to construct sectoral taxonomies of innovation in services that are closer to reality. The analytical perspective then shifts as we attempt to develop a biology-inspired approach based on the notion of technological populations.

1. EVOLUTIONARY MODELS OF INNOVATION

Thus our aim in this section is to examine the extent to which the models of innovation outlined in previous chapters are consistent with an evolutionary approach. After a brief summary of the main features of this theory, this question will be considered from two different perspectives:

1. the extended Lancasterian approach and evolutionary theory in general;
2. the presence of evolutionary thinking in each of the modes of innovation identified.

1.1 A Brief Outline of Evolutionary Theory

Drawing on the relationships between various research traditions, in particular the Schumpeterian tradition, biological theories, theories on the thermodynamics of irreversible systems, systems theory and the theory of organizations (Saviotti and Metcalfe, 1991), the evolutionary approach to technical change marks a break with the traditional notion of technology as an infinite set of techniques, which can themselves be reduced to given combinations of production factors. In the evolutionary approach, the content of technology is considerably extended to include 'knowledge that is both directly "practical" (...) and "theoretical" (...), know-how, methods, procedures, experiences of success and failure and also, of course, physical instruments and equipment...' (Dosi, 1982). Thus qualitative change (the production of variety), which is largely ignored in neo-classical theory, occupies a central position here.

From this perspective, innovation is not a conclusive and final outcome whose effects on a 'black box' have subsequently to be evaluated. Rather it is an *(institutionalized) process* of problem resolution, in which *learning* and the multiplicity of *interactions* between the agents in the organization play a central role. The *cumulative* nature of the learning and the *specificity* or *local nature* of the problems to be resolved reflect the existence of *path dependencies* (historicity) and give the process a considerable degree of *irreversibility* ('lock-in'). This process does not unfold on the basis of substantive rationality and the maximization principle. Rather, it follows the dictates of *procedural rationality* and the *satisfaction* principle. Behavior patterns, including R&D and innovation, are determined by *routines*: they are *selected* from lists or repertoires of routines on the basis of various principles or *selection environments*.

These hypotheses lead to the formulation of key concepts in evolutionary theory as applied to the economics of innovation:

*   the notion of *technological (techno-economic or socio-technical) paradigm* denotes a set of artefacts (dominant design, technological regimes, technological guidepost) and heuristic problem-solving devices that is stable over a certain period of time;
*   the notion of *technological trajectory* denotes each of the directions or capacities for development opened up by the paradigm. If the trajectory is described as *natural,* these directions are real imperatives;
*   the notion of *national innovation system* is based on the interactive nature of innovation processes. It denotes a set of actors (firms, govern-

ments, research centres) that interact through financial, legal and political, technological, social and informational flows (cf. Niosi et al., 1992).

1.2 The Extended Lancasterian Approach and Evolutionary Theory

The approach we have developed is evolutionary because it constitutes an attempt to break into the 'black box'. The point of entry chosen is the 'product' and not, as in neo-classical theory, the process. In our concept of the product, competences [C] and tangible and intangible technical characteristics [T] are mobilized in order to provide services [Y], that is *to solve problems* (this is particularly evident in the case of consultancy services). Thus there is some degree of consistency between our concept of the product and the evolutionary definition of innovation as a problem-solving activity. A new 'product' is nothing other than a new or more effective way of providing services, that is of solving old or new problems (not just technical problems but organizational, strategic and social problems as well).

This approach explicitly takes into account the notion of interaction (particularly with clients, as represented by the [C'][C] linkage), which occupies an important position in evolutionary theory. According to Dosi (1991), 'evolutionary models seek to model economic systems characterized by a wealth of interactions'.

In the approach developed by Saviotti and Metcalfe (1984), the 'technological regime' (in Nelson and Winter's sense of the term) or the 'dominant design' (as defined by Abernathy and Utterback) equate to a given list of technical characteristics X_j. A 'technological trajectory' denotes a path of gradual improvement in these technical characteristics X_j.

The amendments we made to the approach have consequences for the definition and content of technological paradigms and trajectories in services. It is to these consequences that we now turn. The main amendments can be briefly summarized.

1. The set of technical characteristics has been extended in order to take account of intangible techniques.
2. The approach now explicitly includes a set of service provider's competences that links up with that of the client to symbolize the interface at which the service is provided.

Thus in the case of services, the notion of technological trajectory takes on a particular meaning, since it also (or exclusively) relates to 'service technologies', such as financial, actuarial or human resource management techniques. These technologies are also characterized by 'lock-in' and irreversibilities; for example, it seems difficult to envisage a return to Taylorism in situations in which other modes of work organization have been tried out.

Similarly, the notion of technological paradigm encompasses not only material artefacts and heuristic problem-solving devices relating to those artefacts but also intangible products with less clearly defined frameworks (methods, etc.).

Furthermore, the notion of dominant design, or the related notions of technological regime and technological guidepost, will be defined for a given period of time by a stable set of technical characteristics [T], in which the share of intangible technical characteristics will vary depending on the type of service. The notion of dominant design applies not only to cars and tractors but also to fast food restaurants, retail outlets or even consultancy. The rise to prominence of the 'object-based approach' in IT services can be seen as a change of intangible technological regime. In extreme cases, the technological regime may be identifiable only because its intangible technical characteristics have a certain degree of stability. Another extreme situation can also be envisaged, namely that of the 'pure' service, whose service characteristics are obtained solely through the mobilization of competences.

In the case of the 'purest' services, it is also possible to introduce *cognitive trajectories* corresponding to the gradual improvement of the competences [C_k] as a result of individual and collective learning processes and the accumulation and exploitation of expertise. A cognitive trajectory in which combinatory competences predominate will tend to foster the recombinative model of innovation (and to some extent the incremental model) and, indirectly, the formalization models. A cognitive trajectory in which scientific and technical competences related to components predominate will tend to foster the ameliorative and ad hoc models.

If it is accepted that the model in which the service provider's competences [C_k] are gradually improved equates to a *learning-driven cognitive trajectory*, then the model in which the combinations [C'_k][C_k] are improved can be described as a *learning-driven cognitive trajectory applied to interaction or the service relationship*. The combination of service provider's and clients' competences [C'_k][C_k] can be the object of forms of interdependencies which, by analogy with technological lock-in, can be denoted by the term *cognitive lock-in*.

In this case, the term *cognitive or competence regime* can be used to denote a general set of competences formalized in a list of cognitive characteristics (C_k). A 'competence regime' is a set of competences C_k that remains stable over a certain period. A change of competence regime requires the destruction of old competences and their replacement by new ones.

We conclude this point with the following observations.

1. It would seem that all the previous analyses can be applied to the 'post-Fordist' manufacturing sectors, particularly the most knowledge-intensive ones.
2. Technological or cognitive trajectories are generally considered in their

totality. In the case of any given 'product', therefore, they account for the evolution of all its technical or cognitive characteristics. However, it might also be interesting to focus on 'micro-trajectories', that is changes taking place in individual characteristics considered in isolation. These various characteristics may have different capacities for evolution. If the overland transport of goods or people, for example, is compared with the transmission of information through computer systems, it is clear that, for reasons determined by natural laws, the service characteristic 'transport speed' attains its maximum value very rapidly in the first case but not in the second. Similarly, the service characteristic 'space' of a car cannot decrease indefinitely. The corresponding micro-trajectory is characterized by a low potential for development.

3. The evolutionary concepts of dominant design, technological regime and technological paradigm are considered in terms of the technical characteristics (T_j) and, more generally, independently of the service characteristics. Particularly in the case of services, where technical inertias are sometimes weaker, it would also seem possible to consider them in terms of service characteristics, with a dominant design being defined as a stable set of service characteristics. After all, it would be sufficient to move from one (third world) country to another to become aware of how indispensable some aspects of services have become to us.

4. The fourth and final observation flows from the previous one. It may be that Saviotti's suggestion (Saviotti, 1996) that the discontinuities in technological evolution are attributable more to the structure of the technologies than to that of the services they provide applies more to goods than to services. In the case of services, indeed, significant qualitative changes (production of variety) may result from manipulation of the service characteristics without any intervention in the structure of the 'technologies', which in some cases are not even present (absence of technical characteristics [T]).

1.3 Evolutionary Theory and the Individual Modes of Innovation

Our purpose in this section is to examine the extent to which each of our models of innovation can be said to come within the scope of an evolutionary approach. In evolutionary theory, as we saw earlier, innovation is defined as a 'problem-solving model'. It is clear that the six models of innovation examined in this book fit perfectly with this definition, since they describe various basic problem-solving mechanisms: improvement, addition, elimination, association, dissociation, objectification, 'formatting', etc.

Turning now to the biological analogies so beloved of evolutionary theorists, we can say in general terms that the various models of innovation equate to (more or less significant) mutations. They create variety. More generally, the various key concepts in evolutionary theory that draw on biology are found in our various models: as we have already noted, each of them creates variety. Reproduction (cell division), genetic continuity and adaptive capacities (fitness) are all found in the models. Routines that can be likened to genes combine with other components of the product (tangible technical and even process characteristics) to define a genotype, while the environment influences the phenotype (the service characteristics).

1.3.1 The radical model
The radical mode of innovation helps to produce what Abernathy and Utterback (1978) call a new 'dominant design'. According to Dosi (1991, p. 354), 'the evolutionary approach does not necessarily imply gradualism: it is just as compatible with the notion of abrupt change, instability or revolution (just as in biology, evolutionism admits of discontinuities).' The radical model is the one that produces the greatest variety within the system. In this radical model, the genotype, that is the system {[C'], [C], [T]}, is always completely modified.

1.3.2 The ameliorative model
Ameliorative innovation as we have defined it has its roots in the various cumulative learning processes that evolutionary theory has done much to reveal (learning by doing, use, interaction). It is not restricted to mere reductions in production costs but also changes the quality of the competences and of the technical characteristics and in consequence that of the service characteristics as well.

1.3.3 The incremental model
The incremental model, and the previous one, help to extend the dominant design. The purpose of both of them is to enhance the 'fitness' (degree of adaptation or suitability) of an innovation for its environment. Incremental and ameliorative innovations modify the phenotype (the service characteristics) in order to deal with a minor change in need (environment) by drawing on minor modifications of the genotype (the competences and the technical characteristics), in contrast to the complete modification brought about by the radical model. The ameliorative and incremental models (and the recombinative model as well to some extent, at least in its dissociative variant) are expressions of (or contribute to) what is known in evolutionary theory as the 'path dependency'. To use a biological analogy, we can say that in these two models (the ameliorative and incremental ones) the various species are each other's heirs, that is they are characterized by a certain degree of genetic continuity. The biological analogy could also be used here in a negative sense by alluding to the hypertely (that is, the extreme development of a characteristic beyond the degree to which it is apparently useful) from which innovations produced by the incremental model (or through the addition of characteristics)

may suffer from a certain point onwards. The particular case of the hybridization of a good with the service characteristics of a service could also be envisaged.

1.3.4 The ad hoc model

This model is also closely linked to cumulative learning processes. It is the product of a non-optimizing procedural rationality (innovation is produced but it is not necessarily reproducible in the traditional sense of the term). It triggers a process of codification and recording of knowledge, with a view to ensuring the reproducibility, if not of the ad hoc innovation itself, then at least of certain elements of it.

1.3.5 The recombinative model

This model has its origins in Schumpeter's definition of innovation (cf. Chapter 3, note 8). However, it is important not to reduce these combinative processes to combinations of the (tangible or intangible) 'elements' of a product, whether it be a good or a service. The recombinative mode of innovation has also to be considered from the point of view of its capacity for bringing different elements together: actors, agents of innovation, firms and organizations. This recombination can be considered at various levels of analysis (micro, meso, macro). It is present in various concepts used in evolutionary theory and in other theoretical traditions that are compatible with it, at least in part: networks in the sense of the term used by Callon (1991) and in the sociology of innovation and local or national innovation systems, in Lundvall's sense of the term (Lundvall, 1985).

1.3.6 The formalization model

A biological analogy already alluded to (cf. Chapter 3, Figure 3.6) can be used to characterize the formalization (or objectifying) and recombinative modes of innovation, namely that of the multifunctional, undifferentiated original cell which, through a process of division, produces autonomous, differentiated cells with their own specific functions. The original service (service function) gives birth to autonomous service products. The aim of the formalization mode of innovation is to control the ensuing variety and, in particular, to reduce the corresponding information costs. In services, after all, the 'product' can be found in an infinite number of configurations (just as the environment and the customers can be found in an infinite number of 'states'). The aim, therefore, is to reduce them to a finite number. To the extent that it is a form of innovation produced, as it were, by 'standardizing' engineers, the purpose of the formalization mode of innovation is to reduce the entropy of the system.

2. THE CHARACTERISTICS-BASED APPROACH AND THE DIVERSITY OF INNOVATION TRAJECTORIES IN SERVICES

The evolutionary taxonomies of technical change we examined in Chapter 1 have certain disadvantages, particularly when it comes to explaining innovation trajectories in services. They reduce the diversity of forms of innovation, which is paradoxical for analyses that identify themselves with a theoretical school that attaches great importance to the notion of diversity (Saviotti, 1988, 1996; Metcalfe and Gibbons, 1989). They establish rigid, one-to-one relationships between types of industries or firms and technological trajectories.[1] A characteristics-based approach to the product may, as we shall see, help to enrich and extend trajectory-based taxonomic analyses.

2.1 The Functional Breakdown of the 'Product' and the Characteristics-Based Approach

In order to attempt this exercise in extending trajectory-based analyses, we need slightly to modify our initial concept of the product as a system for establishing correspondences between characteristics and competences (representation A in Figure 5.1). In representation B, the set of technical and process characteristics [T] is broken down into three new sets representing different technological 'families':

1. logistical and material transformation technologies (mechanics, robotics, for example) [M];
2. logistical and information processing technologies (IT and telecommunications) [I];
3. intangible knowledge-processing technologies (formalized methods), what Bell (1973) calls 'intellectual technologies' [K].

Each of these three vectors or sets of technical characteristics equates to an internal function (or group of activities) of the 'product' in question, in accordance with the functional breakdown of the 'product' advanced by Gadrey (1991).

Thus the vector of 'tangible' technical characteristics [M] is associated with the logistical and transformative operations through which tangible objects are 'processed', that is transported, transformed, maintained, repaired, and so on.

The vector of 'informational' technical characteristics [I] equates to the logistical and information processing operations by means of which 'codified' information is 'processed', that is produced, captured, transported, etc.

The vector of 'methodological' technical characteristics [K] is associated with the operations or functions related to the processing of knowledge by means of methods (codified routines, intangible technologies).

These various operations (and the associated technologies) can be distinguished from each other by the medium which the service in question is based on. These are, respectively, (obviously tangible) material, codified information and knowledge.

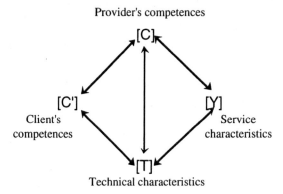

A : *Initial representation*

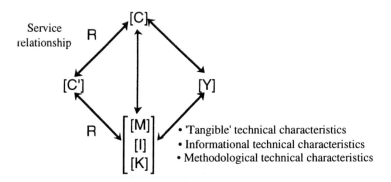

B : *Extended representation*
(through [T] breakdown)

Figure 5.1 Extending the general concept of the 'product' by incorporating the nature of technologies

However, as Gadrey (1991) points out, the medium of service delivery can also be the client himself. The associated operations can be described as relational or 'contactual' service operations. Their relationship to the technologies is more complex, since they can draw on each of the families of technologies [M], [I], [K] identified above. They can also (in the ideal-typical case) make direct use of the competences [C] that are considered here independently of the technologies in which they might be incorporated. In representation B in Figure 5.1, these contactual operations are denoted by the figure R. Thus R denotes the service relationship, that is the direct link between the service provider's competences [C] and/or his technical resources ([M], [I], [K]) and the client symbolized by the set of competences [C'].

Depending on the importance of the role played by material, informational and methodological operations, each service activity may draw to varying extents on the technologies [M], [I], [K]. Thus in insurance companies, for example, in which the informational element and information technologies are generally considered to be dominant, those aspects of the product associated with the relational service are assuming considerable importance: examples might include preventive procedures and the improvement of settlement times, which rely on the reorganization of work and formalized 'methods'. The material logistical element and the associated technologies are also playing an increasing role (the organization of transport systems in assistance services; supply of authorized service providers to repair damage in the case of property insurance).

In addition to these various sets of technical characteristics, representation B in Figure 5.1 also includes the vector of competences [C] and the vector of service characteristics [Y]. The inclusion of competences allows us to consider the provision of service (or use) characteristics without any technological mediation (that is, through the deployment of competences), which is feasible not only in high-level services but also in manual services (for example, cleaning when virtually no technologies are deployed). This particular service transaction will be written C(Y). Similarly, the technical characteristics (and the associated operations) will be written henceforth as follows: M(Y), I(Y), K(Y), in acknowledgement of the fact that the various types of operations and the associated technologies contribute to the realization of the service functions or characteristics [Y].

This concept of the 'product', which takes account of the nature of the technologies deployed, makes it possible to envisage different innovation trajectories. Indeed, our idea is that each of the components of the product and of the associated characteristics (or any combination of them) gives rise to or is capable of giving rise to, firstly, specific innovations which, secondly, may follow their own specific innovation trajectories.

- *The logistical and material transformation trajectory* $\Delta M(Y)$ operates in that part of the service relating to logistics and material transformations. This is a traditional (or 'natural', to use the term proposed by Nelson and Winter, 1982) trajectory based on increasing mechanization and exploitation of economies of scale. This trajectory accounts for the evolution of transport and materials-handling technologies: transport vehicles, handling and sorting systems, cooking and refrigeration systems, etc.
- *The logistical and data-processing trajectory* $\Delta I(Y)^2$ is at work in the logistical/informational component of the service. Its principal characteris-

tic is a trend towards a reduction of communication costs, the establishment of networks, the production of new information and new ways of using that information. It corresponds, self-evidently, to the dynamic of information and communication systems, etc.

- *The trajectory which we will call the methodological or intellectual methods trajectory* $\Delta K(Y)$ takes account of the production and evolution of formalized methods of processing knowledge. This trajectory is encountered mainly, but not exclusively, in intellectual services.
- *The ('pure') service trajectory* $\Delta C(Y)$ is an ideal type which describes service innovations that evolve independently of any technological medium (in the sense of the tangible, informational and methodological technologies envisaged above), that is through the direct mobilization of competence C to provide the service functions or characteristics Y.

The service relationship R can evolve as well. However, it does not follow a trajectory in the sense of the four outlined above. The analytical perspective here is different. The interface or contactual service can rely solely on competences (relational competences, of course, but also theoretical, technical, methodological and ethical competences, in accordance with the distinction made by Charlon and Gadrey (1998)). They may also draw on any of the technologies identified above. Thus, depending on the nature of the principal technical characteristics that are mobilized, the relational trajectory (which is not considered here in its own right) may merge with the various other trajectories, that is the (pure) service, material, informational and methodological trajectories.

The first four trajectories $\Delta M(Y)$, $\Delta I(Y)$, $\Delta K(Y)$ and $\Delta C(Y)$ can be classified on a descending scale of 'materiality'. The (pure) service trajectories $\Delta C(Y)$ are relatively more immaterial or intangible than methodological ones $\Delta K(Y)$, while the role played by software may well mean that the logistical and data-processing trajectories $\Delta I(Y)$ should be regarded as having a lower level of 'materiality' than the logistical and material transformation trajectories $\Delta M(Y)$. In sum, it can be said that $\Delta M(Y)$ and $\Delta I(Y)$ are technological trajectories in the strict sense, $\Delta K(Y)$ is an immaterial technological trajectory and $\Delta C(Y)$ is a service trajectory in the strict sense.

These various trajectories are 'generic trajectories' within which a certain number of other trajectories may be contained. In the case of Pavitt's taxonomy, for example, there would be a set of technological trajectories corresponding respectively to science-based firms, supplier-dominated firms, etc.

Whether applied to the manufacturing or service sector, Pavitt's taxonomy is concerned solely with material and informational trajectories. The first version of Pavitt's analysis (1984) is underpinned by the implicit hypothesis that service activities are limited essentially to undifferentiated technological components (no distinction is made between material and informational logistical technologies and trajectories). Basically, service-sector firms buy vehicles for land sea or air transport, cooking and refrigeration equipment, cleaning machines, mail sorting machines, cash registers, conveyor belts, computers, etc. All technologies originating in manufacturing firms tend to mechanize the service and, in many cases, to generate economies of scale.

Soete and Miozzo's analysis, as well as the revised version of Pavitt's taxonomy (1989), introduce very clearly the distinction between material logistical operations and informational logistical operations. This time, computers, peripherals and software, as well as telecommunications systems, are at the centre of the analysis.

The service trajectory $\Delta C(Y)$ is not considered at all in any of these different taxonomies. Several arguments could be put forward to explain this 'omission':

- a technologist conception of innovation as a material artefact;
- the inability of existing innovation indicators to take account of certain forms of innovation in services (Djellal and Gallouj, 1998, 1999; Evangelista and Sirilli, 1995; Gault, 1998);
- the lack of databases on innovations in services, such as those which exist for the manufacturing industry;
- the difficulty in separating out the service component $C(Y)$ in the strict sense from the other components, and particularly from the technological components denoted by the terms logistical and material transformation $M(Y)$ and logistical and data-processing $I(Y)$, to which they are very closely related.

2.2 Different Innovation Trajectories within a Single Service Activity

If the functional breakdown outlined above and the corresponding innovation trajectories are accepted, it becomes possible to construct analytically a number of evolution profiles. This leads us to reject the establishment of one-to-one relationships between a given firm or industry and a given trajectory. There are in fact many possible relationships (or configurations), all of which are consistent with the hypotheses of evolutionary theory, while at the same time avoiding determinism and confinement in a given trajectory. In other words, several trajectories can operate within the same firm or industry, and they may mutually reinforce each other, compete with each other or coexist without affecting each other at all.

If we take the term 'configuration' to denote a mode (or group of modes) of establishing relationships between trajectories, three different types of configuration can be envisaged (see Table 5.1). However, care must be taken to distinguish between those configurations that result from the researcher's analytical choice (and simplifications) and those that denote the nature of a product or firms' behavior and strategies, all of which are empirically verifiable.

Table 5.1 The variety of innovation trajectories in services

Nature of the product or main components and technologies	Configuration	Types of trajectories
Only one of the components or facets of the product (and the corresponding possible technological family) is considered or is important (dominates the others): usually [M(Y)] or [I(Y)], but also [K(Y)], and [C(Y)]	*Unidimensional (one-to-one)*	Each of the generic trajectories (and the corresponding sub-trajectories) is the sole development path in a firm or industry. - 'material' trajectories $\Delta M(Y)$ - 'informational' trajectories $\Delta I(Y)$ - 'methodological' trajectories $\Delta K(Y)$ - 'service' trajectories $\Delta C(Y)$
The various product components or facets (and the corresponding possible technologies) are considered	*Combinatory (fixed coefficients)* • *separate*	The various generic trajectories (and corresponding sub-trajectories) coexist within a firm or industry, without affecting each other. $[\Delta M(Y) + \Delta I(Y) + \Delta K(Y) + \Delta C(Y)]$
	• *hybrid*	The trajectories are complementary and indissociable $(\Delta [M(Y) + I(Y) + K(Y) + C(Y)])$
The various product components or facets (and the corresponding possible technologies) are considered in terms of the evolution of their relative importance over time	*Evolutionary (variable coefficients)* • *by sedimentation*	The increased importance of one trajectory does not exclude the others. $\Delta M(Y) ---> [\Delta M(Y)] + \Delta I(Y) ---> [\Delta M(Y) + \Delta I(Y)] + \Delta K(Y) ---> [\Delta M(Y) + \Delta I(Y) + \Delta K(Y)] + \Delta C(Y)$
	• *by exclusion (or substitution)*	The rise of one trajectory excludes the others. $[\Delta M(Y) ---> \Delta I(Y) ---> \Delta K(Y) ---> \Delta C(Y)]$
	• *by causality or determination*	The evolution of one trajectory determines that of another. E.g. $[\Delta M(Y) => \Delta I(Y)]$ or $[\Delta C(Y) => \Delta I(Y)]$

It is not our intention here to provide a new taxonomy of trajectories, but simply to illustrate in different ways (from different, not necessarily unconnected perspectives) the great wealth of innovations and innovation trajectories and the relationships between them. For example, the configuration which we describe as 'evolutionary' amounts to nothing more than the adoption of a dynamic perspective towards the other configurations, the object of which is no longer simply innovation trajectories but also, and above all, 'the trajectories of innovation trajectories'.

2.2.1 'Unidimensional' (or one-to-one) configurations

In these configurations, the 'product' is considered from the perspective of just one of its components or facets. In many cases, the facet in question is the material or informational component, that is $M(Y)$ or $I(Y)$; even more frequently, these two components are not distinguished from each other but considered simply under the general heading of technological innovation. More unusually, the 'product' can also be considered from the point of view of the methodological component $K(Y)$, or the service component in the strict sense $C(Y)$, that is independently of the other operations, and particularly of the corresponding technologies.

If the 'product' of the firm or industry is considered solely from the perspective of one of these components or representations, the trajectories operating in that firm or industry will be exclusively material $\Delta M(Y)$, informational $\Delta I(Y)$, methodological $\Delta K(Y)$ or service-oriented $\Delta C(Y)$, depending on the component or representation selected. Thus there are firms or industries that evolve solely in accordance with the material logistical trajectory, others that follow a logistical and data-processing trajectory only and yet others that are dominated by the service trajectory (although this case is not considered in Pavitt's study or in that of Soete and Miozzo).

Furthermore, each of the 'generic' trajectories (and the corresponding 'sub-trajectories') constitute the sole development path for a given firm or industry. Thus in Pavitt's taxonomy (1984), which, as we have already indicated, seems to reduce the product to its undifferentiated material and informational components, the various corresponding sub-trajectories (those of science-based, production-intensive and supplier-dominated firms) are associated in a unilateral and deterministic way with given firms and industries. The same applies in Soete's and Miozzo's taxonomy.

This type of configuration, which, in our view, has its roots in the analytical simplification that characterises the taxonomies developed by Pavitt and Soete and Miozzo and reflects their interest in technological innovations only, can, nevertheless, be empirically verified. For example, it can readily be accepted that the transport industry was for a long time dominated by a material technological trajectory based on a 'product' in which material logistics were the main service component. Although this configuration still exists in some SMEs, the nature of the product is generally changing and the other components are becoming more important (see Section 2.3.2).

2.2.2 'Combinatory' ('fixed-coefficient') configurations

In this type of configuration, the product is considered from the perspective of its four possible facets and the corresponding technologies: material logistical M(Y), informational I(Y), methodological K(Y) operations and technologies and service functions or characteristics unmediated by technology, that is 'pure' service functions C(Y). This concept of the product allows innovation and innovation trajectories to be considered in a more complex, non-deterministic way that is often closer to reality.

'Combinatory' configurations make it possible to envisage the existence of different trajectories within the same firm or industry, thereby linking in various ways the different innovation trajectories that exist within that firm or industry. Thus this configuration may take several different forms:

- *Separate coexistence* within the same firm or industry. If all the possible trajectories are considered to be operating (which is not necessarily the case), this configuration could be 'represented' as follows: [ΔM(Y) + ΔI(Y) + ΔK(Y) + ΔC(Y)]. This 'separate coexistence' configuration is an extreme case, which probably occurs only rarely, in which each of the various generic trajectories (and possibly the corresponding sub-trajectories) are operating simultaneously within the same firm or industry, without really affecting each other. It reflects a situation in which trajectories are being extended independently of each other, that is one in which autonomous innovation trajectories are at work in the various functional components of the activity. The more a firm's products differ from each other, the more likely this configuration becomes. Thus, for example, innovation trajectories in standard insurance activities and those in the so-called *sociétés d'assistance* (which provide services rather than monetary compensation if the insured risk materializes) may in some cases provide an illustration of precisely this kind of separate coexistence (cf. Section 2.3.4). From the point of view of 'sub-trajectories', this separate coexistence may signify, for example, that a given firm can be 'supplier-dominated' in certain aspects of its activity and 'science-based' in others.

- *Hybridization of trajectories.* Once again, in the most general case, this too can be formalized in the following terms: (Δ[M(Y) + I(Y) + K(Y) + C(Y)]). In this form, which is more common than the previous one, trajectories can intertwine and become inseparable and complementary rather than coexisting in isolation. Thus there are many examples of mergers not only between material and informational logistical trajectories (Δ[M(Y) + I(Y)]) but also between informational and service trajectories (Δ[I(Y) + C(Y)]). Indeed, microelectronics and IT have gradually pervaded all material logistical operations. Medical instrumentation can no longer be envisaged without these technologies; the transport of goods is now highly dependent upon the transmission of information, and will doubtless be even more so in the future. This trend is particularly marked in mail order, parcel services and container transport, etc. In this last case, it is now possible to ascertain at any time the owner of each container, its contents, its position, its origin and initial destination, its new optimal destination (once empty), the type of container, the nature of any possible repairs and their cost, conditions of conveyance, etc. (Ernst, 1985).

2.2.3 'Evolutionary' (or 'variable coefficient') configurations

In this case, the product is still considered in terms of its different components but the relative importance of each one in the definition of the product is considered to be variable over time. Thus we are dealing here with a situation in which, depending on the relative importance of each component over time, there is a shift from one trajectory to another (extreme case) or from the predominance of one trajectory to that of another.

These configurations are those in which the whole set of trajectories (or just some of them) constitute the different stages in the evolution of a given firm or industry. Thus we are dealing with what might be called a 'trajectory of trajectories'. These configurations mark an analytical break with the previous ones. Depending on how their operations and activities have evolved, therefore, some firms or industries can be seen to have moved from a material logistical trajectory $\Delta M(Y)$ to an informational logistical trajectory $\Delta I(Y)$ and then to a service trajectory $\Delta C(Y)$, while others have shifted from a service trajectory to an informational technological trajectory, and so on.

In reality, evolutionary configurations can take different forms:

- *Sedimentation*, which could be represented in a general ideal-typical case as follows: $\Delta M(Y) \longrightarrow [\Delta M(Y)] + \Delta I(Y) \longrightarrow [\Delta M(Y) + \Delta I(Y)] + \Delta K(Y) \longrightarrow [\Delta M(Y) + \Delta I(Y) + \Delta K(Y)] + \Delta C(Y)$. In this form, the increased importance of a given trajectory does not exclude the others; on the contrary, the new trajectory is added to the existing ones. Obviously, an evolutionary configuration that develops through a process of 'sedimentation' does not usually follow the whole path mapped out above, but only some of its stages.

- *Exclusion (or substitution)* $[\Delta M(Y) \longrightarrow \Delta I(Y) \longrightarrow \Delta K(Y) \longrightarrow \Delta C(Y)]$. As certain product components become less important and others become more important, some trajectories disappear. New trajectories replace the old ones. Here again, the path mapped out in the 'formalization' above is only a general case. It is the longest path, but shorter ones are also possible.

- *Causality or determination*: e.g. $[\Delta M(Y) \Rightarrow \Delta I(Y)]$ or $[\Delta C(Y) \Rightarrow \Delta I(Y)]$. This form of evolutionary configuration (which also comes within the scope of the combinatory configuration) represents situations in which the evolution of a given trajectory determines that of another. This is the case, for example, when the evolution of technological trajectories gives rise to certain changes in service trajectories or vice versa.

To sum up, the taxonomies of Pavitt and of Soete and Miozzo are only particular forms of the configuration which we have called 'unidimensional' or 'one-to-one'. They do not account for the multiplicity of trajectories that a single firm can follow. Regardless of sector, a firm can evolve in accordance with any one of the configurations presented above, or indeed with several of them.

2.3 Examples Taken from Different Service Industries

The aim of this section is to provide some illustrations of the various configurations examined above. The examples are taken from the following industries, all of which have been the subject of empirical investigations: contract cleaning, transport, distribution, financial services (banking and insurance) and consultancy. These different industries illustrate the variable proportions of the different 'components' or facets of the 'product' and of the corresponding technical characteristics and competences $M(Y)$, $I(Y)$, $K(Y)$, and $C(Y)$, as well as the variable evolution of these proportions over time. In contract cleaning, and particularly in transport and distribution, the logistical material component and the corresponding technologies $M(Y)$ can be said to occupy a central position, while in insurance and banking the logistical informational component and technologies $I(Y)$ predominate; in consultancy, it is the service component $C(Y)$ that predominates, while in the large networks where the process of service provision is structured around highly formalised methods, it is the methodological component $K(Y)$ that occupies the central position.

In Pavitt's taxonomy, as has already been emphasized, the various services considered belong to the category of 'supplier-dominated' firms. In Soete and Miozzo's taxonomy (see Chapter 1, Figure 1.2), contract cleaning and retail distribution belong to the category of 'supplier-dominated' firms, transport to 'large-scale physical networks', banking and insurance to 'informational networks', and consultancy to 'specialized suppliers and science-based firms'.

However, our empirical studies suggest that innovation behavior in each of these industries is more varied, with a multiplicity of possible and mutually dependent innovation trajectories. It is not statistical representativeness which is important here, but the highlighting of new trends, of turning points in the evolution of firms' behavior.

2.3.1 Contract cleaning

In essence, the activity of small cleaning firms can be said to be limited to the material logistical component of the product $M(Y)$ (based on elementary cleaning tools, the simplest form of which would be a broom). Little use is made of informational technologies, and very few new 'relational' or service functions see the light of day in cleaning. Innovation trajectories are limited, irrespective of the medium (material, informational, cognitive). As Pavitt and then Soete and Miozzo suggest, these are supplier-dominated firms, although in reality this domination is relatively limited since the equipment used generally has a low, or even very low technological content (brooms) and suppliers of this type of tool are particularly numerous.

The situation, however, is very different in the largest contract cleaning firms (Sundbo, 1996; Djellal, 2001b). Indeed, these firms' product must be considered at least in terms of its three material, informational and service components or facets. Thus the service trajectories are far from stagnant, and operate in these large firms alongside the material and informational trajectories, with which they can maintain the whole range of relationships outlined above.

It would seem that the (long-term) evolution of these firms can be mapped out in terms of what we have described as the evolutionary configuration, which can be represented here as follows: $\Delta M(Y) \dashrightarrow \Delta M(Y) + \Delta C(Y) \dashrightarrow \Delta M(Y) + \Delta C(Y) + \Delta I(Y)$. These firms started out as providers of a service that was highly labor-intensive but with low capital intensity, out of which emerged a material logistical trajectory ($\Delta M(Y)$) of limited scope (a trajectory characteristic of supplier-dominated firms). They subsequently changed the nature of their product by strengthening the logistical and material transformation component and the corresponding technologies $M(Y)$. This change took place or progressed in accordance with the principle of 'supplier domination' to the extent that the firms had recourse to the market in order to introduce technical systems (sophisticated cleaning machinery). In the subsequent phases, the service facet $C(Y)$ of the product and the corresponding innovation trajectory rose to prominence, followed by the informational trajectory $\Delta I(Y)$ (linked to the strengthening of the informational component of the product). Although this general long-term evolution corresponds to what we have called the 'evolutionary configuration by sedimentation', we will see that other forms of the evolutionary configuration can also be envisaged.

Djellal (2001b) gives many examples of innovations that illustrate the evolution of different trajectories in the largest contract cleaning firms. The service trajectory $\Delta C(Y)$, for example, is reflected in the proliferation of new services (considered here independently of the technologies on which they will subsequently rely). These new services are characterised by increased complexity and strategic content. Thus these firms progressed from the provision of standard labor-intensive cleaning services with an unskilled workforce to the provision of high-skill services, including biological cleaning in hospitals, cleaning as an integral part of the production process and of bacteriological controls in the food-processing industry, 'computer cleaning', etc.

The material logistical trajectory $\Delta M(Y)$ can be illustrated by the use of robots in some cleaning processes and the installation of specialized cradles and trolleys adapted to particular environments. The informational logistical trajectory $\Delta I(Y)$, a more recent phenomenon in cleaning firms, can be illustrated by the design and use of many software systems, for example for quality control, task description, etc.

There are manifold relationships between these different trajectories, and they represent several of the configurations already described above. For example, the cleaning of computer equipment (an innovation in the service component) is the source (evolutionary configuration by causality or determination) of further innovations relating to informational and material trajectories $[\Delta C(Y) \Rightarrow \Delta I(Y) + \Delta M(Y)]$. Indeed, in order to be able to provide such a service, it was necessary to develop various new tools relating to the material component of the 'product': e.g. special chemical products, instruments for blowing air and sucking up dust and a trolley specially adapted for use in confined spaces.

2.3.2 Road haulage

Taking as a starting point a functional definition of the product, Djellal (2001a) gives an account of the diversity of possible innovation configurations in the road haulage industry. The historical evolution of the industry is characterised by the increasing prominence of, firstly, the informational and methodological components and, subsequently, of the service components of a "product" which was limited initially to its material logistical component in the strict sense. The evolution of the corresponding innovation trajectories (evolutionary configuration) is thus as follows: $\Delta M(Y)$ ---> $[\Delta M(Y)] + \Delta I(Y)$ --->$[\Delta M(Y) + \Delta I(Y)] + K(Y)$ ---> $[\Delta M(Y) + \Delta I(Y) + \Delta K(Y)] + \Delta C(Y)$. It reflects the rise to prominence first of informational and subsequently of methodological and service innovation trajectories. Overall, the configuration thus produced is of the sedimentary type. However, it can also take other forms (exclusion, for example) if a particular firm is considered, rather than the industry as a whole.

According to Djellal (2001a), this general evolution serves to explain the current structure of the road haulage industry. Thus there are still firms today that are dominated by the material trajectory $\Delta M(Y)$. These are usually small firms, organized according to a craft model and dominated by suppliers of transport equipment.

However, there are also firms in which the four trajectories considered above, or at least two or three of them, are combined. This is the case with the largest transport firms that are integrated into large-scale networks. These firms have the capacity to extend each of the components or 'facets' of their product, either separately (separate combinatory configuration) or in close interaction with each other (hybrid combinatory configuration and causal evolutionary configuration). Thus a transport firm can be, at the same time or alternately, 'dependent on suppliers' of transport vehicles, 'dependent on suppliers' of computer and telecommunications equipment or 'science and engineering based' when it is capable of designing and introducing its own information and telecommunications systems (e.g. computer systems for monitoring the progress of goods) or the balance of power shifts in its favor. It can also follow a service trajectory if it introduces new service functions, or extends the 'pure' service facet of its product. At the same time, however, relationships can be established between these different trajectories. Computer systems have been introduced into road haulage systems to such an extent that the corresponding innovation trajectories are now merged and indissociable. The introduction of sophisticated communication and data processing systems has been partly responsible for creating new services such as 'tour operator' services.

Finally, Djellal (2001a) highlights the existence of firms following informational, methodological and service trajectories, or just methodological and service trajectories or even solely service trajectories. These tend to be firms classed as 'tour operators' which resemble travel agencies or even consultancy firms. They manage information, organizational knowledge, methods and coordinating competences relating to transport. Viewed from the perspective of the long-term evolution of the road haulage industry, this type of firm can be seen as the culmination of an evolutionary configuration that has ousted some of the initial components of the product (namely the 'material', 'informational' and 'methodological' components).

2.3.3 Distribution

Focusing on large-scale retailing and adopting a long-term perspective, it can be recalled that the innovation model at work was for a long time based firstly on the material logistical function and technologies of the product $M(Y)$ (introduction of Fordist logistical systems) and then on the informational logistical function and technologies $I(Y)$. Thus there are many examples of new informational technologies being used in distribution (Zeyl and Zeyl, 1996; C. Gallouj, 1997a): data generators (point-of-sale terminals), decision-making tools (information points, labels, etc.), point-of-sale management tools, computerized sales kiosks, self-scanning, etc.

For a number of years in the United States, and more recently in France, a trajectory that might be described as a service-oriented trajectory is being superimposed on to the old material and informational trajectories which are still operating: addition of numerous new services and new 'social relations' improvement methods (see examples in Section 2.3, Chapter 3).

It should be pointed out that material and informational trajectories have become interconnected (particularly through EDI and, more recently, ECR, Efficient Consumer Response), and that this has given rise to hybrid configurations. However, there is an even more pronounced process of hybridization in the service relation (R), in that many new contact services are incorporated in or closely linked to material or informational logistical systems, and are inconceivable outside of those systems. This is the case with interactive information and advice points, new fax services, tele-shopping and home shopping services by fax, telephone or Internet, automatic vending machines, etc.

2.3.4 Financial services (banking and insurance)

Although informational technological trajectories undeniably operate in banking and insurance companies, and indeed play a central role, these activities are also characterized by the rise of what we have called service trajectories, a fact which is obscured by some theoretical analyses. This has led to a modification in the nature of the product (or in our perception of it). In other words, the 'banking product' is not limited to its informational logistical function but contains an important service dimension, which is itself the locus of certain developments.

Thus, for example, Barras' reverse cycle theory (1986, 1990) satisfactorily accounts for informational trajectories by describing an initial phase of incremental innovation linked to back-office computerization, a second phase of radical process innovation linked to front-office computerization (e.g. ATMs) and a third phase in which new products are introduced (e.g. online banking). However, it ignores service trajectories, which account for the evolution of services (new financial products, new insurance contracts linked to new risks or events, ad hoc or tailor-made solutions, etc.).

Thus although some banking and insurance companies do operate on the basis of a dominant unidimensional configuration (because size of firm differs, as does area of specialisation), most of them are underpinned by combinatory and evolutionary configurations. Innovation, whether involving the material logistical, informational or service components, can evolve along different paths which may remain separate, interconnect or influence each other, depending on the case in question.

For example, through the time savings generated, informational innovation trajectories (introduction of different generations of computers) determine the rise to prominence (causal evolutionary configuration) of service functions C(Y) such as sales activities, consultancy, ad hoc solutions. Home banking is undoubtedly a good illustration of this particular form of the combinatory configuration which we have labelled hybrid. Indeed, technological and service trajectories are closely interlinked here, which is why Barras feels justified in describing this technological development as a genuinely new service.

The combinatory configuration in its 'separate coexistence' form manifests itself in large insurance companies, or in the insurance industry as a whole, through the creation of subsidiaries (the so-called *sociétés d'assistance* referred to above*)* that have developed a new area of specialisation in which the product components (material, informational and service logistics) have, from the outset, been relatively evenly balanced. The services provided by these subsidiaries make use of different technologies from those used in traditional insurance activities. As well as computer systems, various telecommunication and transport systems are used. The service components are also fundamentally different: it is no longer a question of paying financial compensation when the insured risk materialises, but rather of providing different functions or services (transport, catering, hotels, health, etc.). Thus innovation trajectories can follow paths parallel to those in the traditional insurance sector (separate coexistence).

2.3.5 Consultancy

In this heterogeneous group of activities, the M(Y) component occupies a relatively limited place. The long-term trajectory can be represented by the following terms: $\Delta C(Y) \longrightarrow \Delta C(Y) + \Delta K(Y) \longrightarrow \Delta C(Y) + \Delta K(Y) + \Delta I(Y)$, which describe the rise to prominence of the methodological and informational trajectories in a service activity that could initially be described as the mobilization of competences and expertise in order to provide service functions or characteristics C(Y).

This type of evolution must not be interpreted as an industrialization trajectory. Indeed, the emergence of the trajectory $\Delta K(Y)$ does not reflect the emergence of an increasingly important trend towards industrial rationalization but rather a tendency towards professional rationalization (in accordance with the distinction made by Gadrey, 1994b). Furthermore, $\Delta I(Y)$ and $\Delta K(Y)$ trajectories rarely dominate $\Delta C(Y)$ trajectories. On the contrary, these trajectories usually coexist and maintain dialectical relationships with each other.

The empirical studies we have carried out in different areas of consultancy suggest that multiple configurations exist. It is not unusual to encounter unidimensional configurations. Thus the service trajectory $\Delta C(Y)$ may be the only trajectory operating in some firms or industries: this is often the case in legal consultancy and strategic consultancy, where innovation turns on cognitive trajectories linked to the accumulation of knowledge and expertise and can take particular forms (ad hoc, tailor-made, etc.). This stems from the predominance of the service 'facet' in activities which are often referred to as ideal types of 'pure' service. The $\Delta K(Y)$ trajectory illustrates the rise to prominence of methodological innovation within firms, a frequent occurrence in large international audit and consultancy firms.

However, in computer services, for example, informational trajectories are closely linked to service trajectories because the service medium is the information system.

2.4 Conclusion

Sectoral models of technological behavior, developed at the interface between economics and management sciences and underpinned by evolutionary theory (Pavitt, 1984; Soete and Miozzo, 1990) constitute a significant step forward in our understanding of innovation phenomena. These various forms of behavior are determined by firms' technological bases, regarded as potential for evolution and subject to a certain degree of irreversibility ('path dependency'), and by firms' learning processes and absorption capacities (in the sense defined by Cohen and Levinthal, 1989).

These sectoral taxonomies and the corresponding trajectories introduce specificity and idiosyncrasy or, in other words, *history* into firms' behavior, just as they introduce *variety*. Technological behavior is not homogeneous and governed by a substantive rationality (of techniques choice) but heterogeneous and shaped by the 'trajectory' operating at any given time and the non-transparency of knowledge and its costs.

While adhering to the general principles of this approach, this article has sought to reveal the limitations of existing taxonomies when dealing with innovation in services. Indeed, evolutionary sectoral taxonomies are technologically determined, although non-technological trajectories, which we will describe as service trajectories, are conceivable. They attribute standard behaviors and trajectories to firms and sectors, whereas in reality the same firm can evolve along different trajectories.

In sum, we have shown that a functional breakdown of the service activity, relocated within the framework of competences mobilized and final service functions or characteristics, allows variety to be introduced on a number of levels: 1) on the static level: in the forms and nature of innovation; 2) on the dynamic level: both in the multiplicity of trajectories, i.e. in the evolution of these innovations, and in the multiplicity of the possible relationships between these trajectories. In other words, and without calling into question evolutionary taxonomic approaches, our approach reveals a far greater degree of complexity in innovation phenomena (several trajectories within one firm, with multiple possible relationships between them), of which the taxonomies in question are only particular cases.

Thus the proposed approach, which would benefit from greater empirical validation, makes it possible to overcome the determinism inherent in traditional approaches and to introduce greater variety and dynamics. Beyond the service sector, it can also be applied to all manufacturing firms, since the functional breakdown is equally relevant to their product. In the last part of this chapter, we extend this line of thinking by changing the analytical perspective and introducing an 'approach' that focuses on the analysis not of a single product but of a technological population.

3. THE POPULATION APPROACH AND EVOLUTIONARY THEORY

In a recent study, Saviotti (1996) enriches the approach based on vectors or sets of characteristics with one derived from biology that is consistent with evolutionary theory, namely the *population approach*. The basic idea of this approach is that the various *product models* (that is, the different variants of each product) are distributed within a characteristics 'space' in such a way as to form *technological populations*. We will attempt here, firstly, to transpose this approach to our modified concept of the 'product' and, secondly, to reconsider some of the evolutionary concepts examined above in the light of this new approach.

3.1 The Population Approach and its Mechanisms

The population approach, which emphasizes the variance in the characteristics of the members of the same population, stands in contrast to typological approaches, which are concerned with representative average 'individuals'. As applied to innovation phenomena, this population approach has two advantages: 1) it enhances our understanding of certain concepts, such as regime, paradigm and trajectory, and of the significance of the differences between technologies or of those between radical and incremental innovations...; 2) it provides a basis for mapping technologies, that is for tracing the evolution of technical populations within the characteristics space.

This population approach seems to us to have a third advantage, which is that it may offer a way of effecting the transition from an approach focused on individual products to one that focuses, at the micro level, on the output of a single firm or even, at the macro level, on that of an entire nation. Figure 5.2 depicts a technical characteristics space consisting, for simplicity's sake, of two technical characteristics (X_1 and X_2). Each point in this space corresponds to a 'technological model' represented (here) by a pair of 'values' (or levels) of the two characteristics X_1 and X_2. The clouds of points represent technological populations, that is subsets of goods (technological models) with identical or virtually identical technical characteristics.

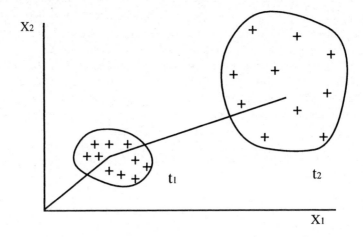

Figure 5.2 The change in the position and density of the technological population between t$_1$ and t$_2$
Source: Saviotti (1996).

Saviotti highlights three types of change that may affect a given technological population.

1. *A change in the position of the population in space.* This change is
    explained (in this hypothetical case) by an improvement in the 'levels' of
    the technical characteristics X_j. The path thus travelled equates to what is
    called a 'technological trajectory'.
2. *A change in the density of the population.* Changes in density equate (or
    give rise) to changes in the intensity and shape of the technological com-
    petition. Thus a high technological density (that is, a low level of pro-
    duct differentiation) is associated with perfect competition, whereas a low
    density (that is, high product differentiation) reflects competition of the
    Schumpeterian kind.
3. *Fragmentation of the technological population.* Fragmentation of this
    kind (cf. Figure 5.3) may be brought about by the intensity of the techno-
    logical competition in period t_2, which might in turn encourage some
    firms to differentiate their output in order to gain control of market niches
    in which they enjoy a certain monopoly.

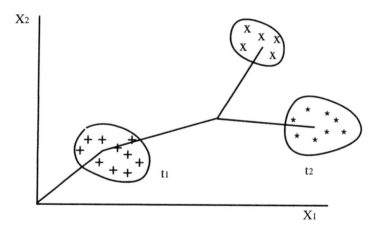

Figure 5.3 Specialization/fragmentation of the technological population
Source: Saviotti (1996).

We propose to add two other types of change apparently not included in
Saviotti's analysis. The first of these, the association or combination of
technological populations, is just as important in goods as in services, while
the second, technological or service 'regression', seems to be particularly
prevalent in services.

1. *The association or combination of technological populations.* This is the
    obverse of the previous type of change (technological fragmentation) and

equates to the recombinative mode of innovation in its 'associative' variant. Two technological populations that are autonomous in t_1, that is occupying different parts of the characteristics space, merge in time t_2 (Figure 5.4).

2. *Technological or service 'regression'*. This equates to some extent to the dissociative or (reverse or negative) incremental modes of innovation, in which characteristics are removed[3] rather than added or their 'weight' is reduced rather than being increased (Figure 5.5). It would apply, for example, to charter flights, fast-food restaurants and the new, 'no-frills' hotels.

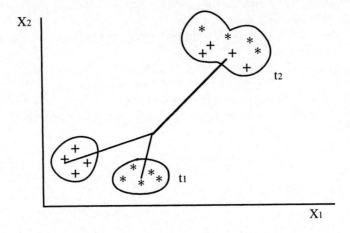

Figure 5.4 Combination of technological populations

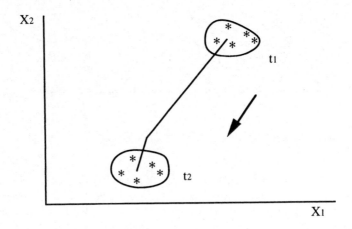

Figure 5.5 Regression in technological populations

Once again, our hypothesis is that this population approach can be transposed to services. If we ignore, for simplicity's sake, the client's competences, this means applying the approach to systems of the {[C], [T], [Y]} type or, in accordance with the distinction made in the previous section, to systems of the {[C], [M], [I], [K], [Y]} type which equate, respectively, to the service provider's competences, to the tangible technical characteristics [M] and [I], to the methodological characteristics [K] and to the service characteristics. However, since the vectors on the side of the 'structural' elements are different (and no longer just [X]), it is necessary, for simplicity's sake, to consider a population approach for each of them, that is for the competences, for the intangible technical or methodological characteristics and for the tangible technical characteristics (this last case will not be considered here since it corresponds to that put forward by Saviotti). The analytical decompositions undertaken here are, of course, considerably simplified. In reality, as we showed in the previous section, albeit at a different level of analysis, the various spaces overlap with each other and the resultant configurations are both complex and hybrid.

3.2 Populations of Competences

By analogy with technological populations, *cognitive populations* can be identified. In a space represented, for simplicity's sake, by three axes representing levels of values of competences C_1, C_2 and C_3, the clouds of points are here equivalent to cognitive populations, that is subsets of services that draw on the same or very similar competences and knowledge.

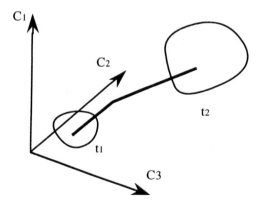

Figure 5.6 Trajectory of cognitive populations

These cognitive populations display the same behavior patterns as technological populations (Figure 5.6).

• They can change position in space and follow, between t_1 and t_2, a trajectory that we will describe as a *cognitive trajectory*. This cognitive trajectory may be 'competence-enhancing' (Tushman and Anderson, 1986), that is it will tend to increase the 'weight' of the competences. Conversely, it may be 'competence-destroying'.

- An increase in population density will be equivalent to a strengthening of the *cognitive regime* (or of the *dominant cognitive design*).
- Cognitive populations may also fragment or combine with each other, or they may undergo processes of cognitive regression characterized by the disappearance of certain 'axes' of competences or by a drop in the 'value' or 'weight' of certain characteristics of competences. Where applicable, this includes the situation, already alluded to, in which 'competence-destroying' trajectories or innovations develop.

This competence space, which is generally only one of the elements in a more complex, hybrid configuration, occupies a central position in the case of 'pure services' (ideal type) (certain consultancy transactions, for example), since the only 'technologies' deployed to provide the service are competences. In this case, this cognitive population space acts as a technological population space.

In order to illustrate this population approach, we can attempt to apply it to the evolution of the legal competences of representative law firms. Let us assume, for example, that t_1 denotes the decade after the Second World War, t_2 the current period, C_1 commercial law, C_2 divorce law and C_3 inheritance law.

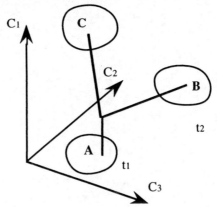

Figure 5.7 A population approach applied to legal competences

Figure 5.7 can be interpreted as follows. In the decade immediately following the Second World War (in t_1), most of the knowledge deployed in the dispensing of legal advice related to domestic disputes such as divorce and inheritance. The cloud of points A is made up of 'cognitive service models' in which the main competences deployed are C_2 and C_3, that is divorce and inheritance law. The 'weights' of C_2 and C_3 are high, whereas that of C_1 is close to zero. In t_2, commercial law C_1 has become essential. As far as legal services are concerned, the cognitive trajectory from t_1 to t_2 is characterized by the rise to prominence of commercial law in all its forms and a decline in private law.

It might also be hypothesized that the population has fragmented, with the result that there are now two separate cognitive populations: a population of commercial lawyers (C) and a population of specialists in civil law (B).

If we remain with the provision of legal services and the competences and knowledge deployed to that end, shrink the time-frame and concentrate solely on business legal services, then different cognitive trajectories can be revealed (Figure 5.8).

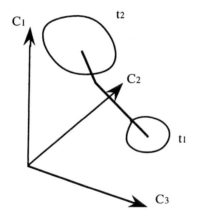

Figure 5.8 A population approach to the competences deployed in a commercial law firm

For example, if it is assumed (imaginary example, cf. Figure 5.8) that C_1 represents computer law (or environmental law or even EC law), C_2 tax law and C_3 the law relating to river navigation, then it is evident that computer law, which did not exist a short while ago ('weight' of C_1 close to zero in t_1), has today (in t_2) become an important competence and area of activity, as have environmental and EC law. On the other hand, the law relating to river navigation has declined in importance considerably and is close to zero in t_2. The path followed between t_1 and t_2 is a cognitive trajectory.

Similar examples can undoubtedly be found in other service activities. In insurance, for example, a new discipline known as cyndinics (or the science of danger) has risen to prominence in recent years. In cleaning services, new competences have been constructed around the cleaning of strategic assets, such as computer systems.

3.3 Populations of Intangible Techniques

In Chapter 2, we sought to make a distinction between tangible technical characteristics and intangible (or methodological) technical characteristics [K]. Saviotti's analysis takes account only of the former. As with competences, there is no difficulty in extending the population approach to intangible technical characteristics. In other words, all previous analyses (Section 3.1) can be applied to intangible technical characteristics (methods). Thus we will confine ourselves here to one example, namely recruitment consultancy. In this area, there are various methods, that is sets of intangible technical characteristics, that are associated with various aspects of the 'service characteristics provided' (cf. Chapter 2):

1.   methods for analysing need: K_1,
2.   methods of approach: K_2,
3.   selection methods: K_3,
4.   monitoring and follow-up methods: K_4.

In order to simplify the graphical representation, Figure 5.9 includes only the first three methods. Each axis or dimension of the intangible technical characteristics space represents different levels or degrees of quality of the characteristic in question.

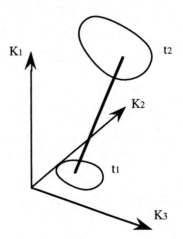

Figure 5.9 The population approach applied to recruitment consultancy methods

It can be assumed that at the outset (t_1) most recruitment consultants did not really have any methods for analyzing need and that they relied instead on client recommendations and made use of non-formalized competences [C]. On the other hand, it can be assumed that they did have methods for approaching and selecting candidates and for monitoring their integration (the population is concentrated in the plane (K_2, K_3) and the 'value' attributed to the characteristic K_1 is close to zero). In period t_2, recruitment consultants have improved the various intangible technical characteristics, namely the methods for analyzing need K_1, the methods for approaching candidates K_2 and the methods of selection K_3. The path followed between t_1 and t_2 can be termed the *(intangible) technological trajectory.*

In the case of recruitment consultancy, a population approach may even uncover a technological 'specialization', in the sense of revealing that the 'service' provided by a single one of these technical characteristics has developed. This is what is shown in Figure 5.10, which takes account of the four intangible characteristics. In other words, the technological population A equates to recruitment consultancy services (or companies) that mobilize each of the four technical characteristics. The populations B, C, D and E, for their part, represent services or firms that draw on only one of these techniques.

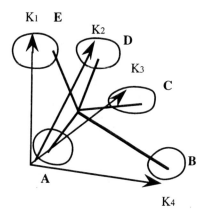

Figure 5.10 'Technological' specialization

For reasons of clarity and simplicity, the various vectors representing the service have been decomposed. In reality, these various spaces would have to be combined in order to capture the true complexity and specificity of the 'product' in question.

To conclude this point, we can say that in this population approach:

- the radical innovation model equates to the emergence of a new characteristics space that is different from any preceding space;
- the incremental model equates to the addition of an axis T_j, C_k...;

- the ameliorative model is equivalent to an increase in the 'value' of some of the existing axes;
- the ad hoc model equates to the development of certain levels of competences [C] towards certain levels of intangible technical characteristics [K];
- the recombinative model corresponds either to the merger of two populations or their break-up;
- the formalization model makes the axes 'clearer' by reducing them from an infinite quantity to a limited number. It changes the nature of certain variables or axes, with competences [C], for example, being transformed into intangible technical characteristics [K].

CONCLUSION

It has been our aim in this chapter to advance, in various ways, the notion that our extended approach to the product and the models of innovation that flow from it come within the scope of the evolutionary approach to innovation. We have also sought to enrich that approach, in particular by highlighting the full diversity of innovation trajectories in services

Thus the evolutionary approach proves itself able to account for innovation in services without reducing it solely to its technological manifestations. This is hardly surprising in view of the conceptual overlaps between this theory and the service sector, the service activity and, more generally, the service relationship as a mode of coordination among economic agents. For example, in evolutionary theory, innovation is not an outcome but a process, an act; the provision of a service is also an act. Evolutionary theory is concerned with systems with an abundance of interactions; service provision is, by definition, often interactive. Evolutionary theory is based on the principle of procedural rationality; in many services, the coordination of the actors and the establishment of a market are part of an 'economcs of quality' (in Karpik's sense of the term) in which networks and conventions play an important role. In the next chapter, we consider the way in which convention theory might illuminate a socio-economic analysis of innovation.

NOTES

1.   For a more detailed analysis, cf. Chapter 1, Section 1.2.
2.   This trajectory, which we class as informational to distinguish it from the previous ('material') trajectory, also covers the evolution of technologies which are, themselves, largely 'material' (computer systems)
3.   In order to account more rigorously for a removal in the strict sense of the term, we should, in reality, envisage the disappearance of one of the dimensions of the characteristics space (disappearance of Xj).

6. Characteristics, Worlds of Production and Worlds of Innovation

INTRODUCTION

It is possible, and it is the aim of this chapter, to advance the approach to the product developed in Chapter 2, and the models of innovation rooted in evolutionary theory derived from it (cf. Chapters 3 and 5), by interpreting it within the framework of the *economics of conventions*. In so doing, we are seeking to link two bodies of theoretical writings: evolutionary theory and convention theory. This chapter, it must be emphasized, occupies a particular position in the book. Naturally, we cannot claim that it constitutes an exhaustive examination of such a difficult question. Our objective is the much more modest one of putting forward a certain number of hypotheses and lines of thought that might in future warrant further investigation and greater empirical and theoretical validation.

Our attempt to reconcile the evolutionary approach to innovation and convention theory – an exercise which, as we will see, particularly enriches our understanding of the nature of the 'product' and of the mechanisms of innovation in services – will be a three-stage process. We will begin by providing a broad-brush outline of some of the general principles of convention theory, at least in the variants of it dedicated to highlighting the plurality of worlds (or states of worlds) in which human activities can be performed and *justified* (Section 2.1). Without concerning ourselves at this stage with the question of innovation, we will then go on (Section 2.2) to examine the way in which the extended concept of the product advanced in Chapter 2 can be enriched with a 'conventionist' perspective, that is by introducing the diversity of possible worlds of production and the corresponding quality conventions. Finally (Section 2.3), we will examine the way in which the various enrichments proposed can help to reinvigorate our approach to innovation and the nature of the models of innovation derived from a characteristics-based approach.

1.   CONVENTIONS AND WORLDS OF PRODUCTION

Convention theory claims to replace the traditional market mode of coordination with a new mode of coordination based on the existence of pre-existing shared rules that provide a framework for behavior; these rules are construed as 'conventions'.

Within this theory, which is still being constructed and consolidated (as is evolutionary theory, incidentally), P-Y Gomez (1994) identifies two sub-schools:

1.   a sub-school which he terms *functionalist* (micro-socio-economic), whose efforts are directed towards detailed examination of concrete actions and interactions, which are regarded as essential to an understanding of the construction and functioning of the social framework, and
2.   a *structuralist* sub-school, whose objective is to construct a fixed analytical framework that can be used to examine phenomena in the real world and to interpret them from a number of different perspectives.

In the arguments developed here, we will draw principally on two theoretical constructs developed by the structuralist sub-school within convention theory:

1.   Boltanski and Thévenot's worlds (Boltanski and Thévenot, 1991);
2.   Salais and Storper's worlds of production (Salais and Storper, 1993).

Although they are not unrelated and are based on similar hypotheses, these two constructs are not, as we shall see, one and the same thing. What sets them apart from each other in particular is that the first has its roots in political philosophy and seeks to characterize value systems, whereas the second is concerned with the more economic characteristics of production, markets and work. Examining the two in succession should not be seen as a superfluous exercise. Rather, it will enable us to highlight different aspects of the innovation dynamic.

1.1 The Worlds of the 'Economies of Grandeur'

Boltanski and Thévenot (1991) are the authors of a theoretical construct which, largely through its metaphorical power, has succeeded in bursting the boundaries of individual disciplines to gain for itself a remarkable audience and rate of diffusion in the academic world, without for all that escaping sometimes bitter criticism (Tréanton, 1993; Economies et Sociétés, 1997).[1]

In order to resolve the question of the coordination of agents (the production of agreements), Boltanski and Thévenot advance the notion that there exist a number of 'pure' worlds that operate according to different principles.

The principal characteristics of each of these worlds are summarized in Table 6.1. Membership of one world or another is determined by reference to a *convention* relating to a certain number of principles, and in particular the following:

- the higher common principle, which establishes equivalence between beings;
- the state of 'grandeur' (greatness or worthiness), which defines the 'great beings' that ensure that the previous principle is upheld;
- the state of 'smallness', which is defined by contrast with the state of greatness;
- the dignity of individuals: this is a convention defining what confers dignity on beings in a given world (work, interest, etc.);
- the repertoire of subjects, that is the list of the individuals that characterize a given world;
- the repertoire of objects, that is the list of the main objects that characterize a given world;
- the investment formula, which expresses the sacrifice required to change state;
- the order of grandeur, that is the relative ranking of the 'states of greatness'.

The arguments developed in this chapter will draw for the most part on the four worlds that seem to be best suited to our purpose of defining and qualifying the product (in the sense attributed to it in this book, that is one that also encompasses processes) and its (various forms of) renewal:

1. the industrial or technical world: that of volumes and technical operations;
2. the market or financial world: that of worth and of monetary and financial transactions;
3. the domestic world: that of interpersonal relations, empathy and relations of trust built up over time;
4. the civic world: that of social relations based on a concern for equality of treatment, fairness and justice.

It may seem paradoxical, in an analysis of innovation, to exclude the world of inspiration, that is the world of creativity and creation. The reason is that we are concerned here with innovations that affect the economy and markets. In such innovations, moments of independent, free creation unrelated to commercial or industrial considerations are very much the exception. In other words, the type of creation that interests us here (the one that is of interest to economists rather than to gourmets, aesthetes or music lovers) is not the province of a single world but can be expressed in terms of the 'value systems' of the four other worlds adopted here. By the same token, we should not in theory exclude the opinion-based world (as we do here for simplicity's sake) from a characteristics-based approach to products. In some cases, indeed, products have an image, a reputation that is one of their characteristics. Thus there are service activities, such as advertising or marketing, from which it is difficult to exclude this opinion-based world.

Table 6.1 The worlds of the 'economies of grandeur'

	Inspirational world	Domestic world	Opinion world
Common superior principle	Inspiration	Personal relations, hierarchy, tradition	The opinion of others
State of greatness	Spontaneous, extraordinary	Kind, wise	Fame
Dignity of individuals	Anxiety of creation, love, passion	Ease of habit, common sense	The desire to be recognized
Repertoire of subjects	Visionaries, artists	Superiors and inferiors	Celebrities and their followers
Rep of objects and mechanisms	Mind, body, dream	Social conventions, gifts	Names in the media, brands
Investment formula	Flight from habit (risk)	Rejection of selfishness, duty	Renouncement of secrecy
Order of greatness	The universal worth of singularity (genius)	Respect and responsibility, subordination, honor	To be recognized, to identify (oneself)
Natural relations between beings	Alchemy of unplanned encounters, dreams, imagination	Keeping company with well-brought up people, to raise, to reproduce	Persuasion
Symbol of the harmony of the natural order	The reality of the imagination	The moving spirit of the household, house, family	Public image, audience
Model event	The rovings of the imagination, adventure, quest	Family ceremonies	The presentation of events
Mode of expressing judgement	Flash or spark of genius	To be able to trust, have faith in	The judgement of the public
Form of evidence	The certainty of intuition	The exemplary anecdote	The obvious fact of success
State of smallness (decline)	The temptation of return to earth, routine	The carelessness of the inconsiderate, vulgar	Indifference and banality

Source: after Boltanski and Thévenot (1991).

	Civic world	*Market world*	*Industrial world*
Common superior principle	The pre-eminence of collective entities	Competition	Performance, efficiency, technical object, scientific principle
State of greatness	As laid down in regulations, representative	Worth	Efficient, functional, reliable, operational
Dignity of individuals	Aspiration to civic rights	Interest, love of things, desire, selfishness	Work
Repertoire of subjects	Collective bodies and their representatives	Competitors, customers	Professionals (experts, specialists)
Repertoire of objects and of mechanisms	Legal forms	Wealth, luxury items	Means/resources (tools, methods, quantity)
Investment formula	Renouncement of the personal and the private	Opportunism	Progress, investment
Order of greatness	Delegatory relationships	Ownership	Control
Natural relations between beings	Working together for a collective purpose	Take a stake, buy, sell, pay	To function
Symbol of the harmony of the natural order	The democratic republic	Market	Organization, system
Model event	Demonstration for a just cause	Deal done, transaction concluded	Test
Mode of expressing judgement	The verdict of the ballot box	Price	'Just so', in working order, functioning
Form of evidence	Legislation	Money	Measurement
State of smallness	Division, isolation	Enslavement to money, loser	Inefficient

1.2 Salais and Storper's Worlds of Production

Another analytical perspective belonging to the structuralist wing of the convention school might usefully be considered here as well. Just like the theoretical construct outlined in the previous section, the notion of worlds of production advanced by Salais and Storper (1993) draws attention to the plurality of possible worlds. Unlike Boltanski and Thévenot, however, it is not Salais and Storper's aim to develop a theory that can be applied to all human and social activities. The scope of their ambition is confined, rather, to accounting for the plurality of productive systems. Consequently, it focuses on conventions relating to products or, more precisely, to product quality (in reality, such conventions also conceal conventions on the quality of work).

The main difficulty in any production and consumption activity is uncertainty about product quality. This uncertainty can be dispelled by two mechanisms that are most admirably described by Knight (1921): *consolidation or grouping* (that is the bringing together within the same category of objects with similar characteristics) and *specialization* (that is having recourse to the work of professionals and experts). It is these two uncertainty-reducing mechanisms that Salais and Storper draw on in order to reveal the various possible types of product quality and the plurality of corresponding worlds of production.

According to these authors, the quality of a product can be measured by two different scales (or conventions); on the one hand, the extent to which demand for it is consolidated, that is the degree of dedication (an echo of the notion of 'fitness' advanced by evolutionary theorists) and, on the other, the extent to which productive activity is specialized. On the basis of these two scales, the following kinds of products can be identified:

1. dedicated products (that is those for which demand is weakly consolidated; these are products specific to the needs of a given customer or group of customers);
2. generic products (that is products that are independent of their users, whose 'destination is anonymous');
3. specialized products (fruits of the work of 'specialists');
4. standard products (fruits of the work of non-specialists).

Combining the degree of dedication of the product, on the one hand, and the degree of professional specialization of the work, on the other, makes it possible to identify four basic types of production worlds (cf. Table 6.2):

1. the market world of standardized dedicated products, that is products that are the fruit of a standardized work process but aimed at a targeted, clearly identified clientele (flexible production);
2. the industrial world of standardized generic products, that is mass products aimed at an undifferentiated clientele that are the fruit of standardized Fordist work processes;
3. the interpersonal world of specialized dedicated products, that is customized or 'made-to-measure' products aimed at a clearly identified customer and satisfying his particular requirements that are created by professionals

in possession of idiosyncratic expertise (craft industries, specialist equipment);

4. the intangible world, in which specialized generic products are produced and consumed, that is anonymous products (in this case, in fact, 'public goods' knowledge) that are the fruit of the labor of high-level experts (research activities).

Table 6.2 The worlds of production according to Salais and Storper

	Specialized products (fruits of specialist work processes)	Standardized products (fruits of standardized work processes)
Dedicated products (intended for identified consumers)	*Interpersonal world of production*	*Market world of production*
Generic products (intended for anonymous consumers)	*Intangible world of production*	*Industrial world of production*

Source: After Salais and Storper (1993).

These worlds differ from those of Boltanski and Thévenot in several respects. Whereas the worlds of Boltanski and Thévenot are worlds of the *discourse of justification* and of *criteria of greatness*, that is different forms of legitimate common welfare, those of Salais and Storper are *worlds of the social and technical relations of production and exchange*.

The worlds of Salais and Storper denote different realities or spaces which, in a way, coexist objectively: they are associated with different types or forms of products. They are worlds that have their own independent existence but it is possible to move between them once a change of product type has been decided.

The worlds of Boltanski and Thévenot (particularly the four best suited to our purpose, namely the industrial, market, domestic and civic worlds) can be analysed as 'different' perspectives on the same world, the same space, the same reality. This does not preclude moves from one world to another, but such a move may involve not so much the physical transformation of a productive system as a change of intellectual or ethical perspective.

2. CHARACTERISTICS-BASED APPROACHES, CONVENTIONS AND THE PLURALITY OF WORLDS

In this section, we will examine the way in which the extended, characteristics-based approach to the product and production can be interpreted and enriched by the two conventionist perspectives briefly outlined above.

2.1 The Characteristics-Based Approach and Boltanksi and Thévenot's Worlds

In Saviotti and Metcalfe's initial concept, the final or service characteristics [Yi] can be likened to the terms of a contract (the engine is obliged to reach such and such a speed, the boot has to have such and such a capacity, etc.). The neoclassical nomenclature hypothesis, applied here not to the product but to the service characteristics, is supposed to be verified. We are dealing effectively with an explicit contract. We attempted more or less successfully in Chapter 2 to apply this general approach to services, that is to proceed as if, here too, the service characteristics could be reduced to the terms of a contract (albeit a less explicit one, since the 'mandates' in services are generally more confused[2] or ill-defined). In particular, we saw that the more one focuses on services with a high informational, cognitive or relational content, the more difficult it is to express the 'product' and its service characteristics in contractual terms. We will now direct our attention to the notion that the service characteristics in set [Y] (and, as we will see, the technical characteristics [T] and competences [C] as well) can be regarded as constructs based on the conventions associated with different worlds and examine the implications of this hypothesis in the field of innovation.

Thus what we are attempting to do here is to enrich the Lancasterian notion of products or services by introducing into it Boltanski and Thévenot's notion of the diversity of worlds. In so doing, we are extending the degree of economic variety still further and, moreover, giving the notion of characteristic a social as well as a technical content.

Taking account of the multiplicity of these worlds is of particular importance in services. In services, after all, as Jean Gadrey (1994b) notes, a product's qualities are justified in ways that are more diverse, more mutually opposed and, in many cases, more ambiguous than in any other area of economic activity. This tension, which is the reason for the diversity of explicit or implicit products, can be explained in various ways. Firstly, some services are based on a very particular medium, namely individual persons or groups of persons whose lives have a number of different facets (domestic, civic, economic). Secondly, the service sector includes a large number of activities namely public and social services, in which the civic world plays, or is supposed to play, a fundamental role.

Gadrey (1994b) uses Boltanski and Thévenot's framework to show that there are several justifiable definitions (and therefore several families of descriptive characteristics or criteria) of service products, depending on the situation, the actors and their understanding of the meaning of the output. We adopt the same analytical perspective here, since we are interested in the totality of (service and technical) characteristics and competences which, together, define the product.

In order to incorporate the diversity of worlds into our extended Lancasterian approach (and thereby extend it still further), we can juxtapose several sets of (service and technical) characteristics and competences associated with different worlds (as defined by Boltanksi and Thévenot). Thus our (simplified) initial representation of the product (Figure 6.1), which indicates that the service characteristics (which fall within the domain of world I, the industrial or technical world) are obtained by drawing on competences and technical (and process) characteristics, is replaced by a new representation (Figure 6.2) in which the indices I, II, III, IV represent each of the worlds under consideration (the industrial, market, domestic and civic worlds).

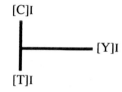

Figure 6.1 The initial representation of the product

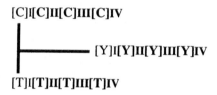

Figure 6.2 A representation of the product taking into account the plurality of worlds

It may seem paradoxical to suggest examining technical and process characteristics from the perspective of the different worlds. The general tendency would be to regard such characteristics as falling solely within the domain of the technical world. Our hypothesis is that technologies are not neutral and that their relevant characteristics may fall within the domain of separate worlds. As far as their potential for producing service characteristics is concerned, technologies can be implemented in accordance with different rationales and value systems. Thus there are technical solutions that are fairer (or considered fairer) than others. As far as intangible technical characteristics are concerned (methods, modes of organization), there can be no difficulty in accepting that certain organizational arrangements might fall within the domain of the domestic and civic worlds (arrangements intended to ensure anonymity, confidentiality, discretion, fairness in the order in which cases are dealt with, etc.). As far as tangible technologies are concerned, examples might include the introduction in French post offices of cash machines adapted to take the cash cards issued in conjunction with the savings accounts intended for socially and economically disadvantaged customers.

The same applies to competences. The set of competences must be able to take account of those that might be described as *social and civic competences*, that is the ability to provide a service for, or simply to maintain a relationship with, customers who may be seriously disadvantaged socially and economically. Such social and civic competences may be accepted or even given an enhanced status (this is generally the case in the French post office, for example) or suppressed (as is usually the case in traditional banks). The competences of some customers [C'k] may be particularly weak (socially and economically disadvantaged customers, cognitive and cultural handicaps in the case of postal services, for example). The balance can be redressed by mobilizing the social and civic competences of staff dealing with the general public ([Ck]ᵢᵥ) so that they can empathize with disadvantaged customers and effect the 'translation' of their needs.

In the enriched configuration, the Lancasterian approach advanced by Saviotti and Metcalfe is reduced to an analysis of *products³ from the perspective of the industrial or technical world*. What counts is that the product fulfils the terms of the contract, in other words that it achieves the levels of technical performance specified in the contract. Thus a car, for example, must be able to reach a speed of 75 mph and to carry five people in a certain degree of comfort, the boot must have a certain luggage capacity, etc.

Confining ourselves for simplicity's sake to products or the final or service characteristics [Y], we can cite by way of illustration a certain number of situations that highlight the diversity of worlds. Thus public services, for example, are usually considered from the perspective of the industrial or technical world. However, the market world is playing an increasingly important role here, particularly in organizations involved in financial activities, and it is undoubtedly in the public services that it is easiest to put into practice and to identify final or service characteristics that fall within the domain of the civic world.

Table 6.3, which is limited to the set of characteristics [Y], illustrates the multiplicity of 'products' or final or service characteristics provided by the French Post Office, the French family welfare offices (CAF) and the French public employment service (ANPE).

Table 6.3 The multiplicity of 'products' or final service characteristics [Y] in different service organizations*

	Products or 'corresponding final service characteristics' falling within the domain of the:			
	Industrial world [Y]$_I$	Market world [Y]$_{II}$	Domestic world [Y]$_{III}$	Civic world [Y]$_{IV}$
The Post Office: postal and financial services	- basic technical operations relating to the logistics of postal services (delivery, collection, sorting) and to banking and financial transactions - industrial quality indicators (errors, malfunctions, adherence to deadlines, etc.)	- yield, earnings, anticipated projected value of the various financial assets held by customers	- production of personal relations - individualization of services - interpersonal arrangements	- equal treatment for users (at counters and on delivery rounds) - equal accessibility - non-discrimination - assistance for marginalized groups - 'social' rates - 'social banking' services
Family welfare offices	- standardized services provided for anonymous citizens - diversified ranges of standard services - punctuality and correctness of payments	- benefits (allowances) paid (amount, diversity)	- emphasis on the economics of the service relationship - original (innovative) solutions to individual problems	- equality of treatment - non- or positive discrimination - external inform. using the various media - discovery of 'potential' clients - social manag. of benefits (flexible manag. of adm. proof, continuity of payment) - social induction
Public employment service	- making available information (on vacancies : displays of job vacancies, electronic information services, voice information services, self-service equipment - speed, accessibility	- Financial assistance (to firms[4]) as part of employment promotion programs	- personalized responses (advice, adjustment of demand to supply, training) - monitoring, support for those who find employment	- individualized support for disadvantaged job-seekers. - certain services offered free of charge (e.g. photocopies, electronic inf. services, travel costs) to ensure accessibility and universality.

Note : *Examples restricted to Y characteristics.
Source: After Gallouj, Gadrey, Ghillebaert (1996); Adjerad (1997); Delfini (1997).

Several general observations can be made in respect of this analysis.

1.   We have attempted in Table 6.3 to identify individual 'products' and their

characteristics from the point of view of users (that is on the basis of the criteria favored by customers). We have not viewed 'products' and their characteristics from the perspective of the producing organization. As soon as we abandon the neo-classical market perspective, in which there is identity since the (market) value of a service is the same, in equilibrium, on both sides of the market, significant differences emerge between the two points of view (particularly as regards the numerous free services not traded in the market). In the market world, for example, the (real) return on the funds invested by customers is undoubtedly, from their point of view, an important use or service characteristic of products of the 'savings account management' type. On the other hand, the net banking proceeds (or other indicators of financial results over the course of the financial year) is not, even though it is certainly one of the possible 'direct products' of the Post Office's banking function.

2.   In the case of financial services, we must not, of course, confuse the following two elements: on the one hand, the price of the 'product' and of the corresponding characteristics and, on the other, the monetary gains that these 'products' might generate, what they 'bring in'. Elements of the latter type (profits or gains) belong to the service characteristics category. In this respect, reference might usefully be made to the general definition of any monetary and financial instrument put forward by Tobin.[5] This definition is based on the following set of service characteristics: liquidity, divisibility, reversibility-substitutability, yield, earnings, anticipated projected value, ease of exchange, risk, etc. On the other hand, the elements of the first type (price) are not use values but exchange values. In theory, they have no place in a concept of the product that has its roots in Lancaster's work. Nevertheless, it might be asked whether such a theoretical principle might not be called into question in certain particular situations, namely those in which the price seems to constitute a genuine 'use' characteristic. This might be the case, for example, with some of the 'social rates' applied by the French Post Office, which seem to be much more than the price that has to be paid in order to obtain a 'service' or service characteristic. Thus, as Gadrey (1996c) notes, 'if certain charges are kept fairly low in order to maintain a "universal" service, they determine the social accessibility of the products in question. The quid pro quo for the cost thus incurred is a 'product' (a result), namely access to postal services for a segment of the population that would be deprived of them if the charges were "normal".[6]

3.   In the light of the previous two observations and of the fact that, in Table 6.3, it is the services provided by the organizations and not their production processes that are being evaluated, it would seem that, with the exception of financial services (insurance, banking, financial services provided by the Post Office, etc.) and to a lesser extent services that give rise to the payment of cash benefits, the 'market' world should in general be

excluded from any representation of product characteristics.

4.   As far as the Post Office is concerned, our own analyses have gone much further in revealing service characteristics that fall within the domain of the civic world ([Y]$_{IV}$). If the service transaction is defined as a problem-solving or 'repair' operation, it becomes possible to construct a framework for analyzing the various service characteristics or products. This framework revolves around two variables (cf. Table 6.4):

   •   the source of the problem to be rectified (the analogy with the definition of innovation in evolutionary theory as a problem-solving activity has to be noted). The problem may be cognitive or cultural (illiteracy, difficulty or impossibility of communicating), economic or financial, related to housing difficulties, isolation or behavioral difficulties linked to poverty;

   •   the nature of the service (or service characteristics) provided in order to rectify matters.

Some 20 services (provided at post office counters or on the telephone) or service characteristics falling within the domain of the civic world can be identified in this way: translation, reception, training, document drafting, listening in confidence, advice on problem solving, intermediation with the social services or voluntary organizations, advice on job placement or recruitment, humanized penalties, acceptance of frequent withdrawals of very small sums ('purse-counter service'), psychological assistance, exemption from administrative proof, settlement of disputes, etc. These various service characteristics or services (depending on the level of analysis adopted) are summarized in Table 6.4 and juxtaposed with the types of problem to which they are supposed to respond.

The opportunities for taking account of civic service characteristics in the definition of products are not confined to the public services, nor even to services as a whole. Such opportunities also exist in market services. In an examination of the insurance industry, Gadrey (1996c) identifies as civic characteristics one direct product, namely 'the refusal to go too far in searching out private information on the insured (health, family history)', and one indirect product, namely 'the evening out of premiums, for example between generations or social classes'. Once again, it should be noted that it is not prices that constitute the indirect civic product but rather the accessibility or universality of the service that is ensured by the premiums that are charged. Gadrey concludes that performance according to the criteria of the civic world could be judged by 'the share of policies in respect of which the company agrees to bear additional risks for civic reasons or in order not to discriminate'. Such a strategy can of course be profitable if the costs incurred (excessive segmentation of insurance premiums also gives rise to costs) are offset by reduced transaction costs.

Table 6.4 The service characteristics in the Post Office's activities that fall within the domain of the civic world [Y]IV*

	Cognitive difficulties linked to various social handicaps (illiteracy, etc.)	Poverty, destitution and associated financial difficulties	Spatial characteristics		Deviant behavior of certain groups	
			Specific housing difficulties of disadvantaged groups	Isolation of some individuals (particularly the elderly)	Open disputes, aggressiveness, violence, Damage to equipment and offices, hygiene	Frauds, lies or deceit linked to financial problems of social origin
Sources of the rectification serv. or service characteristics						
Nature of repair or rectification, ie of the service provided or of the service characteristics [Yi]Iv	- Reception, assistance, explanations, advice, translation - Training and individual self-sufficiency - Forms filled in by officials - Drafting of documents: (tax return, claim forms for medical expenses)	- *Social welfare* measures not directly linked to Post Office services: listening, compassion, discretion (barriers and yellow lines to maintain privacy); links with social services and voluntary organizations; advice, job placements, recruitment - *Social measures* linked to Post Office services: humanized penalties (extension of payment times); acceptance of passbooks or cash cards for frequent withdrawals of small sums	- Search for addresses - Redirection of mail	- Home services, home visits for elderly people wishing to withdraw money - Psychological assistance - Exemption from the need to provide proof of identity	- Prevention, management and calming of disputes	- Limitation and prevention of incidents - Advice

Note: *Financial and counter services, excluding mail delivery, collecting and sorting.
Source: After Gallouj, Gadrey, Ghillebaert (1996).

176

Similarly, the addition of 'free' service characteristics to some goods or services falls within the domain of the civic world when accessibility and universality are thereby increased and within that of the domestic or relational world when loyalty is strengthened. There are very many examples of this latter type in retailing and some forms of rental services: making available a free information and advice line following the purchase or hire of an item (for example, do-it-yourself materials and equipment), allowing customers to purchase items on a sale-or-return basis, and so on.

This enrichment of the definition of the product through the integration of new worlds is just as valid in the case of goods. Indeed, the incorporation of environmental or ecological characteristics into certain goods can also be interpreted in terms of civic justifications, even though other justifications can of course be sought in the market world, such as fears of direct or indirect economic penalties (poor brand image). In some cases, technical characteristics and competences of the same kind (that is falling within the domain of the civic world) can be linked to these ecological and environmental civic service characteristics. Moreover, the civic dimension of the use characteristics of technologies (particularly information technologies) can be said to find expression in the respect paid to the ethical dimensions and confidentiality of the information that is gathered and processed.

Finally, it should be noted that the introduction of civic service characteristics into both goods and services can take place on the initiative of service providers or be enforced. Legislation can clearly stipulate the material conditions that will ensure access to certain services for disadvantaged populations (for example handicapped people). It can impose norms (levels of service characteristics) in areas such as pollution (noise, smoke, etc.), safety and security and hygiene (for example in hospitals, where it is necessary to combat nosocomial diseases) that have their counterparts in the technical characteristics.

2.2 The Characteristics-Based Approach and Salais and Storper's Worlds of Production

Salais and Storper's construct poses a certain number of difficulties that have already been identified by Gadrey (1996b). These difficulties can be divided into three categories:

1. a theoretical difficulty: the first criterion adopted by Salais and Storper in constructing their typology of worlds of production contrasts specialized 'products' with standardized 'products' (cf. Section 1.2). In reality, the starting point here is not the *product* but rather the degree of specialization or standardization of the *labor* that goes to create the product;
2. several semantic difficulties: the adjective 'market' cannot just denote the world in which 'standardized dedicated' products are made. In fact, the

market dimension is present throughout the other worlds (with the possible exception in certain cases of the intangible world). Moreover, the distinction that is drawn between an intangible world, on the one hand, and an industrial world, on the other, is a source of ambiguity when it comes to dealing with service activities and industries that are widely agreed to be characterized by a certain degree of intangibility;

3. a difficulty with the application of the framework to service activities, which is further compounded by the semantic problems alluded to above, although they are not the sole cause of the difficulty. Salais and Storper construct their analytical framework solely on the basis of examples drawn from manufacturing industry, although they are quite explicit in justifying their use of the notion of the 'product' in terms of their concern to break with the good-service dichotomy, since for them 'all products incorporate a service; in extreme cases, the product can consist solely of a service provided by one person for another' (Salais and Storper, 1993, p. 59).

In an attempt to transpose the framework to service activities, Gadrey (1996b) suggests that these difficulties (cf. Table 6.5) might be resolved by:

*   abandoning labor specialization or standardization as a criterion while retaining the product as the starting point for analysis;
*   introducing the relative balance of power between supply and demand as a criterion, expressed as the varying opportunities or abilities to exercise the 'voice' or 'exit' options (Hirschman, 1970);
*   renaming the worlds. Thus the market, industrial, interpersonal and intangible worlds would be known, respectively, as the world of flexible production, the Fordist world, the professional and personalized services world and the world of creation.

Our task once again is to translate these configurations into the terms of our concept of the product as a system of characteristics and competences. In order to perform this task, we will replace the criteria of specialization and dedication adopted by Salais and Storper and Gadrey's criteria of product 'flexibility' and the balance of power between supply and demand with the following three criteria (cf. Table 6.6):

1. the extent to which the service characteristics [Y] are formatted (that is the degree of standardization);
2. the importance accorded to the technical characteristics [T], which we will denote by the term technological intensity. For simplicity's sake, the technical characteristics vector [T] includes tangible and intangible technical characteristics as well as process characteristics (for a discussion of this convention cf. Chapter 2, Section 3.2);

3. the 'strength' or intensity of the service relationship symbolized by [C']
[C].

Table 6.5 The worlds of service production

	Non-standardized, 'customized' products or services	Standardized products or services
Customers/users in a relatively favorable position from the point of view of supply choice (voice + threat of exit) *Production tends to be demand-driven,* with exceptions (de facto local monopolies, profession controlling clientele, etc.)	THE PROFESSIONAL AND PERSONALIZED SERVICES WORLD Services produced by the 'consultative professions' (Freidson, 1970) as well as craft workers and small traders, 'made-to-measure' services to individuals - Economics of professional quality (Karpik, 1989) and of profession - Type of product: personalized service, 'made-to-measure' products	THE WORLD OF FLEXIBLE PRODUCTION Diversified ranges of standardized goods or services, driven by demand. Just-in-time, 'certified' industrial standards relating to product quality, delivery times and processes (industrial quality). Firm J, bank in the 1990s - Economics of flexible production and post-Fordist industrial quality - Type of product: diversified product ranges delivered on a just-in-time basis
Customers/users in a relatively subordinate position being able to choose only between 'captivity' or (in some cases) exit. *Production tends to be 'pushed' on to the market* (or towards users)	THE WORLD OF CREATION The world of research and innovation, of original creation. 'Learned professions' (Freidson), artistic and literary creation, creative design, advertising, etc. - Economcs of reputation and prestige - Type of product: 'creations'	FORDIST WORLD 'Mechanistic' manufacturing or service-sector bureaucracies (Mintzberg, 1982). Mass production of goods and service for anonymous customers or users (or 'citizens'). Low level of differentiation. Absence of 'voice'. Firm A, Mintzberg's (mechanist) M model. - Economics of Fordist production - Type of product: standardized, mass produced

Source: According to Gadrey (1996b).

These various elements [C'], [C], [T], [Y] equate to the various components of the 'product' as defined in Chapter 2. Thus the 'product' remains the starting point for our analysis but the definition adopted here is one particularly suited to services since it also takes account of the process. We are not merely changing the terminology but also the analytical perspective: the formatting of [Y] reflects the way in which standardization is expressed at the level of the service characteristics, the concept of technological intensity takes account of the importance of the technical and process characteristics [T] and the use of the service relationship symbolized by [C'] [C] introduces a fundamental aspect of service delivery.

Linking the formatting of [Y] and technological intensity criteria produces the following three alternatives that express an increasing degree of product formatting or standardization.

1. The service characteristics [Y] are weakly formatted and the technological intensity (in the sense of the tangible, intangible and process technologies) is low. The extreme case would be a 'pure' service, in which the service characteristics are obtained merely by mobilizing competences without any technological mediation.
2. The service characteristics [Y] are weakly formatted but the technological intensity is strong, that is the tangible or intangible technical characteristics [T] play an important role.
3. The service characteristics [Y] are strongly formatted and the technological intensity is high, that is the technical characteristics [T], particularly in their tangible and process variants, play an important role.

In this way, six worlds of service production can be identified. They are depicted in Table 6.6 below.

The professional and relational world of production is characterized by weakly standardized services or service characteristics [Y] and a strong service relationship [C'][C]. It can be divided into two separate sub-worlds depending on the degree of technological intensity (importance of [T]):

1. the world in which technological intensity is low. It equates to the 'pure service' configuration in which the service characteristics [Y], which are difficult to format, are obtained through the mobilization of the customer's competences in tandem with those of the service provider (service relationship [C'][C]). Small management or legal consultancy firms, ordinary medical consultations and local services (for the elderly[7], for example) belong to this world.
2. the world in which technological intensity is high. In this case, the vector [T] comprises intangible technical characteristics for the most part (methods, etc.). Compared with the first sub-world, the increase in tech-

nological intensity can be said to some extent to reflect the increased formatting of competences (the crystallization of methods, etc.). Examples might include consultancy in new technologies and the large international audit and consultancy networks.

Table 6.6 The worlds of service production from the perspective of a characteristics-based approach

Formatting (Standardization) of [Y]	Service characteristics [Y] Weakly formatted		[Y] formatted
Technological intensity (TI) Service relationship	Low TI	High TI	Technological (or capital) intensity still high
	Professional and relational world of production		*Flexible or modular world of production*
	Low TI	*High TI*	
Strong [C'][C]	Voluntary home help services Management consultancy (SMEs) Legal consult (SMEs) Medi consult.	Audit and consultancy (large international networks) Consultancy in new technologies	Collective insurance Hotel trade Transport Local services provided by companies Cleaning (large contractors) Artificial intelligence
	World of creation		*Fordist world of production*
[C'][C] weak, non-existent or restricted to self-service (that is mobilization of [C'] without [C])	*Low TI*	*High TI*	
	Social science research group Advertising (to some extent)	R&D Nuclear physics laboratory	Fast-food restaurants Mass insurance Mass tourism ATMs

The world of creation is similar to the previous world in that the product and the service characteristics [Y] are difficult to format. On the other hand, it differs from it sharply by virtue of the autonomy the 'producer' enjoys vis-à-vis the consumer, which means that the service relationship [C'][C] is weak or non-existent. This world can also be divided into two sub-worlds on the basis of the technological intensity criterion. TI may be low (in the case of human and social science research centres in universities, for example) or high (as in physical science laboratories that rely on heavy equipment).

In *the Fordist world*, the service relationship [C'][C] is very weak (consumption of a service here resembles the purchase of a standard product) and technological or, more generally, capital intensity is still very high. The product, in its various aspects, that is its service characteristics [Y] and its technical and process characteristics [T], is highly formatted (standardized). This is the case, for example, with fast-food restaurants, mass insurance, mass tourism, the use of automated self-service systems in banking, postal services and the use of information terminals.

The last world is that of *flexible or modular production*, in which the products supplied are made up of varying combinations of highly formatted modules of characteristics, with the precise choice of combinations requiring active participation on the part of the client. Technological or capital intensity is also very high. This is the case, for example, with certain aspects of insurance, the hotel trade, the transport of people, the cleaning services provided by some large international firms (cf. Sundbo, 1996), the introduction of artificial intelligence, etc.

It is not always easy to find examples of services associated with each of these worlds. The particular tropisms may very well be thrown back into question very quickly by institutional variables (size of firm), cultural variables (there seems to be a greater affinity for formatting or standardization in the English-speaking world) and strategic variables. We will see furthermore in Section 3.2.3, for example, that strategies are put in place to facilitate the transition from one world to another.

3.   CONVENTIONS AND WORLDS OF INNOVATION

In the final stage of our argument, we will attempt to link in various ways the conventionist approaches outlined above (that of Boltanski and Thévenot, and then Salais and Storper's) with the question of innovation and the modes of innovation we have already defined in evolutionary terms.

3.1 Innovation and Boltanski and Thévenot's Worlds

We will begin with a general investigation of evolutionary theory in the light of Boltanski and Thévenot's worlds before examining, more specifically, the implications of integrating these worlds into our various models of innovation.

3.1.1 Evolutionary theory in the light of Boltanski and Thévenot's worlds

In standard neoclassical theory, innovation can be regarded as falling solely within the domain of the industrial and market worlds (cf. Table 6.7). Technical change, reduced in scope to process innovations alone, is considered implicitly through the notion of the production function, in which inputs and outputs are assumed to be homogeneous and anonymous. Analysis focuses on the effects of technical change on a certain number of major economic variables, the most important of which is productivity, which has to be increased (industrial world). However, this increase in productivity has its counterpart in the market world, since it leads to cost reductions. The domestic and civic worlds have no place here, since the various relationships that are formed or are revealed and the behavior of individuals in the process of production and innovation are of no concern here. The 'black box' remains resolutely shut. Thus the absence of relations (the non-interaction hypothesis) gives rise to a linear notion of innovation, in which the R&D, production and sales phases follow on from each other without feedback. The various professional groups involved in the different phases move in specialized 'worlds' that are more or less isolated from outside interference or influence.

In evolutionary theory, on the other hand, the black box is breached. The various concepts of innovation may find their justifications not only in the industrial and market worlds, as in neoclassical theory, but also, in our view, in the domestic and civic worlds as well. Various types of (non-exclusive) relations can be identified and linked to concepts and analyses that play an important role in evolutionary theory. The following list is by no means exhaustive.

1. *Human beings' relations to the product and to other objects (means of production).* This type encompasses all forms of learning, that is to say, in the order in which the concepts emerged: learning by doing, using, searching and, more recently, trying. These relations are also reflected or manifest themselves in the product's lack of anonymity (in other words, its service characteristics are very dependent on those who produce them and those who consume them), in the idiosyncrasy of tasks and in the tacit nature of the knowledge and competences deployed.

2. *Interpersonal relations.* This type includes part of the previous category when the relations between human beings unfold as part of a relationship to the product. Thus we are dealing here primarily with the learning relationships listed above, to which should be added learning by consulting and, more generally, learning by interacting. This is also the site at which sympathy and empathy manifest themselves and at which conflicts develop and are resolved. Evolutionary economics would not appear to be really concerned with this aspect of conflict. In the economics of conven-

tions, on the other hand, it occupies a central position.[9] The notions of tacit knowledge and competences might also be said to fall within the domain of an interpersonal relationship, albeit one with a specific configuration, namely the relationship of a human being to him or herself (reflexivity). They are, after all, aspects of his or her personality and cannot be dissociated from it.

3. *The relations of products to other products.* Such relations can be expressed through the notions of combinations, systems and networks. In the case of goods, these relations fall within the domain of the industrial and technical world (the production of a good involves the combination of a certain number of technical characteristics [T]). In the case of services, they also fall within the domain of the civic and above all the domestic worlds, to the extent that combinations of products are also combinations of systems of social relations (combinations [C'][C]). These inter-product relations can also be considered over time. From this perspective, they reveal product 'lineages' and provide a basis for introducing the concepts of technological trajectories and path dependency (historicity).

4. *The relations of human being to organizations.* These relations are expressed in particular through the following concepts and phenomena: organizational learning, the feeling of belonging to a company (company culture), corporate memory and idiosyncratic knowledge and competences.

5. *The relations of organizations to other organizations.* These relations are reflected in the following concepts: cooperation, interaction, local or national innovation system and techno-economic networks.[10]

The linear model of innovation derived from neoclassical hypotheses is called into question here. It is replaced by a model characterized by a wealth of interactions, namely the chain-link model which, it will be remembered, comprises several possible paths leading to innovation (rather than just one) and a multiplicity of feedback loops of varying lengths between the various phases of the process (Kline and Rosenberg, 1986).

Overall (cf. Table 6.7), the various concepts referred to above can be said to fall, to some extent, within the domain of the domestic and relational world, as broadly conceived. We are dealing here not only with the relations that develop between individuals but also with the various relations referred to above that involve human beings, products, organizations, etc. in a multiplicity of different combinations. For example, it might be said, in a way, that tacit knowledge and competences, which reflect the impression that human beings leave on products and vice versa, or the reflexive relationship of human beings to themselves fall within the domain of the domestic world. This explains why they elude neoclassical analysis, whose gaze does not encompass this world.

Table 6.7 The evolutionary theory of innovation in the light of Boltanski and Thévenot's worlds

Reference world / Theory of innovation	Industrial or technological	Market or financial	(Extended)[8] domestic or relational	Civic
Neoclassical	- process innovation - increase in production - decrease in inputs - product anonymity - non-interaction hypothesis, linear model of innovation	- decrease in production costs		
Evolutionary	- technological regime - dominant design - technological guide post - technological paradigm	- techno-economic paradigm - market selection environment	- learning by doing, using, searching, trying, consulting, interacting - organizational learning, company culture, corporate memory - routines - interactive model of innovation - absence of product anonymity, - idiosyncrasy of tasks, tacit knowledge and competences - 'made-to-measure' innovation - techno-economic networks - local and national innovation system - technological trajectory, path dependency (relation over time, historicity) - externalities of networks	- socio-technical paradigm, - principle of social acceptability (exclusion of the nuclear paradigm because of social unacceptability) - non-market selection environment

On the other hand, notions such as technological regime, dominant design, technological guide post and technological paradigm (as defined in evolutionary theory[11]) fall in our view within the domain of the industrial and technological world. After all, they have strong connotations of permanence and materiality. However, as we began to do in Chapter 5, we can consider transposing some of these concepts to more intangible characteristics. This process of transposition can be advanced by hypothesizing, for example, that civic dominant designs might exist or that characteristics falling within the domains of other worlds than the industrial and technological worlds, might contribute to the definition of these concepts. For example, there is not yet a (civic) 'dominant design' defining the notion of 'universal service', and for the moment there are various conflicting concepts (for a discussion of these various concepts, see Gadrey, 1997).

The 'economic' dimension clearly lies at the heart of the notion of techno-economic paradigm. As Freeman (1988, p. 48) notes, 'The expression "techno-economic" rather than "technological paradigm" emphasizes that the changes involved go beyond specific product or process technologies and affect the input cost structure and conditions of production and distribution throughout the system'. This concept clearly has echoes of the market world. Finally, it seems to us that certain aspects of the civic world are present in the notions of social acceptability and of non-market selection environment and in the concept of socio-technical paradigm, which emphasizes the social and institutional dimensions. The reasons for the failure of nuclear technology to fulfil its hopes of constituting a paradigm in its own right are not to be found in the market world (costs) or in the technological world (range of possible applications) but rather in a social disapproval that has its roots in ecological and environmental concerns.

3.1.2 The various models of innovation and the worlds

Our purpose here is to attempt to link our various models of innovation (radical, incremental, ameliorative, ad hoc, recombinative and formalization innovation) with an approach that incorporates the plurality of possible worlds (industrial, market, domestic and civic worlds). If, as we saw earlier (Section 2.1), a product and its product characteristics can be associated with different worlds, the same applies to the 'renewed' version of that product, that is the result or aims of the innovations.

It should be noted that, by excluding the world of inspiration from our analysis, we have already rejected an initial solution, whereby innovation would be associated solely with the world of inspiration. This means that analysis of innovation cannot be reduced to analysis of inspired intuitions and of 'men and women of genius'. According to Callon (1994), there is no such thing as a world inhabited by clearly identifiable geniuses, the creators of innovations whose begetters are always undisputed and which are the product of strokes of genius – contrary to the notion peddled by a certain mythologizing tradition. Innovations are always produced by networks of hybrid actors that are linked in space and time and interfere with the reference *'grandeurs'* of these actors and their objects.

For the same reasons as those given in Section 2.1 (namely the frequently human nature of the medium of service delivery and the importance of public and social services), it is undoubtedly in services that innovation can most readily be associated with the domestic and civic worlds. The introduction of a conventionist perspective (that of Boltanski and Thévenot's worlds) into our models of innovation rooted in evolutionary theory lays bare some interesting phenomena, and it is to these that we now turn.

3.1.2.1 'Pure' models of innovation that can take different forms in different worlds. Our various models of innovation can come into being in each of the worlds under consideration here, and not just in the industrial or technological world. In other words, the civic, domestic and market worlds can accommodate the various modes of innovation in just the same way as the industrial or technological world. Those innovations that we will describe as civic, domestic or market, depending on the objectives they set themselves, their outcomes and their justifications, will be defined in the same terms as innovations of the same type emerging in the industrial or technological world (cf. Chapter 3). For example, a radical innovation (in the strict sense of the term) falling within the domain of the civic world will be defined as a new system of competences, technical characteristics and service characteristics {[C'], [C], [T], [Y]} that has no element in common with any existing system. It would appear, for example, that the French family welfare offices (CAF), the public employment service (ANPE), local social services departments, among other bodies, have put in place a number of schemes with the aim of providing new services to their 'clients'. In the case of the family welfare offices, Adjerad (1997) cites the examples of the 'social funds for water' and the 'social funds for electricity', which are multilateral agreements between the welfare offices (generally the initiators of such schemes), local authorities and water and electricity suppliers, in which the welfare offices undertake to pay part of the water and electricity bills of users (or customers) experiencing difficulties and to guarantee them access to these services during certain time slots. Other examples can be cited, such as the involvement of family welfare offices in the establishment (some time ago now) of 'consumer schools', which teach people in difficulty to manage their spending more effectively. This is a genuine educational service that goes beyond the welfare offices' normal sphere of activities (new [Y]) and requires the training of skilled staff deploying specific knowledge and competences [C] and possibly techniques [T]. There is absolutely no difficulty in accepting that radical (civic) innovations can subsequently be improved in various ways: natural learning processes (ameliorative innovation), addition of new civic service characteristics (incremental innovations), various processes leading to the formatting of characteristics (formalization innovation), etc. The transformation of the traditional French 'holiday vouchers' into 'leisure vouchers' (a scheme that funds access to certain local leisure facilities, such as swimming pools, cinemas, etc.) by the family welfare offices can undoubtedly be described as the improvement and adaptation to social realities of a scheme that was radically innovative in its time[12].

Innovation in police services, for example, can be considered in various ways, but one important model of innovation at work in this area equates to what we have described as the ameliorative model. As we have already noted, it leaves the structure of the characteristics and competences system that defines the service unchanged but changes the 'weight' or value of some of those characteristics and competences. This model falls within the domain of the civic world when the innovation in question reduces the weight of certain service characteristics, such as the degree of brutality, of arbitrariness, etc., or – and this amounts to the same thing – increases the weight of the corresponding positive characteristics (courtesy, fairness, etc.). In other words, improvements in quality can impact on civic and ethical service characteristics (cf. Payson, 1994). The same argument can be applied to the administration of justice. One obvious way of attaining these objectives is to improve the competence of police officers and judges [C] while at the same improving the knowledge and competences of users [C'] in their dealings with this type of service and those who provide it (awareness of their rights, opportunities to appeal, etc.).

3.1.2.2 New sources or mechanisms of innovation: hybridization and institutionalization. Even in non-market services, where increasing attention has been paid to considerations of cost and efficiency that often conflict with concerns of a civic nature, models of innovation seldom manifest themselves in their 'pure' form. In other words, they hardly ever give rise to innovations whose characteristics all fall within the domain of one given world. There are other possible scenarios. One that would seem to be more common, particularly in market services, is that in which modes of innovation manifest themselves not in their 'pure' form in one single world but rather in a hybrid way (hybridization). Another is that in which characteristics falling within the domain of one world migrate to another world; for want of a better term, we will call this migration of characteristics (which usually denotes the transition from the domestic or civic worlds to the industrial or market worlds) a process of institutionalization. These are two new mechanisms that lead to new, 'justifiable' forms of innovation.

1. Hybridization mechanisms in the worlds of production and innovation. Innovation can be produced by adding characteristics or manipulating them in some other way; this might involve, for example, the combining, the splitting up or the objectification (formalization) of service characteristics that fall within the domain of a different world from that which dominates in the product in question. Several examples can be cited to illustrate what might be called the hybridization of worlds. In addition to all the service characteristics of the traditional bank account, the Giro accounts operated by the French Post Office, for example, also have a certain number of characteristics that fall within the domain of the civic world. Such accounts are open to all without discrimination, they allow frequent withdrawals of very small sums of money and the penalties for going overdrawn are not particularly harsh. A post office that makes the services of an interpreter available to its foreign customers is introducing into its 'product' a civic service characteristic that is lacking in other offices (see Table 6.4 for other examples in the case of the Post Office).

In the case of the French national gas and electricity companies (EDF-GDF), civic service characteristics manifest themselves (and constitute innovations) when the procedures for cutting supplies to customers in arrears take account of certain social or civic criteria, in particular the time and place of the disconnection. Civic characteristics can also be introduced into telephone services. This is the case, for example, when subscribers in arrears are blocked from making outgoing calls but can still receive incoming calls and are still able to dial certain emergency numbers. In this example and the previous one, the civic characteristics are based on the adaptation of technical systems.

2. Institutionalization mechanisms. Innovation can manifest itself through what might be called the institutionalization of characteristics. This is a process by means of which a characteristic or set of characteristics, often belonging either to the domestic world or to the civic world, move from being implicit to explicit, gain recognition, become institutionalized and are sometimes sold. As a result of this process, they change reference world and enter the industrial or market worlds. This institutionalization mechanism might be said to fall within the domain of the formalization mode of innovation.

More specifically, the informal civic services (together with the corresponding service characteristics) that are provided in the course of certain service activities can be institutionalized, thereby becoming integral elements of the service (service characteristics) that may be provided free of cost or charged for (the latter case would constitute a migration from the civic to the market world). Sessions for those requiring assistance with filling in their tax returns or the introduction of interpreting services in some post offices are examples of this formalization of the informal and of the encroachment of the industrial and technological world, if not of the market world, into the civic world.

Other examples of this phenomenon of 'institutionalization' can be cited. Some of the services offered free of charge by voluntary organizations working with the elderly or handicapped can be provided by commercial companies. In this case, they would constitute 'product innovations'. The change of service provider also means a change of world. In a study of innovation in the insurance industry (Gadrey and Gallouj, 1994), we highlighted a form of innovation that we dubbed 'informal management or makeshift innovation'. These are innovations produced unofficially (sometimes surreptitiously, particularly when they involve attempts to bypass central computer systems) by employees with a view to performing certain operations within their particular sphere of expertise (in a way the domestic sphere) more efficiently. The institutional recognition of this type of innovation and its migration towards the category of innovation that we describe as 'formal management innovation' is another example of such a process of institutionalization. More generally, the various mechanisms introduced to gather ideas from front-line workers (suggestions boxes and so on) in manufacturing and service companies can be interpreted as strategies for institutionalizing elements from the domestic world and integrating them into the industrial or market world.

3.1.2.3 New arguments in justification of certain 'non-standard' models of innovation. Some of our models of innovation find their justification more in some worlds than in others. The ad hoc model and also, to some extent, the 'made-to-measure' or customized model, find their justification in the domestic and relational world. The innovations they produce come into being at the point of interaction between customer (user) and provider. Their relations to the market world are not the usual ones. In particular, they may not be reproducible as such. This characteristic, which is undoubtedly problematic in a strictly market world, poses no problems in the domestic world. Moreover, these innovations are difficult to appropriate by virtue of the fact that they are co-produced by clients and providers. Once again, the tools of convention theory can help to shed new light on this question of the appropriability regime when the innovation is jointly produced. Thus it would seem possible to extend Gadrey's notion of loyalty conventions (Gadrey, 1994b) by adding what we might call non-imitation and non-diffusion conventions.

Overall, the introduction of the domestic world allows us to loosen some of the constraints that lie heavily on our theoretical concepts of innovation (the need for innovations to be reproducible, for example). In the case of the French family welfare offices, Adjerad (1997) shows that, as far as social welfare is concerned:

> each time a new problem arises, attempts are made to innovate, to devise new solutions. Thus the basic *'grandeur'* structuring this world is creativity. The schemes put in place may concern an individual, the family or a collective entity (a district of a town, for example). (...) The particular difficulty lies in the fact that they are very often unique cases.

3.1.2.4 Arguments for a 'non-standard' justification for certain types of innovation. This is the familiar argument that some innovations that affect human life or survival (in the medical field, for example, or in that of nuclear technology) cannot be defined and evaluated on the basis of service characteristics falling solely within the domain of the industrial or market worlds.

Moreover, as we have already noted, there are innovations, particularly but not solely in the public services, falling within the domain of the social and civic world (for example, products specific to certain physical or social handicaps) that should not be evaluated solely by reference to the market world.

Although these innovations do have a cost, they also generate a form of value added that cannot be quantified or valued but is best described as social value added. In evolutionary terminology, this type of innovation, like the previous one, refers to a non-market selection environment.

Similarly, new services (particularly financial allowances or benefits) should not be considered solely in terms of costs. It is necessary to identify potential beneficiaries and to arouse their interest. In the case of the French family welfare offices, for example, Adjerad (1997) shows that some offices are setting up working groups whose task it is to analyze the characteristics of the populations in their area and to identify individuals who are not claiming benefits to which they are entitled. Payment of these benefits (civic world) is paradoxically perceived by the family welfare offices as an increase in market share (market world).

3.1.2.5 Highlighting some of the 'unspoken aspect' of innovation (in the sense of conflicting justifications)

a) Some technological, organizational or service innovations may be intended to reduce (or even to eliminate) the 'weight' of service characteristics falling within the domain of the civic world. For example, when the Post Office issues a cash or credit card to a disadvantaged Giro account holder, it is contributing to his or her social integration (he/she has a credit card 'like everyone else' and 'he/she gains a certain pride from it'). In reality, however, the objective of the exercise falls not so much within the domain of the civic world as in that of the industrial and market worlds, since the intention is also to remove this 'undesirable' customer from the queue, and even from the office altogether. In other words, the aim is to separate him from 'wealthier' customers by encouraging him to use automatic cash machines. Thus the industrial and technological world (installation of automatic cash dispensers and giving disadvantaged customers access to them) can be said to produce social and civic externalities.

The introduction of interpreters into certain post offices in disadvantaged areas with large immigrant populations can be interpreted in the same way. The rationale behind the provision of this social service is also industrial and technical in nature: because of the difficulties they have in communicating, customers of foreign origin waste counter clerks' time, make the queues longer and distort productivity statistics. Consequently, they have to be removed from the queues and isolated.

The use of private cubicles by financial postal consultants in order to give advice in confidence to 'problem' clients (courtesy register) can be interpreted in the same way by changing register (technical and market registers).

These same arguments associated with the civic world, which ultimately conceal *'grandeurs'* that fall within the domain of the industrial and technical or market and financial worlds, are found in other enterprises as well. When the French National Railway company opens some of its stations to the homeless (Strobel, 1995), they are merely ratifying and rationalizing an un-deniable fact that has negative market consequences, including damage to property and a bad image in the eyes of 'normal' travellers. It is a way of concentrating all the homeless in one station.

b) Some technological innovations have the opposite effect to the previous one. At the same time, paradoxically, technologies (electronic communica-tions, computer systems) lead some service providers to maintain direct ser-vice relationships only with their 'problem' clients. Here too, the industrial and technological world (that of machines in this case) can be said to 'give rise to' the social and civic world. This time, we are dealing with a perverse effect. These 'problem' clients have little aptitude for using these technolo-gies, or rather they use them but continue to feel a need to communicate with human operators. Thus they will use automated telephone systems to find out their account balance but will also telephone the service provider for confirma-tion. In the case of these customers, these technologies tend to increase the workload rather than substituting capital for labor.

3.2 Innovation and Salais and Storper's Worlds of Production

Here too, it seems to us erroneous to seek to associate innovation with a single world (the intangible world) which we have renamed, following Gadrey, the world of creation. The question of innovation and its relationship with Salais and Storper's worlds of production can be considered from two different perspectives:

1. as a productive activity in its own right (involving the creation of varying degrees of novelty or originality), innovation can itself be examined in terms of the worlds of production framework;
2. innovation can also be examined as the force driving the shift from one world of production to another.

Before investigating these two points, we will try to identify possible links between the evolutionary theory of innovation and Salais and Storper's cons-truct.

3.2.1 Sectoral taxonomies of technical change and worlds of production

Analogies between the evolutionary theory of technological change and Salais and Storper's construct can be made. It would seem, for example, that links can be established between certain types in the sectoral taxonomy of technolo-gical trajectories developed by Pavitt (1984) and Salais and Storper's worlds (cf. Table 6.8).

Thus the 'production-intensive' category, which comprises in particular continuous process activities such as steel and glass-making and mass production activities, equates to the Fordist world, while the 'science-based' category, which includes firms in the electronics, electrical and chemical industries, equates to the intangible world or the world of creation. The 'specialized suppliers' category, which includes firms specializing in precision instruments and mechanical engineering, falls within the domain of the interpersonal world, since these firms supply products that are the fruit of specialist work processes and are dedicated to clearly identified customers.

The 'supplier-dominated' category, on the other hand, is more hybrid. According to Pavitt, it includes all service firms which, as we have seen, can in reality be associated with the four worlds of production (depending on their type), as well as manufacturing activities, such as textiles, clothing, leather goods, printing and publishing, which are more difficult to associate with any one world. Similarly, it is more difficult to establish links between the market world as defined by Salais and Storper and any particular type in Pavitt's taxonomy.

Table 6.8 Salais and Storper's worlds of production and Pavitt's sectoral taxonomy of technical change

Evolutionary theory Pavitt's taxonomy	Convention theory Salais and Storper's worlds
Production-intensive firms	Fordist world
Specialized suppliers	Interpersonal world
Science-based firms	Intangible world
Supplier-dominated firms	
	Market world

3.2.2 The worlds of innovation production

Our various models of innovation (that is radical, incremental, ameliorative, etc.) can be associated with various worlds of innovation production (or innovation worlds) (cf. Table 6.9). These associations denote particular tropisms rather than rigid and deterministic relationships. They enable us to identify the dominant models of innovation in any given world.

However, if these associations are to be successfully established, it will be necessary, largely because of the specificity of some of the models of innovation already put forward, to accept a more flexible interpretation of the service relation criterion [C'][C]. Depending on the case in question, we will take it to represent the client's involvement in the production of innovation, that is to say the extent to which the innovation is co-produced by the client (*dimension 1*), the place allocated to the client, and therefore to the service relationship, in the new service (*dimension 2*) and, finally, in Salais and Storper's terms, that is as the dedicated product/generic product dichotomy, which can be translated into the terminology of evolutionary theory as the degree of 'fitness' (vis-à-vis the client) displayed by the 'product' that emerges from the innovation process (*dimension 3*). It will be noted that dimension 2 is a particular case of dimension 3, since in services any weakening or strengthening of the service relationship helps to increase or, conversely, to reduce the 'generic' nature of the 'product'.

Table 6.9 The models of innovation integrated into the worlds of production framework

Formatting (or standardizaton) of Y	Service characteristics [Y] weakly formatted		[Y] formatted
Technological intensity (TI) Service relationship or equivalent	Low TI	High TI	Technological (or capital) intensity still high
	Professional and relational world of production		*World of flexible or modular production*
	Low TI	*High TI*	Recombinative innovation
[C'][C] (dimension 1,2,3)* strong	Ad hoc innovation Fully customized innovation	Formalization innovation	Adaptive customized innovation Incremental innovation
	World of creation		*Fordist world of production*
	Low TI	*High TI*	(Extreme) formalization innovation
[C'][C] (dimension 1,2,3)* weak	Radical innovation	Radical innovation	Ameliorative innovation (learning processes)

Notes:
* Dimension 1: extent to which the *innovation* is co-produced by the client
Dimension 2: place allocated to the client (and hence to the service relationship) in the new service
Dimension 3: degree of 'fitness' of the 'product' that emerges from the innovation process.

Thus if we examine the service relationship criterion as it manifests itself in dimensions 1 and 3, it becomes clear that the ad hoc and fully customized innovation models[13] can be associated (in the sense of the word outlined at the beginning of this section) with the professional and relational world. As we showed in Chapter 3, these models are at work particularly in highly intangible services (weakly formatted characteristics) and highly relational services (in which the service relationship, that is the combination [C'][C], is strong). They are the source of co-produced forms of innovation (strong [C'][C]) which, like the products of this world, are difficult to standardize, even though efforts to record and codify expertise and experience (which is essential if the result of this innovation is to be reproducible to some extent) tend to push them towards another dimension of this world (the one in which technological intensity in the broad sense of the term, that is the use of technologies [T], is high).

The adaptive customized (cf. note 13), recombinative and additive (incremental) models are clearly flexible or modular modes of innovation production. They belong to the flexible world of production. Their objective is to adapt products to a specific clientele (dedication, search for 'fitness', cf. Chapter 5). The service relationship is considered here as it manifests itself in dimension 3. Thus the fast food industry, which arose out of the unbundling of the characteristics of the traditional restaurant trade, seeks to provide a response adapted to the needs of customers in a hurry, while charter flights, which arose out of the unbundling of the service characteristics of the traditional airline industry, seeks to meet the expectations of passengers who are less time-constrained and less demanding as regards service characteristics but more sensitive to price. On the other hand, the innovation corresponding to these models does not need to be co-produced (at least not in the sense of the term as it applies to ad hoc innovations and dimension 1 of the service relationship).

The radical innovation model can be associated with the world of creation. It is the source of innovations whose characteristics are new and weakly (or not yet) formatted, such that there is a certain degree of flexibility in the pre-paradigmatic phase, that is before the emergence of the dominant design. If this time we adopt dimension 3 of the definition of the service relationship, innovations of this type can be said to be generic (the degree of 'fitness' tends to be low), in the sense that they are seeking to create their own market (and not always succeeding).

The ameliorative model (based on learning effects) and the formalization model (often in its most tangible manifestations) equate to the Fordist world. The place allocated to the client in the new service arising out of the innovation process is reduced or strictly defined (dimension 2). The product that emerges from the innovation process is generic and its degree of 'fitness' is low (dimension 3).

The formalization model is compatible to some extent with the professional and relational world of production (when the latter is characterized by high technological intensity). In some cases or with certain types of service, it may fall within the domain of the Fordist world. In the professional and relational world of production, the formalization model affects the formatting of the intangible technical characteristics [T] (methods, etc.). This formatting has little effect on the service characteristics [Y] but does impact more, and in various ways, on the service relationship ([C'][C]). It can strengthen it (interface methods) or weaken it (in which case the focus is on the back-office technical characteristics). In both cases, but particularly in the second one, the aim is to strengthen the product's 'generic' dimension (dimensions 2 and 3 of the service relationship). For its part, the formalization mode of innovation associated with the Fordist world of production relies on technical systems and contributes to the formatting of 'products' and of the corresponding service characteristics.

The various worlds of innovation production can also, in our view, be associated with the various models of the organization of innovation outlined in Chapter 4 (cf. Table 6.10). Thus the professional and relational world of production (I) can be associated with the professionals in partnership model and the craft model (in its professional variant) in which, it will be remembered, expertise, that is the set of individual competences [C], and the interface [C'] [C], the combination of service providers' and clients' competences, play a fundamental role in producing innovation. The ad hoc model of innovation occupies an important place here.

The managerial model seems to be compatible with the professional and relational world of production (II). It will be recalled that, in this model of innovation organization, the set of technical characteristics [T], and particularly its intangible elements (methods, etc.), and the set of competences [C] energized by various strategies (organized training, recruitment, 'up or out' strategies) are important levers of innovation. It will also be recalled that, while all the models of innovation can be mobilized within the framework of the managerial model, the formalization model plays a central role.

The traditional industrial model can be associated with the Fordist model. It is the vector of technical and process characteristics [T] that is the main lever of innovation here, deployed in departments specializing in the design, maintenance, improvement or introduction of technical systems (departments of production techniques, IT departments).

This traditional industrial model has a tendency to develop into a more flexible model (as in some banks and insurance companies) that we have labelled the neo-industrial model; this more flexible model can be associated with the flexible world of production. Responsibility for innovation no longer lies with a single specialist entity but is distributed among various actors interacting with each other (interactive model of innovation versus the linear model).

The entrepreneurial model, finally, which characterizes firms set up to exploit the radical innovation, falls within the domain of the world of creation.

Table 6.10 Models of innovation organization and worlds of production

Professional and relational world of production		Flexible or modular world of production
(I)	*(II)*	
Professionals in partnership model Craft model (experts)	Managerial model	Neo-industrial model

World of Creation		Fordist world of production
(I)	*(II)*	
Entrepreneurial model	Entrepreneurial model	Traditional industrial model

3.2.3 Models of innovation and the dynamic of the worlds of production

The various models of innovation can also be regarded as instruments that effect the transition from one world of production to another. This dynamic can take a variety of forms, which we propose dividing into two categories: formalization-industrialization trajectories and 'service intensification' trajectories.

3.2.3.1 The formalization-industrialization trajectories. The trajectories running from left to right in Figure 6.3, that is those converging towards the flexible and Fordist worlds of production, are formalization-industrialization trajectories. They represent the gradual rise to prominence of the formatting or standardization of characteristics. They are the result of the separate, successive or simultaneous implementation of the formalization, recombinative, incremental and radical models.

Trajectory n° 2 (which, to stretch the terminology somewhat, we will call the 'industrialization diagonal'), which links the professional and relational world (I) with the Fordist world by way of the professional and relational world (II), corresponds precisely to the process of 'industrialization' in services as defined in Chapter 3:

- the professional and relational world (I) can be associated with the 'pure service' configuration, in which co-production plays a very important role and the technical characteristics are absent;
- the professional and relational world (II) equates to the 'intermediate service' situation, in which the customer's role in the service relationship tends to be more 'controlled' (development of scripts defining each actor's

role in the process of service delivery) and technologies play an increasingly important role. The technologies in question here are essentially intellectual ones, involving the processing of knowledge;

- the Fordist world is associated with the rise to prominence of tangible technologies, the disappearance of the competences deployed in direct customer contact and the growing importance of self-service.

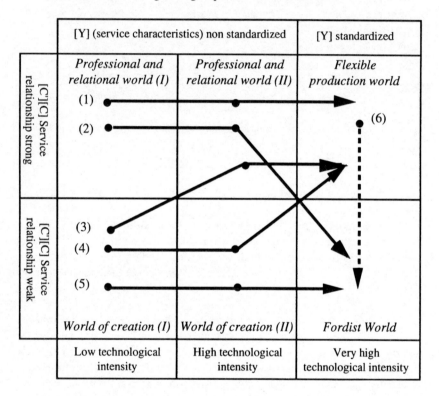

Figure 6.3 The formalization-industrialization trajectories

This formalization-industrialization trajectory could be extended by making a detour via the flexible world of production before reaching the Fordist world (dotted line, trajectory n° 6). This would link the professional world (I), the professional world (II), the flexible world of production and the Fordist world.

The formalization-industrialization trajectory can unfold while the service relationship remains constant. This is the interpretation to be given to the horizontal lines originating in the professional world (I) and the world of creation (I) and ending up in the flexible world of production and the Fordist world respectively, possibly by way of the professional world (II) and the world of creation (II) respectively (trajectories 1 and 5). It is also compatible with a certain increase in the level of the service relationship, provided that this increase goes hand in hand with the formatting or standardization of the service characteristics. This is the case with trajectory 3, which links the world of creation (I), the professional world (II) and the flexible world of production, and with trajectory 4, which links the worlds of creation (I) and (II) with the flexible world of production.

3.2.3.2 The service intensification trajectories. All the trajectories that converge towards the professional and relational world (north-west quadrant of Figure 6.4) are 'service intensification' trajectories; they are characterized by the rise to prominence of the service relationship and/or a decline in the level of the standardization or formatting of characteristics, together with a decrease in technological intensity. They can be based on the following innovation models: ad hoc, customized, incremental and radical.

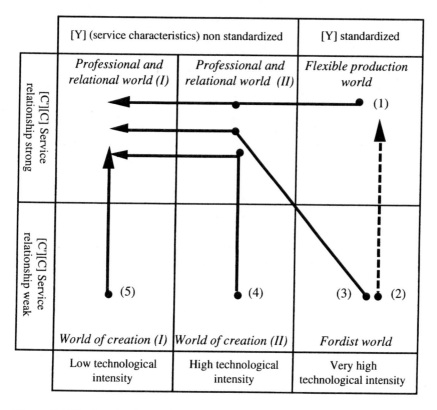

Figure 6.4 The 'service intensification' trajectories

To misuse the terminology once again, Figure 6.4 shows the converse of the industrialization 'diagonal', namely a service intensification 'diagonal' (trajectory 3), which does not exclude the previous trajectory (as already noted in Chapter 3) and is based on the radical, ad hoc and incremental models of innovation...

In discussing Figure 6.3, it was noted that the industrialization trajectory could be extended by making a detour via the flexible or modular world of production. In reality, the opposite phenomenon is more commonly observed, namely the transition from the Fordist world to the flexible world of production, that is a shift in the service intensification 'diagonal' (cf. dotted line, trajectory 2, Figure 6.4).

Other 'service intensification' trajectories can be envisaged, such as trajectories 4 and 5, which the link the world of creation (I and II) with the professional and relational world (I), by way of (in case of trajectory 4) the professional and relational world (II). This would describe, for example, the case of an IT researcher who leaves his laboratory to become an IT consultant in a large consultancy firm, where methodologies are used to ensure overall consistency, before joining an organization and strategy consultancy where methods are not so all-pervasive.

By way of conclusion to this section, let us point out once again that these two dynamics or trajectories are not mutually contradictory. They have already been examined in the context of the retail trade, banking, consultancy (cf. Chapter 3, Section 2.3) and software development (Horn, 1997).

CONCLUSION

The purpose of Saviotti and Metcalfe's analysis is to introduce quality and variety into the concept of technical change which, in standard neo-classical theory, is confined to the analysis of quantities. Our aim in this chapter has been to extend these notions of quality and variety by taking into account aspects brought into play by introducing a plurality of worlds into the concept of the product.

Thus the introduction of convention theory into evolutionary models of innovation based on the dynamic of characteristics has several consequences. It extends the variety or scope of the system and reveals other justifiable forms of innovation: innovations that find expression in worlds that elude traditional economic theory and innovations produced through the hybridization and institutionalization of worlds...

NOTES

1. The reference here is to a special issue of the journal *Economies et Sociétés* entitled 'Régulation et conventions' (n° 10, December 1997).
2. To use the expression adopted by Girin (1994).

3.   For simplicity's sake, we have ignored here the important distinction that Gadrey makes between direct products (the act of service delivery) and indirect products (long-term results).

4.   It should not be forgotten that the French public employment service provides services for two types of users: job-seekers and firms.

5.   Unpublished manuscript on monetary theory, Chapter 2, 'Properties of Assets', cited in Greenbaum and Haywood (1971).

6.   Even though, in this case, the price itself is not a characteristic of the product. This characteristic is the generalized access.

7.   Although in this case, detailed analysis of the functional and institutional diversity of this type of service allows us to divide the various forms of service between several worlds.

8.   i.e. not confined to interpersonal relations.

9.   Some commentators take the view that the economics of conventions emphasizes the moment of agreement rather than conflicts or disagreements.

10. 1In reality, the notion of the techno-economic network, in Callon's sense of the term (Callon, 1991), which encompasses the relations between scientific, technological and market poles, covers all the other types of relations.

11. The definitions of these concepts are given in Chapter 5.

12. These examples were suggested by S. Adjerad, the author of a thesis that analyzes the output of the family welfare offices in particular in terms of 'worlds'.

13. It will be remembered that, in the insurance industry for example, the fully customized model equates to the design of a genuinely new policy that is specific to a given client (often a large company). There is a strong ad hoc element. The fully customized model contrasts with the adaptive customized model, which involves adapting the standard policy to a particular client by changing the premiums and introducing additional clauses. This model is very similar to incremental model.

Conclusion

If the approach to innovation developed in the course of this book were to be summed up in a single phrase, then it could be described as being (or seeking to be) *integrative*, *evolutionary* and *conventionist*, in that its constant points of reference have been the characteristics of products and of productive systems.

AN INTEGRATIVE ANALYSIS

This first term is, in our view, of the utmost importance. There is increasingly less reason to retain the goods/services dichotomy, since it can be reconciled by defining the service relationship as a mode of coordination among economic agents.

However, the integrative nature of our analyses of the product and of innovation can be considered at several different levels.

Our analyses of the product in terms of characteristics also encompasses the process dimensions (including competences). Thus our apparent reversal of the standard neo-classical approach, with products rather than processes being the starting point, is not what it appears to be, since in our approach processes in fact lie at the heart of the analysis of products.

One of the consequences of our concept of the product is that our analyses of innovation encompass the various forms and kinds of innovations. They account for process, organizational and product innovations, for technological and more intangible innovations.

Above all, however, our analyses can be applied to both goods and services. The first reason for this is that they have their roots in an adaptation of a formalization, that of Saviotti and Metcalfe, originally developed for the analysis of goods. The second is that goods themselves produce lasting effects, which are in effect services. The third and final reason is that the 'service model' has long been at work in the production of many goods and that a large number of goods can now be defined as good-service hybrids made up of various combinations of service characteristics relating to the artefact itself (that is the good) and of service characteristics that exist independently of the good's internal technical specifications (the service characteristics of a service).

Finally, our analyses attempt to link evolutionary theory and convention theory and thereby to enrich the socio-economic analysis of innovation.

AN EVOLUTIONARY ANALYSIS

Like the neo-classical theory, the evolutionary theory of innovation has developed by emphasizing technological and process innovation within the framework of industrial economics.

In both cases, the treatment of services has suffered from a technologist bias that can be attributed largely to the inertia of our conceptual apparatuses and analytical priorities (on this point cf. Gallouj, 1997).

As we have tried to show in this book, evolutionary theory can extricate itself from this inertia and provide a satisfactory account of innovation in services (without setting it against innovation in goods but rather enhancing our understanding of it). Thus if it is accepted that innovation can be defined as a problem-solving activity, as it is in evolutionary theory, and particularly if it is agreed that this definition can be applied to services, then it becomes possible to uncover a multiplicity of forms of innovation, intangible as well as tangible, ad hoc as well as institutionalized. At the same time, the central concepts of evolutionary theory (trajectories, paradigms, regimes, dominant designs, guide posts...) are themselves enriched, since they can also explain innovation in services by taking where necessary more intangible or cognitive aspects.

It is not surprising that evolutionary theory should be able to account for innovation in services. After all, some of its basic concepts and hypotheses could be said to be 'in phase' with the analytical categories that usually define services and, more generally, the service relationship, whether it manifests itself in goods or services. For example, just like the evolutionary definition of innovation, which emphasizes movement (process) and interaction at the expense of maximization, a service is itself an act, a relationship to which it is often difficult to apply the principles of optimization. Our attempt to apply evolutionary theory to innovation in services is merely the realization of this potential.

A CONVENTIONIST ANALYSIS

The conventionist perspective adopted in this book is structuralist in nature (it uses fixed reference frameworks that explain different facets of the real world). The arguments developed here could profitably be rounded out with a more functionalist (micro-socio-economic) approach, with actions and interactions being examined in a more concrete way with a view to explaining how the social framework is constructed and functions.

However that may be, the adoption of a conventionist approach facilitates the transition from an economic analysis to a socio-economic analysis of innovation. It enables us to identify new, justifiable forms of innovation and new mechanisms of innovation: 'pure' innovations manifesting themselves in new worlds (radical civic innovations, for example), innovations produced by the hybridization of characteristics originating in different worlds, innovations produced by shifts from one world to another (for example, ad hoc makeshift innovations that become institutionalized). This approach also sheds light on the role of the various models of innovation in the dynamic of worlds (that is the transition from one world to another).

Bibliography

Abernathy, W. and J. Utterback (1978), 'Patterns of Industrial Innovation', *Technology Review*, **80**, June-July, 41–7.

Adjerad, S. (1997), *Une analyse conventionnaliste du système de protection sociale et de l'évaluation de ses performances : le cas des CAF*, 5th IFRESI Conference, Lille, 20–21 March.

Aglietta M. and A. Brender (1984), *Les métamorphoses de la société salariale*, Paris : Calman-Lévy.

Amable, B. and S. Palombarini (1998), 'Technical change and incorporated R-D in the service sector', *Research Policy*, **26**, 655–75.

Andersen, B., J. Howells, R. Hull, I. Miles and J. Roberts (eds) (2000), *Knowledge and innovation in the new service economy*, Cheltenham, UK, Brookfield, US: Edward Elgar.

Antonelli, C. (1995), *The economics of localized technological change and industrial dynamics*, Boston: Kluwer Academic Press.

Antonelli, C. (1997), *The dynamics of localized technological changes path-dependence and percolation processes in the knowledge-based economy*, SI4S project, European Commission, TSER program.

Argyris, C. and D. Schön (1978), *Organizational learning: a theory of action perspective*, Reading, MA: Addison-Wesley.

Attali, J. (1981), *Les Trois Mondes*, Paris : Fayard.

Auer-Bernet, H. (1986), 'Représentation des connaissances et systèmes experts en droit', *Science, Technique, Société*, **12**.

Bacon, R. and W. Eltis (1978), *Britain's Economic Problem: Too Few Producers*, London: Macmillan.

Baily, M.N. and R.J. Gordon (1988), 'The Productivity Slowdown, Measurement Issues and the Explosion of Computer Power', *Brookings Papers on Economic Activity*, **2**, 347–431.

Bancel-Charensol, L. and M. Jougleux M. (1997), 'Un modèle d'analyse des systèmes de production dans les services', *Revue française de gestion*, **113**, March–April–May, 71–81.

Barcet, A., Bonamy, J. and A. Mayère (1987), *Modernisation et innovation dans les services aux entreprises*, Report for Commissariat Général du Plan, Paris, October.

Barras, R. (1986), 'Towards a Theory of Innovation in Services', *Research Policy*, **15**, 161–73.

Barras, R. (1990), 'Interactive Innovation in Financial and Business Services: The Vanguard of the Service Revolution', *Research Policy*, **19**, 215–37.

Baumol, W. (1967), 'Macroeconomics of unbalanced growth', *American Economic Review*, **57** (2), 415–26.

Baumol, W. (2002), 'Services as leaders and the leader of services', in Gadrey, J. and F. Gallouj (eds), *Productivity, innovation and knowledge in services: new economic and socio-economic approaches*, Cheltenham, UK, Brookfield, US: Edward Elgar (forthcoming).

Bell, D. (1973), *The Coming of Post-Industrial Society*, New York: Basic Books.

Belleflamme, C., J. Houard and B. Michaux, (1986), *Innovation and Research and Development Process Analysis in Service Activities*, IRES, EEC-FAST report, August.

Bessant, J. and H. Rush (1995), 'Building bridges for innovation: the role of consultants in technology transfer', *Research Policy*, **24** (1), 97–114.

Bluestone, B. and B. Harrison (1986), *The Great American Job Machine*, Report for the Joint Economic Committee, December.

Boden, M. and I. Miles (eds) (2000), *Services and the knowledge-based Economy*, London and New York: Continuum.

Boltanski, L. and L. Thévenot (1991), *De la justification. Les économies de la grandeur*, Paris : Gallimard.

Bounfour, A. (1989), 'Vers l'industrialisation du conseil', *Revue française de gestion*, November–December.

Bressand, A. and K. Nicolaïdis (1988), 'Les services au cœur de l'économie relationnelle', *Revue d'Economie Industrielle*, **43**, 141–63.

Callon, M. (1991), 'Réseaux technico-économiques et irréversibilité', in Boyer, R., B. Chavance and O. Godard (eds), *Les figures de l'irréversibilité en économie*, Paris : Edition de l'école des hautes études en sciences sociales, pp. 194–230.

Callon, M. (1994), 'L'innovation technologique et ses mythes', *Gérer et Comprendre*, March, 5–17.

Callon, M. (1995), *Pratiques et enjeux de la démarche qualité dans deux filiales de la Sodexho (Bateaux parisiens, Chèques restaurants)*, CSI, Ecole des mines de Paris, December.

Callon, M. (ed.) (1989), *La science et ses réseaux : genèse et circulation des faits scientifiques*, Paris: La découverte.

Chamberlin, Edward H. (1953), 'The product as an economic variable', *Quarterly Journal of Economics*, February, reprinted in Chamberlin, Edward H. (1957), *Towards a more general theory of value*, New York: Oxford University Press.

Charlon, E. and N. Gadrey (1998), *Professionnalisation et formation : une démarche d'ingénierie dans les secteurs des services de proximité*, CUEEP, University of Lille I.

Clark, C. (1940), *The Conditions of Economic Progress*, London: Macmillan.

Claveau, N., C. Everaere, A.-C. Martinet and F. Tannery (1995), *La dynamique des services à EDF GDF services*, IAE, University of Lyon, July.

Cohen, M. and D. Levinthal (1989), 'Innovation and learning : the two faces of R-D', *The Economic Journal*, September, **99** (397), 569–96.

Cohen, S. and J. Zysman (1987), *Manufacturing Matters*, New-York: Basic Books.

Cohendet, P. (1994), *Relations de service et transfert de technologie*, in J. De Bandt and J. Gadrey (eds), pp. 201–13.

Daft, R.L. and N.B. MacIntosh (1978), 'A New Approach to Design and Use of Management Information', *California Management Review*, **21** (1), 82–92.

De Bandt, J. (1995), *Services aux entreprises : Informations, Produits, Richesses*, Paris : Economica.

De Bandt, J. (1996), 'Coopération, accords interentreprises, concurrence', in J.-L. Ravix (ed.).

De Bandt, J. and J. Gadrey (eds) (1994), *Relations de service, marchés des services*, Paris : CNRS Editions.

Delaunay, J.-C. and J. Gadrey (1992), *Services in economic thought: three centuries of debate,* Dortrecht: Kluwer.

Delfini, C. (1997), *Les services et l'évaluation de la performance à l'ANPE*, mimeo, University of Lille I, May.

Den Hertog, P. (2000), 'Knowledge Intensive Business Services as Co-producers of Innovation', *International Journal of Innovation Management*, **4** (4), 491-528.

Desai, M. and W. Low (1987), 'Measuring the Opportunity for Product Innovation', in De Cecco, M. (ed.), *Changing Money: Financial Innovation in Developed Countries*, Oxford: Basil Blackwell, pp. 112–140.

Desmoutier, H. (1992), 'Un programme pour prendre en compte les techniques dans l'analyse stratégique des entreprises', *Economies et Sociétés*, **18**, July, 7–41.

Djellal, F. (1995), *Changement technique et conseil en technologie de l'information,* Paris : Editions L'Harmattan, Logique économique.

Djellal, F. (2000), 'The rise of information technologies in non-informational services', *Vierteljahrshefte zur Wirtschaftsforschung*, **69**, 646-56.

Djellal, F. (2001a), 'Les trajectoires d'innovation dans les entreprises de transport routier de marchandise', *Revue française de gestion*, **133**, March-April.

Djellal, F. (2001b), 'Innovation trajectories and employment in the cleaning industry', *New Technology Work and Employment*, (forthcoming).

Djellal, F. and F. Gallouj (1998), *Innovation in service industries in France : results of a postal survey,* SI4S project, European Commission, DG XII, TSER program, July.

Djellal, F. and F. Gallouj (1999), 'Services and the search for relevant innovation indicators: a review of national and international surveys', *Science and Public Policy,* **26** (4), 218–32.

Djellal, F. and F. Gallouj (2001), 'Patterns of innovation organisation in service firms: postal survey results and theoretical models', *Science and Public Policy,* **28** (4), 57–67.

Djellal, F. and F. Gallouj (2002), 'What is innovation in services? the results of a postal survey', *European Journal of Innovation Management* (forthcoming).

Djellal, F., Gallouj, F. and C. Gallouj (1998), *Innovation trajectories in French service industries,* SI4S project, European Commission, DG XII, TSER program, July.

Dosi, G. (1982), 'Technological Paradigms and Technological Trajectories', *Research Policy,* **11**, 147–62.

Dosi, G. (1988), 'Sources, procedures and microeconomic effects of innovation', *Journal of Economic Literature,* **XXVI** (3), September, 1120–71.

Dosi, G. (1991), 'Perspectives on Evolutionary Theory', *Science and Public Policy,* December, **18**, 353–61.

Dosi, G. et al. (1988), *Technical Change and Economic Theory,* London and New York: Pinter Publishers.

Dubuisson, S. (1995), *Réorganisation d'une offre de services: codification et ajustement dans la prestation,* CSI, Ecole des Mines de Paris, October.

Dumont, A. (2001), *Innover dans les services,* Paris : Editions Village Mondial.

Easingwood, C. J. (1986), 'New Product Development for Services Companies', *Journal of Product Innnovation Management,* **4**, 264–75.

Eiglier, P. and E. Langeard (1987), *Servuction : le marketing des services,* Paris : Mc Graw-Hill.

Ernst, M.C. (1985), 'Electronics in Commerce', in T. Forester (ed.), *The information technology revolution,* Cambridge, Ma.: MIT Press.

Evangelista, R. and Sirilli, G. (1995), 'Measuring innovation in services', *Research Evaluation,* **5** (3), 207-15.

Eymard-Duvernay, F. (1986), 'La qualification des produits', in Salais, R. and L. Thévenot (eds), *Le travail, marché, règles et conventions,* Paris : INSEE-Economica, pp. 239–47.

Eymard-Duvernay, F. (1989), 'Conventions de qualité et formes de coordination', *Revue Economique,* **40** (2), 329–59.

Fisher, A.G.B. (1935), *The Clash of Progress and Security,* London: Macmillan.

Flipo, J.P. (2000), *L'innovation dans les services*, Paris : Editions d'Organisation.

Foray, D. (1993), *Modernisation des entreprises, coopération industrielle inter et intra-firmes et ressources humaines*, report for Ministry of Research and Technology, June.

Foray, D. (1994), 'Les nouveaux paradigmes de l'apprentissage technologique', *Revue d'économie industrielle*, **69**, 93–104.

Forester, T. (ed.), (1985), *The information technology revolution*, Cambridge, Ma.: MIT Press.

Freeman, C. (1988), 'Diffusion: the spread of new technology to firms, sectors and nations', in Heertje A. (ed.), *Innovation, technology and finance*, Oxford: Basil Blackwell, pp. 3–70.

Freeman, C. (1991), 'Innovation, change of technoeconomic paradigm and biological analogies in economics', *Revue économique*, **2**, March, 211–32.

Freidson, E. (1970), *Profession of Medicine*, New York: Harper & Row.

Furrer, O. (1997), 'Le rôle stratégique des "services autour des produits"', *Revue française de gestion*, March–April–May, 98–107.

Gadrey, J. (1990), 'Rapports sociaux de services : une autre régulation', *Revue Economique*, **1**, 49–70 .

Gadrey, J. (1991), 'Le service n'est pas un produit : quelques implications pour l'analyse économique et pour la gestion', *Politiques et Management Public*, **9** (1), 1–24.

Gadrey, J. (1994a), 'Les relations de services dans le secteur marchand', in De Bandt, J. and J. Gadrey (eds), pp. 23–42.

Gadrey, J. (1994b), 'Relations, contrats et conventions de service', in De Bandt, J. and J. Gadrey (eds), pp. 123–51 .

Gadrey, J. (1994c), 'La modernisation des services professionnels : rationalisation industrielle ou rationalisation professionnelle', *Revue française de sociologie*, **XXXV**, 163–95.

Gadrey, J. (1996a), *L'économie des services*, Paris : La Découverte (2nd edition).

Gadrey, J. (1996b), 'Note sur les "mondes de production"', mimeo, Universiy of Lille I, February.

Gadrey, J. (1996c), *Services : la productivité en question*, Paris : Desclée de Brouwer.

Gadrey, J. (1997), 'Service universel, service d'intérêt général, service public : un éclairage à partir du cas des télécommunications et du secteur postal', *Politiques et management public*, **15** (2), 43–72.

Gadrey, J. and F. Gallouj (1994), *L'innovation dans l'assurance : le cas de l'UAP*, Report for UAP and Ministry of Research, Paris.

Gadrey, J. and F. Gallouj (1998), 'The provider-customer interface in business and professional services', *The Service Industries Journal*, **18** (2), 1–15.

Gadrey, J. and F. Gallouj (eds) (2002), *Productivity, innovation and knowledge in services: new economic and socio-economic approaches*, Cheltenham,

UK, Brookfield, US: Edward Elgar (forthcoming).

Gadrey, J, F. Gallouj and O.Weinstein (1995), 'New modes of innovation: how services benefit industry', *International Journal of Service Industry Management,* **6** (3), 4–16.

Gadrey, J., C. Gallouj, F. Gallouj, F. Martinelli, F. Moulaert and P. Tordoir (1992), *Manager le Conseil,* Paris : Ediscience.

Gadrey, J., F. Gallouj, S. Lhuillery, T. Ribault and O. Weinstein (1993), *La recherche-développement et l'innovation dans les activités de service: le cas du conseil, de l'assurance et des services d'information électronique,* Report for Ministry of Research and Technology, Paris, December.

Gallouj, C. (1997a) *L'innovation dans le commerce et la grande distribution,* SI4S project, European Commission, TSER program.

Gallouj, C. (1997b), 'Asymmetry of information and the service relationship : selection and evaluation of the service provider', *International Journal of Service Industry Management,* **8** (1), 42–64.

Gallouj, C. and F. Gallouj, (1996), *L'innovation dans les services,* Paris : Economica Poche.

Gallouj, F. (1990), *Formation du capital d'expertise et processus d'innovation dans les activités de conseil aux entreprises,* Report for Ministry of Research and Technology, Paris, December.

Gallouj, F. (1991), 'Les formes de l'innovation dans les services de conseil', *Revue d'économie industrielle,* **57**, 25–45.

Gallouj, F. (1994a), *Economie de l'innovation dans les services,* Paris : Editions L'Harmattan, logique économique.

Gallouj, F. (1994b), 'Cycles économiques et innovations de service : quelques interrogations à la lumière de la pensée schumpeterienne', *Revue française d'économie,* **IX** (4), 169–213.

Gallouj, F. (1994c), 'Les déterminants de l'innovation dans les activités de conseil', *Revue française du Marketing,* **149**, 33–51.

Gallouj, F. (1995), 'Le processus de production de l'innovation dans les services de conseil', *Revue Française de Gestion,* March–April–May, 109–19.

Gallouj, F. (1997), 'Towards a neo-Schumpeterian theory of innovation in services?', *Science and Public Policy,* **24** (6), 405–20.

Gallouj, F. (1998), 'Innovating in reverse : services and the reverse product cycle', *European Journal of Innovation Management,* **1** (3), 123–38.

Gallouj, F. (2001), 'Innovation in services and the attendant myths', *Journal of socio-economics,* **30** (5) (forthcoming).

Gallouj, F. (2002a), 'Interactional innovation: a neoschumpeterian model', in Sundbo, J. and L. Fuglsang (eds), *Innovation as strategic reflexivity,* London and New York: Routlege, (forthcoming).

Gallouj, F. (2002b), 'Knowledge intensive business services: processing knowledge and producing innovation', in Gadrey, J. and F. Gallouj (eds) (forthcoming).

Gallouj, F. and O. Weinstein (1997), 'Innovation in services', *Research Policy*, **26** (4–5), 537–56.

Gallouj, F., Gadrey, J. and E. Ghillebaert (1996), *La Poste : Mondes de production, types de produits, contribution à la cohésion sociale*, Report for French Post Office.

Gallouj, F., J. Gadrey and E. Ghillebaert (1999), 'La construction sociale du produit financier postal', *Annals of Public and Cooperative Economics*, **70** (3), 417–45.

Gault F.D. (1998), Research and Development in a service economy, *Research Evaluation*, **7** (2), 79–91.

George, W.R. and C.E. Marshall (eds) (1984), *Developing New Services*, American Marketing Association, Proceedings Series.

Girin, J. (1994), *Les agencements organisationnels*, Condor, Conference 'Contradictions and dynamics of organizations'.

Goffman, I. (1968), *Asiles*, Paris : édition de Minuit.

Goldman, A. (1975), 'The role of trading up in the development of retail system', *Journal of Marketing* **39** (1), 54–62.

Gomez, P.-Y. (1994), *Qualité et théorie des conventions*, Paris : Economica.

Gorz, A. (1988), *Métamorphoses du travail et quête de sens*, Paris: Galilée.

Greenbaum, S.I. and C.F. Haywood (1971), 'Secular Change in the Financial Services Industry', *Journal of Money, Credit, and Banking*, May, 571–89

Greiner, L. and R. Metzger (1983), *Consulting to management*, New York: Heinemann.

Griliches, Z. (1961), *Hedonic Price Indexes for Automobiles : An Econometric Analysis of Quality Change*, Staff Paper 3 in *The price Statistics of the Federal Government*, National Bureau of Economic Research, General Series, n°73.

Guile, B. and J.-B. Quinn (eds) (1988), *Technology in Services : Policies for Growth, Trade and Employment*, Washington: National Academy Press.

Guilhon, B. (1992), 'Technologie, organisation et performance : le cas de la firme réseau', *Revue d'économie politique*, **102** (4), 563–91.

Guilhon, B., P. Gianfaldoni (1990), 'Chaînes de compétences et réseaux', *Revue d'économie industrielle*, **51**, 97–111.

Hales, M. (1997) *Make or buy in the production of innovation: competences, fullness of services and the architecture of supply in consultancy*, SI4S project, European Commission (DG XII), TSER program.

Hamdouch, A. and E. Samuelides, (2001), 'Innovation dynamics in mobile phone services in France', **4** (3), *European Journal of Innovation Management*, 153-62.

Hardouin, J.C. (1973), 'L'apparition de l'innovation financière. Contribution à l'étude de ses éléments explicatifs', Complementary PhD thesis, University of Rennes.

Hatchuel, A. (1994), 'Modèles de service et activité industrielle : la place de la prescription', in De Bandt, J. and J. Gadrey (eds), *Relations de service, marchés des services*, Paris : CNRS Editions, pp. 63–84.

Hauknes J. (1999), *Services in innovation, innovation in services*, OECD forum on 'Realizing the potential of the service economy: facilitating growth, innovation and competition, September, Paris.

Henderson, R. M. and K.B. Clark (1990), 'Architectural Innovation: The Reconfiguration of Existing Product Technologies and the Failure of Established Firms', *Administrative Science Quarterly*, **35** (1), 9–30.

Hill, P. (1997), 'Tangibles, intangibles and services : a new taxonomy for the classification of output', *Canadian Journal of Economics*, **32** (2), 426–46.

Hirschman, A. O. (1970), *Exit, voice and loyalty : response to decline in firms, organizations and states*, Cambridge, Mass.: Harvard University Press.

Hollander, S.C. (1966), 'Notes on the Retail Acordion', *Journal of Retailing*, **42** (2), 24–34.

Horn, F. (1997), *Pluralité et dynamique des mondes de production : l'exemple de la production de logiciels*, miméo, University of Lille I, March.

Horne, D.A and C.R. Martin (1985), 'Service development : a dynamic paradigm', *Working paper* n°451, Graduate School of Business Administration, University of Michigan, November.

Howells (2000), *The nature of innovation in services*, OECD/Australia workshop on innovation and productivity in services, Sydney, October.

Illeris, S. (1996), *The service economy*, Chichester: John Wiley and sons.

Jallat, F. (1992), 'Le management de l'innovation dans les entreprises de services au particulier : concepts, processus et performances', PhD Thesis, University of Aix-Marseille III.

Karpik, L. (1989), 'L'économie de la qualité', *Revue française de sociologie*, **XXX** (2), 187–210.

Kingman-Brundage, J. (1992), 'The ABCs of Service System Blueprinting', in Lovelock, C. (ed.), pp. 96–102.

Kline, S. and N. Rosenberg (1986), 'An overview of innovation', in Landau R. and N. Rosenberg (eds), *The positive sum strategy : harnessing technology for economic growth*, Washington DC: National Academy Press.

Knight, F. (1921), *Risk, uncertainty and profit*, Boston and New York: Houghton Mifflin.

Knight, K. (1985), 'A functional and structural measurement of technology', *Technology Forecasting and Social Change*, **27**, 107–27.

Kubr, M. (1988), *Management Consulting: a Guide to the Profession*, BIT, Geneva.

Kutscher, R. and J. Mark (1983), 'The Service-Producing Sector: Some Common Perceptions Reviewed', *Monthly Labor Review*, April, 21–24.

Lakshmanan, T. R. (1987), *Technological and Institutional Innovation in the Service Sector*, Conference 'Research and Development, Industrial Change and Economic Policy', University of Karlstad, Karlstad, Sweden, June.

Lancaster, K. J. (1966), 'A New Approach to Consumer Theory', *Journal of Political Economy*, **74**, 132–57.

Latour, B. and S. Woolgar (1988), *La vie de laboratoire : la production des faits scientifiques*, Paris : La Découverte.

Le Roy, A. (1997), *Les activités de service : une chance pour les économies rurales ? vers de nouvelles logiques de développement rural*, Paris : L'Harmattan.

Levitt, T. (1972), 'Production line approach to service', *Harvard Business Review*, **50**, September–October, 41–52.

Lorenzi, J.-H., O. Pastré and J. Tolédano (1980). *La Crise du XXe siècle*, Paris : Economica.

Lovelock, C. (1992), 'A basic toolkit for service managers', in Lovelock, C. (ed.), 17–30.

Lovelock, C. (ed..) (1992), *Managing services*, Englewood Cliffs, New Jersey: Prentice-Hall International Editions.

Lundvall, B.-A. (1985), *Product innovation and user-producer interaction*, Aalborg: Aalborg University Press.

Mahar, M. (1992), 'Blue collar, white collar: good jobs are vanishing throughout the economy', *Barron's*, May, **11**, 8–24.

Mayère, A. (1994), 'Relations de service et enjeux d'industrialisation', in De Bandt, J. and J. Gadrey (eds), pp. 101–17.

McNair, M.P. (1958), 'Significant trends and developments in the post war period', in A.B. Smith (ed.) *Competitive Distribution in a Free High Level Economy and its implication for the University*, Pittsburg: University of Pittsburgh Press, pp. 1–25.

Meisenheimer, J.R. (1998), 'The service industries in the " good " versus " bad " jobs debate', *Monthly Labor Review*, February, 22–47.

Metcalfe, S. and I. Miles (eds) (2000), *Innovation systems in the service sectors: measurement and case study analysis*, Dortrecht: Kluwer Academics Publishers.

Metcalfe, S. and M. Gibbons (1989), 'Technology, variety and organisation : a systematic perspective on the competitive process', *Research on Technological Innovation, Management and Policy*, **4**, 153–93.

Miles, I., N. Kastrinos, K. Flanagan, R. Bilderbek, P. den Hertog, W. Huntink and M. Bouman (1994), *Knowledge-Intensive Business Services: Their Role as Users, Carriers and Sources of Innovation*, PREST, University of Manchester.

Mills, P. K. (1986), *Managing service industries : organizational practices in a postindustrial economy*, Cambridge, Ma.: Ballinger Publishing Company.

Mintzberg, H. (1982), *The structuring of organization, Englewood Cliffs,* New Jersey: Prentice-Hall.

Monnoyer, M.C (2002), 'Les composantes servicielles des systèmes d'offres électroniques', in Djellal, F. and F. Gallouj (eds), *Nouvelles technologies et innovation dans les services : approches économiques et socio-économiques,* Paris : L'Harmattan (forthcoming).

Moulaert, F., F. Martinelli and F. Djellal (1990), *The Role of Information Technology Consultancy in the Transfer of Information Technology to Production and Service Organizations,* Nederlandse Organisatie voor Technologisch Aspectenonderzoek, Lille.

Muller, P. (1991), 'Quel avenir pour l'agriculture et le monde rural ?' *Economie rurale,* n°202-203, May–June, 67–70.

Mustar, P. (1993), *La création d'entreprise par les chercheurs. Dynamique d'intégration de la science et du marché,* PhD, Ecole des Mines de Paris.

Mustar, P. (1994), 'L'entrepreneur schumpeterien a-t-il jamais existé ?' *Gérer et Comprendre, Annales des Mines,* March, 30–7.

Nelson, R. and S. Winter (1982), *An Evolutionary Theory of Economic Change,* Cambridge, Ma. and London: Belknap Harvard.

Niehans, J. (1983), 'Financial Innovation, Multinational Banking, and Monetary Policy', *Journal of Banking and Finance,* 7, 537–51.

Niosi, J., Bellon, B., Saviotti, P. and M. Crow (1992), 'Les systèmes nationaux d'innovation : à la recherche d'un concept utilisable', *Revue française d'économie,* 7, 215–49.

Noyelle, T. (1986), *New Technologies and Services : Impact on Cities and Jobs,* mimeo, University of Maryland, College Park.

OCDE (1996), *The OECD jobs strategy : technology, productivity and job creation,* Paris.

Pavitt, K. (1984), 'Sectoral Patterns of Technical Change: Towards a Taxonomy and a Theory', *Research Policy,* 13, 343–73.

Pavitt, K., M. Robson and J. Townsend (1989), 'Accumulation, diversification and organisation of technology activities in UK companies, 1945-83', in Dodgson, M. (ed.), *Technology Strategy and the Firm : Management and Public Policy,* London: Longman, pp. 38–67.

Payson, S. (1994), *Quality Measurements in Economics,* Aldershot, UK, Brookfield, US: Edward Elgar.

Petit, P. (1986), *Slow growth and the service economy,* London: Frances Pinter.

Petit, P. (ed.) (1998) *L'économie de l'information : les enseignements des théories économiques,* Paris : La Découverte.

Pilat (2000), *Innovation and productivity in services: state of the art,* OECD/Australia workshop on innovation and productivity in services, Sydney, October.

Preissl, B. (2000) 'Service innovations: what makes it different', in Metcalfe, S. and I. Miles (eds), *Innovation systems in the service sectors:*

measurement and case study analysis, Dortrecht: Kluwer Academics Publishers, pp. 125–48.

Ravix, J.-L. (ed.) (1996), *Coopération entre les entreprises et organisation industrielle*, Paris : CNRS Editions.

Reboud, L. (1997), 'Les implications d'une relation de service ignorée : l'exemple du monde agricole' in Reboud, L. (ed.) *La relation de service au cœur de l'analyse économique*, Paris : L'Harmattan, pp. 133–53.

Salais, R. and M. Storper (1993), *Les mondes de production*, Paris : Edition de l'Ecole des Hautes Etudes en Sciences Sociales.

Saviotti, P.P. (1988), 'Information, variety and entropy in technoeconomic development', *Research Policy*, **17**, 89–103.

Saviotti, P.P. (1996), *Technological evolution, variety and the economy*, Cheltenham, UK, Brookfield, US: Edward Elgar.

Saviotti, P.P. and Metcalfe, J.S. (1984), 'A theoretical approach to the construction of technological output indicators', *Research Policy*, **13** (3), 141–51.

Saviotti, P.P. and S. Metcalfe (eds) (1991), *Evolutionary Theories of Economic and Technological Change: Present State and Future Prospects*, Reading: Harwood Publishers.

Schumpeter J. (1934), *The Theory of Economic Development*, Cambridge MA: Harvard University Press [1st edition 1912]).

Shostack, G.L. (1981), 'How to design a service', in Donelly, J.H. and W.R. George, *Marketing of services*, Chicago, American Marketing Association.

Shostack, G.L. (1984), 'Service Design in the Operating Environment', in George, W.R. and C. Marshall (eds), *Developing New Services,* American Marketing Association, Proceedings Series, pp. 27–43.

Smith A. (1960). (First Edition 1776) *The Wealth of Nations*, The Modern Library, New York: Random House.

Soete, L. and M. Miozzo (1990), 'Trade and Development in Services : a Technological Perspective', mimeo, MERIT, Maastricht, Netherlands.

Solow, R. (1987), 'We'd better watch out', *New York Times Book Review*, 12 July.

Strobel, P. (1995), 'Services publics et cohésion sociale', *Recherches et Prévisions*, (42), 7–16.

Sundbo, J. (1992), 'The tied entrepreneur', *Creativity and innovation management*, **1** (3), 109–20.

Sundbo, J. (1993), *Innovative Networks, Technological and Public Knowledge Support Systems in Services*, mimeo, Roskilde University, Denmark.

Sundbo, J. (1994), 'Modulization of service production and a thesis of convergence between service and manufacturing organizations', *Scandinavian Journal of Management*, **10** (3), 245–66.

216 *Innovation in the Service Economy*

Sundbo, J. (1996), 'Development of the service system in a manual service firm: a case study of the Danish ISS', *Advances in Services Marketing and Management*, **5**, 169–91.

Sundbo, J. (1998), *The organisation of innovation in services*, Roskilde, DK: Roskilde University Press.

Sundbo, J. and F. Gallouj (2000), 'Innovation as a loosely coupled system in services', in Metcalfe, S. and I. Miles (eds), *Innovation systems in the service sectors: measurement and case study analysis*, Dortrecht: Kluwer Academics Publishers.

Tarondeau J.C. and D. Xardel (1992), *La distribution*, Paris: PUF, Que sais-je.

Tether, B. and C. Hipp (2000), 'Competition and Innovation amongst knowledge intensive and other service firms: evidence from Germany', in Andersen et al. (eds), *Knowledge and innovation in the new service economy*, Cheltenham, UK, Brookfield, US: Edward Elgar, pp. 49-67.

Thévenot, L. (1986), 'Les investissements de forme', in *Conventions économiques*, Paris : CEE-PUF.

Thurow, L. (1985), *Towards a high-wage, high productivity service sector*, Economic Policy Institute, Washington DC.

Tréanton, J.-R. (1993), 'Tribulations de la justice', *Revue française de sociologie*, **XXXIV** (4), 627–56.

Triplett, J. (1986), 'The economic interpretation of hedonic methods', *Survey of Current Business*, January, 36–40.

Tushman, M.L. and P. Anderson (1986), 'Technological discontinuities and organizational environments', *Administrative Science Quarterly*, **31**, 439–65.

U.S DEPARTMENT OF COMMERCE (1996), *Service industries and economic performance*, March.

Warrant, F. (2001), *Favoriser l'innovation dans les services: un rôle pour les pouvoirs publics*, Paris: L'Harmattan.

Wind, J., P.E. Green, D. Shifflet and M. Scarbrough (1992), 'Courtyard by Marriott: Designing a Hotel Facility with Consumer-Based Marketing Models', in Lovelock, C. H. (ed.) *Managing Services*, Englewood Cliffs, New Jersey: Prentice-Hall International Editions, pp. 118–37.

Zaltman, G., R. Duncan and J. Holbek (1973), *Innovation and Organization*, New York: John Wiley and Sons.

Zarifian, P. (1987), *La production industrielle comme production de services*, Conference 'Dynamics of services and Economic theory', University of Lille I, January.

Zeyl, A. and A. Zeyl (1996), *Le trade marketing ou la nouvelle logique des échanges producteurs-distributeurs*, Paris : Vuibert.

Zimmerman, J.B. (1995), 'Le concept de grappes technologiques', *Revue économique*, **46** (5), 1263–95.

Index

functional description 31
functional innovation 26
functionalist sub-school 164
functions, products as a combination of
32-3

general formulation
of a product 58-9
specific applications 59-64
generic products 168, 169
generic trajectories 141, 144
geographical organization 53
Goldman's analysis, retail dynamics 24
goods and services
integrative approach 25-6
Lancasterian approach 28-69

heterogeneity
of behaviour, within industries 8
service activities 8
heterogeneous basic principles,
innovation models 92
heuristic notion, integration of goods and
services 25
high-level services 8
home banking 52-3
hotels and catering
models of innovation 81, 95
models of innovation organization 126
product characteristics 82-3, 84
service characteristics 49-50
service provision 62
human beings' relations
to organizations 184
to products and objects of production
183
hybrid products 66
hybridization mechanisms, production
and innovation 188-9
hybridization of trajectories 143, 145-6
hypertely 136

identity relation 5
imitators, leakage of innovations 127,
128
immediate product 38
incremental innovation 71, 74-7
competence base 113, 114-15, 114
evolutionary theory 136-7
linkages with other models 92, 93
Pavitt's taxonomy 8-9

processes 12, 13
as recombinative innovation 79
in service sector 94, 95
worlds of production 195
indirect product 38, 50
individual competences 56
industrial activity, spaces describing
33-5
industrial model, innovation organization
118, 122
industrial rationalization
consultancy 102-3
operational services 99-100
industrial world 167, 168
evolutionary theory 185
service characteristics 173
industrialization, versus service-
orientation 97-100
informal management innovation
189-90
information, sources of innovation 108,
109
information technologies
capital expenditure 2
impact on services 3-6
innovation organization 123-4
investment, selected industries 3
object-based approach 134
informational networks 10
informational services
incremental innovation 94
service characteristics 46-7
informational technical characteristics
138
innovation
conventionist analysis 203-4
diffusing and protecting 127-9
evolutionary analysis 203
integrative analysis 202-3
sources and determinants of
characteristics-based approach
106-10
the firm as a chain of linked
competences 110-15
see also models of innovation
innovation organization
craft model 121, 122
entrepreneurial model 121, 122
evaluating importance of models
123-7
Fordist model 118, 122